Beriah Gwynfe Evans
Llywelyn

The year is 1262 and Llywelyn ap Gruffydd, Prince of Gwynedd, is about to embark on a daring plan to cast off the yoke of the detested Norman Marcher Lords and unite all of Wales under his banner. But with all the might of the English crown seemingly against him, how can he hope to triumph?

Beriah Gwynfe Evans (1848-1926) was a prolific novelist of the Victorian era in both Welsh and English, particularly associated with the genre of the historical romance. *Llywelyn* was one of a sequence of historical novels he referred to as the 'Gwynfe Novels' covering the breadth of Welsh history, in which he hoped to produce a Welsh equivalent to the *Waverley* novels of Walter Scott.

Melin Bapur Welsh Library
This series re-introduces lesser known works from the English-language literary tradition of Wales.

Cover image:
Detail from a 14th century depiction of a battle in the 2nd Barons' War.

Image status: public domain.

Text copyright:
©Melin Bapur, 2025

All rights reserved. Neither the whole nor any part of the contents of this book may be reproduced for any purposes, except for reasonable extracts as part of a book review.

ISBN:
978-1-917237-46-8

Beriah Gwynfe Evans
(1848-1946)

Llywelyn
or,
The Last of the Welsh Princes
An Historical Romance

Edited by Adam Pearce

Yr eiddoch yn gywir (yours sincerely)
Beriah Gwynfe Evans (1848-1936)

Contents

A 21st century introduction to Beriah Gwynfe Evans and *Llywelyn* vii

Introductory 1

Chapter I The First Four Characters 5

Chapter II The Second Four Characters 14

Chapter III The King's Forest Laws 22

Chapter IV Revelations 30

Chapter V A Brave Lad 43

Chapter VI The Alliance 50

Chapter VII The Night Attack 53

Chapter VIII The Fall of Cefn Llys 64

Chapter IX Historical 73

Chapter X Old Acquaintances 77

Chapter XI English Guile 81

Chapter XII Retributive Justice 86

Chapter XIII Eleanor and Gwen 94

Chapter XIV The Nameless Knight 101

Chapter XV The Combat 108

Chapter XVI The Serenader 115

Chapter XVII The Prophecy 121

Chapter XVIII Love's Trial 127

Chapter XIX English Gold and Welsh Treachery 131

Chapter XX An Unknightly Attack 136

Chapter XXI In England 144

Chapter XXII In Wales 147

Chapter XXIII The Sea Gives Up its Dead 150

Chapter XXIV The Awakening 156

Chapter XXV To Be, or Not to Be............................ 161

Chapter XXVI An Unexpected Revelation................ 165

Chapter XXVII Another............................... 170

Chapter XXVIII A Confession 173

Chapter XXIX Disappointed Hopes 178

Chapter XXX An Unexpected Rescue 184

Chapter XXXI An Unexpected Proposal................... 189

Chapter XXXII A Treacherous Act 193

Chapter XXXIII Hurried Efforts 201

Chapter XXXIV The Prisoner 207

Chapter XXXV 213

Chapter XXXVI A Defeated Plan 219

Chapter XXXVII Caught............................ 223

Chapter XXXVIII Bride or Country 228

Chapter XXXIX Friends and Foes 235

Chapter XL The Page..................................... 241

Chapter XLI All Hope Gone 248

Chapter XLII 251

Notes 258

A 21ˢᵗ century introduction to Beriah Gwynfe Evans and *Llywelyn*

Beriah Gwynfe Evans is a fascinating figure. He was one of a number of nineteenth-century Welsh literary figures whose sheer industriousness was absolutely astounding, yet whose achievements today are, sadly, mostly forgotten. By my count Beriah – a name like his seems destined to be shortened to a personal name – published at least thirteen novels, six in English and seven in Welsh (three of the English novels he later translated into Welsh as well) – most of these in the space of just one decade, and there are almost certainly more – as well as a half dozen stage works and three extensive works of non-fiction, alongside busy careers as first a teacher and then a journalist. It seems many more plays and novels remained unpublished. In amongst all this he also managed to squeeze a lifetime of political activity, including as secretary of the proto-independence movement *Cymru Fydd* during the 1890s.

And yet to the extent Beriah is known today at all, it is probably for either his political activity or his work in drama: his play *Owain Glyndŵr* was performed at the Investiture of the Prince of Wales in 1911 and he is acknowledged as something of a pioneer in Welsh theatre, though even there the term is relative: he produced his stage works have probably not been performed in public since his death. His novels are almost completely unknown and in fact before now only one has ever been published in book form, his 1890s political satire *Dafydd Dafis;* this is the only novel of Beriah's whose existence is acknowledged by his entries in the Dictionary of Welsh Biography (*Y Bywgraffiadur*) and the Companion to Welsh Literature. It is the only novel of Beriah's to have received any real critical attention, in the form of a book chapter by M. Wyn Thomas published as recently as 2017. It is a remarkable book, though rather unrepresentative of Beriah's novels and work in general.

The reasons for this neglect are, on the surface, fairly easy to identify. Partly it is a question of accessibility: unpublished as books, his stories until now could only be read in dusty University archives. Partly his timing was unfortunate: in terms of literature written in *Cymraeg*, there is a well-established critical consensus which dismisses much of the literature of the second half of the nineteenth century (and not without reason). Studies of what used to be called Anglo-Welsh literature (the preferred term these days is Welsh writing in English), in turn, have tended to overlook writers pre-1900 generally as well as writers who wrote mainly in Welsh and only occasionally in English: Beriah fails on both counts. Changing fashions were clearly a factor too, as his works are absolutely of their time: drooping in Victorian sentiment and melodrama, leaning heavily on stereotypical tropes and cliches, and in often florid prose that, in both Welsh and English, shows the influence of the other language in such a way that is guaranteed to irritate purists of either. His work belongs unquestionably to the Romantic aesthetic, and the 20th century reaction against Romanticism was perhaps even stronger in Wales than in England, where Beriah's greatest literary influence, Walter Scott, underwent such a precipitous decline in reputation.

And yet whilst these are all valid criticisms, and Beriah was no great artist, there remains an appeal to these novels: a certain sincerity and earnestness, a passionate belief in the validity of his own endeavours in the face of all indifference, and above all, in the validity and value of the Welsh nation and everything associated with it. For all its cliches his work, in all its variety, also has a very distinctive style in the Welsh context, a tongue-in-cheek boyishness and sense of adventure and fun which means his works are usually at the very least entertaining. It is this earnestness and individuality which lifts the best of his work above mere *kitsch*, and makes him a writer genuinely worth exploring in both languages, at least for anyone interested in writing and the Welsh national consciousness. It is sometimes said that the Welsh lack a sense of national self-esteem, that we possess a kind of collective inferiority complex which leads us to play down our own. This is a charge that could never be placed at the door of Beriah Gwynfe Evans, and yet may also have contributed to his neglect, for his is exactly the kind of loud, unapologetic Welshness that triggers self-consciousness and embarrassment in the insecure. Flawed as they are, there is a spark of joy in these stories. Time perhaps, to re-evaluate, or at least rehabilitate, this neglected figure, much as the once-maligned Walter Scott has in recent decades been at least partially restored to grace.

Born in Nantyglo, now a part of Blaenau Gwent, in 1848, Beriah's unusual biblically-derived given name reflected his Congregationalist Christian background: his father, Evan Evans Nantyglo (1804-1886), was a noted minister and preacher. When his parents emigrated to the United States in 1867, the nineteen-year-old Beriah moved instead to the village of Gwynfe, Carmarthenshire, becoming a schoolteacher and incorporating his new home into his name. Like many teachers of his age in Wales, even the ones who were major cultural figures, Beriah is known to have used the notorious Welsh Not to encourage his pupils to acquire English (a practice he later disavowed and deeply regretted). Though his literary ambitions did not manifest themselves until a little later and he published little if anything for most of the 1870s, he exploded onto the literary scene in 1879 by winning awards in separate Eisteddfodau for a play in Welsh, *Owain Glyndŵr*, and a novel in English on the same subject matter, *Bronwen*, which adjudicator Llew Llwyfo deemed the best of twenty-seven entrants to the competition for 'a novel in English on a Welsh theme'. The following year he established a magazine, *Cyfaill yr Aelwyd*, 'The Household Companion', which he edited until 1891. A great number of novels – many of them serialised in the magazine – followed over the next fifteen or so years; and Beriah quit teaching to pursue journalism and politics in 1885, becoming editor at various times of a number of publications including the *Cardiff Times* in which *Llywelyn* appeared in 1886-7. Politically, Beriah became heavily involved in the *Cymru Fydd* movement for Welsh Home Rule, and his literary output dried up somewhat over the 1890s (it appears that *Dafydd Dafis*, serialised in 1893-4, was his last novel). During the first decades of the twentieth century he returned to drama, publishing a number of plays (including revamping *Owain Glyndŵr* for the investiture of the Prince of Wales in 1911), whilst continuing to be active in politics and with *Cymdeithas yr Iaith Gymraeg* (not to be confused with the later pressure group founded in the 1960s, this earlier organisation promoted the use of Welsh in education). Though he lived until 1926, he remained, in E. G. Millward's words, "a product of the Victorian age in everything he did."

Though being a writer in Welsh from Gwent was not

unique (it is the most linguistically anglicised part of the country; and yet produced Islwyn (1832-1878), perhaps the greatest poet of the nineteenth century in Welsh), it was comparatively unusual. This was just one of several ways in which Beriah stands apart from the typical profile of the 19th century Welsh literary figure. As noted above, he wrote extensively in both languages, and although not a translation as such, *Llywelyn*, originally written in 1886-7, was based on his "drama-cantata" *Llywelyn ein Llyw Olaf*, written in Welsh a few years earlier. Beriah was a passionate defender of the Welsh language, but saw value also in teaching the rapidly growing numbers of anglophone Welsh about the history of their homeland, and in doing so, imbuing them with a sense of Welsh identity which clearly felt threatened. Beriah was also unusual in his dedication to prose, despite the prestige poetry held in Wales during the period; though some of his stage works are in verse, he does not appear to have published any great quantity of poetry (though curiously and ironically he was publicly awarded the Chair, the greatest national award for poetry, at the National Eisteddfod in 1902 – on behalf of his friend T. Gwynn Jones, who, having assumed he would not win, had skipped the Eisteddfod to attend a wedding).

Beriah's novels vary enormously in subject matter and quality. *Owen Hughes* (1883) is a coming-of-age novel with shades of Dickens. *Morfudd Pugh* (1885-1886) is a temperance novel and a mystery novel rolled into one. *Dafydd Dafis* (1898) is a political satire about a man who decides to stand for parliament. Another planned novel, *Ladi Wen y Llyn* (1891), would draw on Welsh folklore, though sadly only the introduction was published. One gets the impression of a man who better understood the potential of the novel as a creative form than any of his Welsh contemporaries, even the great Daniel Owen, and who saw the value in providing a variety of reading materials to his audience. Beriah's creativity and imagination were remarkable, but a tendency to moralisation mars many of these 'contemporary' novels, particularly those written in Welsh (Beriah perhaps perceived a greater need for these works to justify themselves morally). Of greater interest are the substantial number of historical romances Beriah produced, of which there are at least eight, some in Welsh, some in English – *Llywelyn* being one of them – and some with versions in both languages, including *Bronwen*, of which Melin Bapur released the Welsh version in 2025. All these stories draw on formative periods in Welsh history. These are the 'Gwynfe Novels', the "*Waverleys* of Wales," as an advertisement in the *Cardiff Times* put it.

Llywelyn and its sequel *The Widowed Prince*, the final two of the 'Gwynfe Novels' to be published, were serialised from 1886-88 and take as their subject the eponymous last native prince of Wales, who lived c.1223-1282. The first part of the tale begins in 1262 and takes us up to Llywelyn's marriage to Eleanor de Montfort in approximately 1275, whilst the sequel takes the story to its conclusion with Llywelyn's death in 1282. Much as Walter Scott's novels often revolve around characters on the edges of the major historical events being portrayed, the true protagonist of the first part of the story is not Llywelyn himself but rather the fictional Meredydd ab Ednyfed; and as much if not more time is spent with the villains of the piece, the evil Geoffrey de Langley and the treacherous Gruffydd ap Gwenwynwyn, both real historical people. The tropes – betrayals, oaths of vengeance, swooning maidens – are all the standard stuff of the chivalric romance, and the action moves at a rapid pace without stopping for character development. Unlike some of the authors who penned Welsh historical romances in the nineteenth century, Beriah at least pays a reasonable degree of attention to the history, inserting fiction only where it does not contradict known historical facts, though not every time: whilst the real circumstances of Geoffrey de Langley's death, which occurred around 1274, are unknown (enabling Beriah to conjure up the poetic justice of his feud with Hywel), ap Gwenwynwyn in fact outlived Llywelyn's revolt (in which he was one of the most prominent of Edward's supporters) and died sometime later. As per the rules of the genre though, the motivations of the characters are almost entirely black-and-white; the scheming villains motivated by lust, avarice or sheer sadism whilst the heroes are motivated only by national ambition, and loyalty to their friends and women.

It seems it was Beriah himself who made the *Waverley* comparison. In his introduction and foreword to the Welsh version of *Bronwen* – both of which are absent from the English version – he expressed his ambition even more explicitly, and they are worth quoting at some length for the insight they give on Beriah's mindset:

> …it has often concerned the author that no Welshman has ever offered to perform for this branch of the Celtic nation that priceless service Sir Walter Scott performed for the Scots, though there exists in the annals of Wales, in those valuable manuscripts treasured in public and private libraries, a rich vein which, in the hands of a skilled miner, could prove as priceless a treasure to the Welsh nation as the

traditions Scott treated so masterfully proved to the land of his birth...

There is among us a hot-headed class who never tire of praising 'Welshman, Wales and Welsh', men who look at the ancient Welshman as a half-god, and on the modern Welshman as having inherited most of those virtues which crowned his semi-divine forefather with glory; those who consider that Wales was the original Garden of Eden, and those who do not for a second doubt that Welsh will be generally spoken in Paradise! There are also a group who go to the opposite extremes: the debased Welsh. Although the name 'Welsh' is degraded by applying it to such undeserving objects – the Dic Siôn Dafydds of our nation, those who are ashamed of their people, their country, their language; and yet of whom their own nation have rather more reason to be ashamed; people whom, through their undeserving denial of the Land of their Fathers, have done a great deal to foster, indeed, and to spread in the mind of the haughty Saxon that contemptuous scorn of Wales and everything Welsh that the English are always too willing to make apparent. Between these two extremes, however, we find the vast majority of sensible Welshmen, and in particular the enlightened ones... These men bear for their country a love both pure and immortal; and yet though love is proverbially blind, they do not close their eyes to the fact that their country and people are not faultless... Whilst acknowledging that there could be many things associated with our country and its people the less said about which the better, we do not hesitate to claim that there are many other things inseparably connected to Wales and the Welsh of which we can be justifiably proud.*

Beriah's project in his historical novels and plays therefore is very self-consciously a national and political one every bit as much, if not more so, than a literary one: to instil pride and patriotism in his fellow Welshmen. His pleading that this is a moderate stance is a key part of the message, because it heads off the charge of uncritical romanticisation (which is of course a completely fair accusation to level at Beriah's version of history). Whilst they deal with different periods and individuals in Welsh history, the overarching narrative of Beriah's historical romances is of the heroism and nobility of the Welsh and – implicitly – their ultimate national restoration and glory, even when individual heroes may fail.

These stories, then, are fundamentally naïve, but that is a part of their charm, and it is a naivety that is in its own way subversive in a context of the dominant narrative of Welsh submission to English dominance. There are contradictions in such works which can be seen in so much of the Welsh-language literature of the nineteenth century: Victorian optimism sits uneasily with an understandable anxiety about the preservation of Welsh and Welshness (and frequently a pessimism about the future of the language). Wales's past

---

* These extracts are my translations; the originals can be read in Melin Bapur's version of *Bronwen*. Dic Siôn Dafydd was a popular folk character representing the Welshman who turns his back on his Welshness, especially the language.

resistance to England is glorified (often and perhaps tellingly via ultimately unsuccessful figures like Llywelyn and Owain Glyndŵr) even as its contemporary subordinate position within a British Empire with an English monarch is celebrated. These apparent contradictions – which would not have been considered contradictory at the time – should be understood in their context. National identity within Britain would not have been associated with political sovereignty in the same way it might today, and it was not until more sophisticated thinkers like Emrys ap Iwan began to push the envelope that this would really be challenged.

Beriah, as noted, would go on to be a significant player in the *Cymru Fydd* movement which pushed for some form of political independence (albeit within the Empire) and this would have been a period of optimism for Wales's national future, an optimism that is wholly reflected in *Llywelyn*. But perhaps the period in turn reflected the story's naivety: *Cymry Fydd* would fall spectacularly apart before the turn of the century, and even within Beriah's lifetime a romantic story like *Llywelyn* would have seemed old-fashioned. It's certainly a story of its time. But times change, and with Wales perhaps once again taking a greater interest in its history – and in historical figures like both Llywelyn and Beriah Gwynfe Evans – perhaps it's time for the latter to be brought in from the cold.

A. P.   2025

Sources:

E. G. Millward (1991) 'Beriah Gwynfe Evans: A Pioneer Playwright-Producer,' in Hywel Teifi Edwards (ed.) *A guide to Welsh Literature 1800-1900*, Cardiff: UWP. Pp166-185.

Geraint H. Jenkins (1999) 'A Gafodd Cymru Chwarae Teg? Cyfrifiad 1891 a'r Iaith Gymraeg', *Welsh Book Studies* 2

Thomas, M. Wynn (2017) 'Chwarae Rhan yng nghynhyrchiad Cymru Fydd' in Anwen Jones (ed.) *Perfformio'r Genedl*, Cardiff: UWP, pp.91-116.

Note on the Text:

Beriah's text and prose style reflect the period in which this novel was written. In preparing this edition for publication I have been wary of taking too heavy a hand in modifying his prose. Beriah used the once common spelling "Llewelyn" throughout his original novel; here I have substituted "Llywelyn" which is more familiar today and reflects general usage when referring to this particular historical person. I have similarly substituted other names e.g. Einon > Eynon, Owen Glyndwr > Owain Glyndŵr to reflect the spellings most commonly used today, and other rules of modern Welsh orthography. I have left place names as they are in the original text where those names are still in use (e.g. Radnorshire, Abergavenny), but not where the spellings are similarly archaic, whether the name in question is Welsh or English (e.g. "Snowden").

Introductory

Love thou thy land with love far brought
From out the storied past, and used
Within the present, but transfused
Through future time by power of thought.
- TENNYSON

There is no more prominent figure in Welsh history than that of Llywelyn ap Gruffydd. Living, his name was a veritable tower of strength to his oppressed countrymen, and a terror not only to the Lord Marchers and their mercenaries on the Welsh borders, but to the English King surrounded by his nobles, who had spent so much of his country's blood and treasure in vain attempts to reduce the Welsh chieftain. Though long dead, his name is a living memory, enshrined in the heart of every Welshman whatever may be his station in life and the name of *Llywelyn ein Llyw Olaf* never fails to touch some hidden chord in the breast of the Cymro, whether he labours in the depth of the coal pit in his native country, drives his team in the western prairies, hunts the guanaco on the banks of the Patagonian Chupat, digs for diamonds in South Africa, gathers in his wool-crop in Australia, or sits as a member of the first legislative assembly in the world. What Harold was for ages to the oppressed Saxon, what Bruce still remains to the Scotsman, that is what Llywelyn is, and in all probability will ever remain, to the Welshman.

And this is not to be wondered at. That he, with his limited resources and inadequately armed followers should have been able not only to cope with, but to overcome the more numerous, better armed, and better trained forces of the Plantagenet, and to have strained for years the extensive resources of the English King, is far more a matter of surprise than that his country should have been so easily overrun after his untimely death. The consummate tact and military skill he displayed in his numerous contests with the superior forces of the English gained for him not only contemporaneous continental renown, but claim for him an honourable place among the great military leaders of the Middle Ages. Even the bare outlines of his career which jealous history parsimoniously gives us afford sufficient evidence to show that his countrymen have no cause to be ashamed of their great warrior prince; while when these outlines are filled in by song, and tradition, and affection, the inheritance of ages, we can realize for ourselves a personage complete in all that is noblest and best in man, in whose presence his followers might well find the inspiration to enable them to scorn death, and around whose memory the affections of a nation may proudly cling.

The fatal curse of Wales, petty jealousy and internal dissensions, proved throughout his life far more disastrous to him than did the mailed knights, the men at arms, and the archers of the invader. What might have been the final outcome of the struggle had Wales been united, had no Welshmen turned traitor, and had not Llywelyn's brilliant genius been darkened by the death of his wife, it is not for us to consider. It is not with what might have been, but with what actually was that we have to deal.

With Llywelyn died the hopes of a nation; with him fell the independence of Wales; the close of his career proved practically the close of an almost incessant struggle for national independence extending over eight centuries. Welshmen of today may be justly proud of the eight hundred years' stubborn resistance offered by their ancestors to the utmost power of the invader, whether Saxon, Dane, or Norman. During that eight hundred years' war, the nation had no worthier leader than Llywelyn, the last of the Welsh Princes.

It is true that his brother Dafydd to some extent condoned after his brother's death for his treachery to that brother when living, and that he assumed the title of Prince of Wales; it is likewise true that two generations after saw the meteor-like career of Owain Glyndŵr reach its climax in his coronation at Machynlleth as Prince of Wales. But these were only the expiring sparks from the smouldering wick; the flame of the taper had been extinguished at Cefnbedd, and the dynasty of the Welsh princes came practically to an end when the brave but unfortunate Llywelyn fell a victim to the spear of Adam de Francton.

It would evidently be impossible to collect into a single work of fiction all the stirring scenes and remarkable events in the eventful life of the last of the Welsh princes. This impossible task the author has not attempted. In the present work he has only endeavoured to portray a few of the leading events of a limited period – though possibly the most romantic period of a life that was full of romantic incidents from cradle to grave. In a future work the author hopes to be able to complete the task he has, in a manner, only been able to commence in the present story.

I cannot close these introductory remarks without expressing my regret that we have no national memento of any kind to commemorate the greatest of our native princes. It is a national disgrace that the last of the Welsh Princes lies in a grave unmarked by a simple memorial stone, and that the country for which he bled and died has raised no monument and erected no building to commemorate his name and his fame.(1) Still, it is only an additional proof of the lasting influence of his genius that without the aid of mausoleum, monument, or memorial hall, the memory of this great chieftain still lives, and that there is hardly a Cymro who has not heard of, and whose heart does not warm anew with patriotic feelings when mention is made, however casually, of Llywelyn Ein Llyw Olaf – the Last of the Welsh Princes.

Chapter I
The First Four Characters

The strongest still the weakest over-ran.
In every country mighty robbers swayed,
And guile and ruffian force were all their trade
Life was a scene of rapine, want, and woe.
– THOMSON

It was on a fine day in the autumn of the year 1262 that a solitary horseman made his way slowly on a jaded steed along a rough bridle-path that led down a rather steep hill side to the valley of the Ithon, in Radnorshire. Both rider and steed bore the traces of a long and trying journey, while it was evident, from the anxious glances which the horseman threw now and again in every direction, that he was either apprehensive of some danger which he knew might threaten his every step, or that he was in momentary expectation of seeing some long sought-for object.

If it were the former feeling which troubled his breast, he had abundant excuse for it in the unsettled state of the country and the times. The spirit of the natives had been in many places roused by the oppression of the Norman barons, who claimed parts of the country by right of royal grant, but who could only hold them by the power of the sword, and out of sight of whose frowning castles the Welsh peasants not unfrequently dared their power.

It was only a few weeks previously that the governor of Abergavenny Castle, Peter de Montford, had appealed to the king for reinforcements to enable him to withstand the daring onslaughts of the half-naked Welshmen, who had with unexampled audacity thrown themselves on a body of steel-clad knights, and, making up by numbers, daring, and self-sacrificing valour for the lack of suitable defensive armour, had brought many a waving plume to earth, and many a haughty knight to bite the dust. For a whole day he had been obliged to put forth his utmost power to defend the fords of the Usk against what he rightly considered to be only the advanced guard of a more numerous body of the enemy, whose passions were aroused almost beyond the power of restraint by the oppressions and indignities to which they and their families had been subjected by the lords marchers and their followers. Neither age nor sex, inherited right, nor legal justice proved any protection to the Welsh men when the lust or avarice of the invaders prompted any action, and many a roofless dwelling, many a once prosperous home now lying in smouldering ruins, many an orphaned child or widowed wife, or outraged virgin in the neighbourhood of these Norman castles went to make up a sum total of an account which called for a terrible vengeance to meet. And this thirst for vengeance, this sense of injustice, served for these half-naked warriors instead of helm and cuirass, and induced them to throw themselves with the bravery of desperation upon the armour-protected knights and their well-armed and well-trained retainers.

So terrible was the onslaught on Abergavenny that it required the united forces of a Grey, a Mortimer, a Fitz Peter, and a de Bohun to drive the Welshmen even temporarily back.

In other parts of the country, more or less remote, somewhat similar scenes had been, or were being, enacted, so that travelling, unless under the protection of a strong escort, might be considered almost equally unsafe for Welshman, Englishman, or Norman. Possibly it might have been this feeling of insecurity and ever-present danger which caused the rider we have noticed to watch jealously every step of the way he now travelled, though the scene of the deeds we have just recorded was too distant, and the time of their execution too recent, for it to be probable that news of them should yet have reached the romantic valley of the Radnorshire Ithon.

"Mortimer's stronghold of Cefn Llys must be almost in sight," soliloquized he as he approached a turn in the path, "and it behoves me to be doubly cautious. Were I seen by any of his knights I should stand but a sorry chance of flight on this jaded beast. Would that I had my own steed again under me," and the flashing of his eyes and the lighting up of his features showed more of the warrior than was bespoken by his simple traveller's dress.

Scarcely had the thoughts been formed when, turning a slight shoulder of the hill, the castle of Cefn Llys, or Glan Ithon, in all its frowning majesty, stood before him. So suddenly, indeed, did it break upon his view, and so close to him did it appear in the crisp, clear air of the autumn day, that he started and drew rein as though to endeavour to retreat ere the guardians of the castle could sally forth upon him. A moment's consideration reassured him, and a half smile crossed his open countenance as he noticed the folly of his momentary fear. The castle, though apparently so near him, was at least a good hour's journey distant, even had he a far better steed than the poor animal which now carried him.

Crowning the brow of a bleak and lofty peak, more than a thousand feet above the bed of the Ithon, which washed the foot of the mountain, the Castle of Cefn Llys was well adapted for overawing the surrounding country, forming as it did one of the strongest links in the chain of fortresses by means of which only could the Normans hold their precarious sway over even this portion of Wales. So situated, it was a veritable eyrie, from which the rapacious eagles could, almost at will, swoop down upon the peaceful inhabitants of the valley, and retreat with their prey to their mountain fastness, whence they could afford to laugh to scorn the feeble and futile threats of those they had ravaged.

"'Tis indeed a noble building," mused the traveller, as, sitting motionless upon his steed, he gazed with critical eye upon the embattled town which frowned upon him across the valley. "A place that I could undertake to hold with a handful of men against an army, had I but sufficient provender for my men. And yet what gain be strong walls and iron doors, even though perched on the rock above Glyn Ithon, if there be not watchful eyes to guard them day and night? It would not much surprise me were I to take a few score men some dark night, and, led by one who knows the path, I might find the place unguarded, and carry it before its defenders had opened their eyes to their danger. But why talk of this? I want no castle walls and no defences other than those of my own native mountains, though in good sooth such defence as this castle might afford in time of need against these Normans is not to be scorned. But I must on. The sun is already sinking in the west, and night must not overtake me too near my cousin Mortimer," and he again urged his steed forward.

Another half-hour's weary plodding brought him to the banks of the river, which here, winding its way between the steep hills on each side, seemed lost in the depths of the glen, while, a few miles further on, its imprisoning guardians retreated, leaving it to spread itself out more pleasantly in the middle of a beautiful and fertile valley.

Halting on the banks of the stream to give his horse a much-needed draught, the horseman was again about to fall into a fit of musing, when he was suddenly startled by the sound of voices near. His hand unconsciously sought his side as though seeking for his sword-hilt, and the appearance of weariness which hitherto had weighed heavily upon his shoulders seemed to be shaken off in a moment; and anyone watching his countenance at the moment, and versed in reading that tell-tale open page of the inner man, would have recognised in the apparently peaceful traveller one to whom the shout of battle was often the breath of his nostrils, and more accustomed to hold his own by force of arms than to yield it at the call of oppression.

For a second time, however, he found that his fears were groundless. The voices which had startled him evidently came from a group of children, whose forms be could now see glancing through the trees on his left. In another minute they appeared on the open greensward some fifty yards in advance of him.

They were two boys and a girl, the lads apparently eight to ten years of age, while the little maiden, whom they escorted one on either side, might have been two or three years younger.

The horseman smiled as he noticed signs of apparent rivalry between the youthful suitors, and almost betrayed his presence when he saw that one of the two boys was so much more favoured than the other as to arouse the latter's ire.

"I tell thee, Gwen," said the despised one, "thou wilt regret listening to Gruffydd's false speeches and promises. He hath been with his uncle among the English, and hath learned of them to say one thing and mean another."

"Is that so, Gruffydd?" asked the child. "Doth Meredydd say the truth of thee? And dost thou not intend giving me the pair of doves thou spoke of?"

"I am as much of a Welshman as Meredydd," replied Gruffydd, "and what I have said I will do. So tell thou Meredydd to go home. I will come with thee myself to thy father's house."

"If thou wishest it, Gwen," said Meredydd. "I am not one who cares for pushing myself where I am not wanted."

"Thou art ever brawling with Gruff, Meredydd, so thou hadst better go, and leave him to take me home."

Without another word the lad turned on his heel, and left Gruffydd and Gwen to proceed on their childish way alone. The horseman had heard only a portion of this conversation, as every step of the way they took carried the children further out of his hearing, but his quick eye had caught every gesture, and his quick imagination had enabled him to fit in the sense of the words which accompanied them, so that he had little difficulty in recognising a discomfited, honest lover in the lad who now, having turned his back upon his companions, was making his way back towards the place where the horseman still sat motionless.

The lad came forward with a light and springy step, trying to hide his discomfiture under a whistled tune, but his lowering brow and flashing eye showed that this apparent light-heartedness was only a pretence, and that his feelings were far more deeply wounded than he cared to acknowledge, boy though he was.

The horseman now shook his bridle, and forced his steed once more into the path he had left for the riverside a few moments previously. This action brought him almost immediately face to face with the lad, who, satisfying himself with a single glance that the stranger was not one of the Norman knights at whose hands he had seen others suffer, greeted him with a pleasant "Good day."

The greeting being given in Welsh, and returned as readily in the same language, the elder of the two showed a wish to continue the conversation.

"I noticed thee and thy companions part," said he with a smile, "and your parting did not seem to be of the friendliest."

"And little cause hath it to be friendly," replied the lad. "That foolish child believes all that Gruffydd tells her. I know that he promiseth things he can never perform, as is his wont in other things."

"And who mayst thou be, my brave lad?"

"Though I fail to see what right thou hast to ask me the question," replied the boy sturdily, "I perceive by thy tongue thou art a Welshman, and not one of these scurvy Englishmen or haughty Normans who overrun our country, though in good sooth there be some Welshmen whom I am ashamed to call such; and seeing this, and knowing I have no cause to be ashamed of my name, I tell thee I am called Meredydd ab Ednyfed."

"Ab Ednyfed ap Tewdwr?" asked the other eagerly.

"Yes. That is my father's name."

"And a brave Welsh name, borne by a brave and worthy Welshman, I'll be bound," said the horseman. "How far may be his dwelling from where we stand?"

"An' your horse had been fresher I should have said that you could yet reach his house ere the sun sets; as it is, you can yet be there, if it be your pleasure, before it be too dark for me to lead your horse to his stable."

"Thanks, my good lad; I will, then, set out with thee,

if thou wilt lead the way. But tell me, who was thy companion, whom thou sayest will deceive Gwen?"

"He is called Gruffydd ap Gwenwynwyn," replied the boy, brusquely.

"Gruffydd ap Gwenwynwyn? And how comes he here? Hath his father any kith or kin in these parts?"

"The boy came here to a cousin's house some few months since, and hath made little Gwen believe all he says."

"Unless he be more to be trusted than the rest of his family, the less thou hast to do with him the better, lad," said the stranger, gravely.

"Ay? And you, too, know of him, then?"

"I know nothing of the lad, who may be all well so far as I know; but you can hardly make a sheepdog out of a wolf's cub."

"No, nor an honest hound out of a fox," replied the lad, laughing, "and I take Gruffydd to be more of a fox than aught else."

While thus speaking, the lad had led the way along a narrow bridle path which wound its way through the mazes of a scrubby wood which covered the hillside, and which, while it effectually screened them from the view of any who might be watching from the opposite hill, afforded an occasional clear view of the valley beneath, and of its approaches.

Suddenly the boy's quick eye caught a flash on the crest of the hill behind them.

"Stranger," said he, "an' I mistake not, there be the Norman wolves behind us."

The horseman turned in his saddle. His keen eye scanned the road crossing the hill, and approaching the ford which led to Castell Cefn Llys. His practised vision enabled him to understand at a glance that a body of armed men was descending the hill, and in such a direction that had he followed the path he was on when he first saw the children, he must have met them.

"You are right boy, right," said he. "There is a numerous cavalcade making its way for the ford to Cefn Llys."

"Aye, and they will reach it, too, before Gwen can pass on her way to her home," cried the boy. "I must run back and get her to hide in the wood until they are gone."

"They will not harm the child," cried the other in surprise.

"That is more than anyone can say. I have known a baby plucked from its mother's arms and thrown into the Ithon flood ere now," was the reply. "Keep on thy way until this path branches. Take that to the right and it will lead thee to my father's house," and the boy dashed down the steep path, swift as a mountain deer.

The strange horseman watched him disappear, and then slowly and thoughtfully continued his own way, little thinking of what sights the boy would witness before he again met him, and little thinking of the mixed influences for good and evil which the three children he had seen half an hour since would have on his own future eventful career.

Chapter II
The Second Four Characters

*And all the courses of my life do show
I am not in the roll of common men.*
– SHAKESPEARE

The cavalcade whose approach had been noticed by young Meredydd ab Ednyfed, forming quite a numerous party, made its way gaily down the hillside. At the head of it, and evidently the chief personage in it, rode a young knight whose haughty bearing, and the evident respect shown him by his companions, proved him to be a personage of some importance. Bestriding a powerful barb, which he rode with something more than the ease of an ordinary practised rider, he presented to the eye but little in his personal appearance to distinguish him from his comrades, except the air of haughty bearing and habitual command already referred to. Had we seen him, however, some hours previously, when preparing to mount his horse; or could we follow him now until he again dismounted, and seen him standing among other knights, we could not fail to be struck with a marked peculiarity in his appearance. On horseback, as we have said, he presented little to distinguish him from those who surrounded him; standing, he was almost a head taller than most of those by whom he was accompanied. This advantage in height was not due to a general proportionate massiveness in build, for in that case it would have been as evident on horseback as on foot; indeed, the trunk, though strong and well knit, and though fairly broad shouldered, was only that of an ordinary sized man; the legs however were of a length well fitted for a body at least a foot taller than that they bore, and were so much out of proportion to the rest of the figure as to make his appearance on foot almost grotesque. This peculiarity, though it had gained him the title of Longshanks, was not one which could be safely ridiculed, at all events in the owner's presence, as the eagle glance and stern mouth abundantly testified. In justice to him, too, it should be said that no one's gaze would be apt to linger for more than a passing glance at this peculiarity which, in another, would have amounted to an actual deformity: the eye and attention would be naturally drawn to rest upon the dignified, even majestic countenance, and what the eye read there would make one forget the apparent grotesqueness of the extremities. The countenance, naturally broad and open, and wearing the imprint of a spirit at once haughty, noble and generous, was at times obscured by a cloud which materially changed its appearance. This changed appearance would have led an observant reader of character to fancy that the knight was not at all times altogether free from an unworthy spirit of petty jealousy and spite, leading to deeds of malice or revenge really unworthy of his knightly renown and general magnanimity of character. At the moment we first observed him such a cloud as we have endeavoured to describe overcast his countenance, and completely banished its otherwise pleasing appearance.

He was in deep and earnest conversation with two knights who rode on either side of him, sufficiently behind him to pay him marked deference and accord him apparently deserved precedence, and yet near enough to enable the conversation not only to be carried on freely, but to be of a confidential character.

The knight on his right had a bearing scarcely less dignified and haughty than that of the leader, while it was quite free from the appearance of jealousy and spite which at this moment marred the face of the other. He bore the unmistakeable stamp of that high chivalry which was, perhaps, the chief redeeming quality of the better class of Norman nobles of the age. In addition to this, however, there was an indescribable charm in the countenance; the features combining deep thoughtfulness, dignity, and determination and not the least noticeable was the clear, calm, searching grey eye which seemed to read one through and through. The tall, powerful, massive form was that of a warrior tried in many a hard-fought battle; the broad open brow, the thoughtful countenance, and the penetrating eye denoted the statesman while the whole appearance showed the presence of a character of more than ordinary firmness as well as magnanimity.

The knight on the left was of a very different stamp. Ferocity and low-cunning were the most prominent features of the face that would have been considered a type of manly beauty were it not marred by these characteristics. Depraved passions had left their traces, too, still further detracting from the attractiveness of features once handsome, and which were still more than passable when the owner was enabled, as he sometimes was, to hide these defects under the mask of gaiety and bonhomie.

It was not alone in physical appearance that the two knights riding on either side of the more youthful leader differed from each other. While the first of the two we have described paid evident deference to the ostensible leader of the party, it was the deference paid by one who would not sacrifice self-respect even to superior rank; while that of the rider on the left was evidently that of a fawning, cringing, time-server.

In every respect, indeed, the two were typical representatives of what was best and worst in Norman chivalry.

"And you say, de Langley," said the central personage, "that Abergavenny had all but fallen?"

"All but fallen, my Lord Prince," replied he who had been addressed as de Langley. "Had it not been for the timely assistance of Henry de Bohun and his companions-in-arms, my Lord Earl's kinsman, Peter de Montfort, would have a more sorry tale to tell – if, indeed, his tongue had been left him to tell it," and he finished his recital with a half guffaw.

"And what say you, my lord, to this?" asked the Prince of his companion on the right.

"I say, Sir Prince, what I have often said before, in your presence and in that of your royal father, that when the masses of freemen are un-justly deprived of their rights, the limits of forbearance will be reached, and injustice bring a too plentiful crop of troubles."

"You countenance these rebels, then, Sir Earl?" demanded the Prince, sternly.

"I said not so, Sir Prince," answered the Earl with unruffled calmness. "I said not but that it was the duty of Henry de Bohun and of all loyal knights to hasten to the assistance of my kinsman at Abergavenny in his sore distress. I hold that the outbreak having taken place it should be repressed, and with a stern hand. But, in saying this, I say also that my kinsman had no right to arouse the passions of his Welsh vassals by his oppression, and I say, too, Sir Prince, and that in good time, that it will be a part of your duty to see that the wrongs of these poor people are suitably redressed as soon as peace shall have been restored."

"It seems to me, Sir Earl, that you are presuming

beyond your warrant in teaching me my duty," was the haughty reply of the Prince.

"Not so, Sir Prince," was the quiet response. "No loyal knight exceeds his duty as an honest counsellor of the king in warning his liege lord of a threatened danger when he sees it."

"My lord Prince can in this, as in all other matters, disregard danger to his royal person. You, my lord Earl, seem more apprehensive of yours," interposed de Langley.

"No wise man ever disregards danger, though he may not fear it; and you, it seems, Sir Knight, have shown your wisdom in quitting the neighbourhood of Abergavenny in good time."

The knight coloured at this rebuke, and seemed on the point of making some angry reply, but, checked either by the stern light he saw in the Earl's face or by the continuation of the latter's speech, maintained a discreet if pointed silence. The Earl again continued:

"And a Prince, who might be deemed unworthy if he feared personal danger, may be not only pardoned, but justified in fearing danger to his royal prerogatives and supreme powers."

"Come, come, de Montfort, I have had enough of that preaching before at Winchester. I prithee let me have my holiday in Wales free from such lessons," said the prince, half jestingly, half petulantly.

At this moment their further conversation was interrupted by the rapid approach from behind them of a palfrey, whose rider had forced it on from the centre of the cavalcade, which rode some yards in the rear of the three cavaliers.

The child, for the rider who thus fearlessly approached the leaders of the band was little better than a child, was a girl of surpassing beauty. In the regular features might not only be seen traces of noble lineage, but the whole countenance bore a marked resemblance to the knight who had been addressed as Sir Earl, or de Montfort, and whose identity with the great popular leader of the closing years of Henry the Third's reign the reader has doubtless already guessed. It needed no divining power hardly indeed a second glance, to convince even a casual observer that the earl and the maiden stood in the mutual relationship of parent and child. Though the resemblance, however, was so distinct as to be unmistakable, the somewhat stern and haughty countenance of the father was in the maiden's case softened by feminine grace, and toned down into childish beauty.

"My lord earl," she said, in a clear musical voice, "I would have a word with you, with your gracious permission, Sir Prince," bowing slightly to the youthful Edward.

"Would, fair maiden, you had claimed some greater boon, that I might the better prove my devotion to your charms," was the smiling response of the prince.

The earl sat silent, a slight inclination of the head serving both as an acknowledgment of the prince's courtesy, and a command for his daughter to proceed.

"One of the men in the train, a retainer of the Lord Mortimer, says that nearby is a path which is easier to travel though somewhat more circuitous than the one we are now travelling, and that though by taking it my arrival at his lord's castle will be somewhat delayed, it is still more fitting for my poor palfrey's tread and more pleasant for her poor rider's ease."

"And you wish to take that path?" asked the earl.

"If it seemeth fit to you, my lord."

"The day hath been a hard one for thee, my child, and hath doubtless tried thy tender strength sorely.

Since we met you, Sir Prince, somewhat unexpectedly this morning, I have enjoyed your companionship and conversation to the utter forgetfulness of the child's need."

"Though you flatter me, my lord, by saying so, I take much blame to myself that I did not consider ere now that maidens have not the strength to bear such rough journeys as we have. And yet I, too, have my excuse, for the ill news de Langley brought me some time since hath driven all else from my thoughts."

"I have heard the priests tell that there was need of a scapegoat to bear the burdens of other's sins, and if it seemeth good to you, my Lord Prince, to make me such a one, I shall readily sacrifice myself, though I would do aught rather than risk the displeasure of so charming a lady," and de Langley bent to his saddle bow.

The maiden, who had smiled at the first portion of this address, turned away in ill-concealed disgust from the speaker as he gave utterance to the closing sentence, and looked enquiringly at her father.

The prince, intercepting the look, himself replied:

"You, de Montfort, had then better take your party along the easier road, while de Langley and myself, with my Lord Mortimer's men, will hasten forward and have apartments prepared in the castle for your reception."

"I thank you, my Prince, for your courtesy," replied the Earl of Leicester in warmer and friendlier accents than he had yet addressed the prince, "but methinks I told you I am under an oath not to sleep under any other roof than that of a soldier's tent or the freer canopy of heaven, until my daughter sails from Pembroke on her visit to her mother's sister in France."

"True, I had forgotten," replied Edward, while de Langley shot at him a glance full of meaning. "But that is only the greater reason why we should hasten forward

Llywelyn

and provide such accommodation as the castle may afford in the way of shelter and comfort outside its walls."

Thus it was arranged, and in another five minutes the two parties had separated, that of the Earl of Leicester taking a turn to the left, which led, by an easy descent, to a ford a mile lower down the river, while the party of Prince Edward, including his personal followers and the retainers of Roger de Mortimer, who formed for the time an additional guard of honour, descended more rapidly the steep path which led directly to the deeper ford and rougher road which lay immediately below them.

Chapter III
The King's Forest Laws

They choked her cries with wicked might,
And bound her on a palfrey white.
– COLERIDGE

Leaving de Montford's party to pursue their unchecked course, we shall follow the movements of the English prince and his band. They were not destined to cross the ford of the Ithon without interruption. Scarce had they debouched on the narrow strip of greensward which bounded the banks of the river nearest them than the jealous eye of the prince fell upon a dog crouching under one of the bushes, and gnawing a large bone.

"See what the dog hath!" he cried, addressing the nearest retainer, who forthwith, not without difficulty, and in the face of many a threatening growl from the hound whom he despoiled of his prey, drew out and held up to view the hoof and leg-bone of a deer, to which the skin still adhered, and the fresh clots of blood on which testified to its having been but recently slain.

The countenance of the prince lowered still more.

"And is it thus, varlets," demanded he, addressing Mortimer's retainers, "that my forest laws are obeyed? Do you permit every thrall who lists to slay the deer which none have a right to touch but the nobles to whom we ourselves grant the enjoyment thereof?"

These was a moment's silence, and then the leader of Mortimer's men replied,

"An' it please you, my Lord Prince, our good lord

Hywel ap Meurig strictly forbids the killing of any game whatsoever by any but his lord Sir Mortimer himself, or such as he may depute to supply his lord's table."

"That is well," replied the prince, somewhat appeased, "but in proof thereof do me forest law on the hound."

One of the men-at-arms had already seized the hound by the scruff of the neck and held him tight, notwithstanding his snarling teeth. Now, however, in response to a loud whistle from the wood, the dog became almost unmanageable, and it required the utmost exertion of the soldier's strength to hold him. Fancying, and not without cause, that in the present state of the prince's temper his own life might pay the forfeit did the dog escape, he held on to his captive with almost the tenacity of despair.

A pleasant lad from fifteen to eighteen years of age, barelegged, bareheaded, and barefooted, now appeared suddenly on the scene and, after gazing in mute surprise at the numerous company he had thus unexpectedly fallen upon, was about to turn away when his eyes fell upon the still struggling dog. In a moment his whole aspect changed. The slouching loutish gait was transformed into a bounding eager step, as, running up to the man who held the dog captive, he said in Welsh:

"What wantest thou with my dog? I tell thee let him go."

The man grinned, but without replying. At a nod from the prince, de Langley now approached. "Thy dog hath been caught gnawing the leg-bone of a freshly-killed deer," he said.

"Well," asked the lad, "and what of that?"

"By my honour, what of that?" echoed de Langley in great surprise. "What of that but that it will cost him his life!"

"Cost my dog's life?" asked the lad with an incredulous laugh.

"Aye, cost thy dog's life," was the reply.

"Not while these two eyes see the deed done, nor while these two ears are open to his whine," replied the boy sturdily. "Here, Crafanc, hi, good dog!" and he turned as though to go.

Three or four pairs of hands, however, detained him, while the dog which had all but succeeded in his frantic efforts to escape was now more firmly secured by the passing of a strong leather thong around its neck.

"Ha! Sayest thou so?" said de Langley with a scowl. "Well, 'twere a thousand pities such an honest-looking lad as thou shouldst be guilty of a falsehood which might lie heavy on thy conscience. What say you, my lord prince? Are we to let the Radnor men have the freedom which resulted in nearly costing you your royal castle of Abergavenny? Or are we to learn and take to heart the godly lesson of our father confessor, Simon de Montfort?"

The countenance of the prince, which had somewhat softened at the evident affection existing between dog and boy, hardened again at this malicious thrust, and he replied in a cold voice:

"Do as thou listest, but let not the forest laws be broken."

A fierce joy lit up de Langley's face at these words, and making a sign for one of his men to approach, he again turned to the lad, and said:

"'Twere a thousand pities, as I said, that thou shouldst burden thy conscience with a heedless lie."

"What meanest thou?" asked the lad, trying in vain to preserve a steady, unquivering voice.

"Thou said'st that the dog should not be slain while thy two eyes could see the deed, and thy two ears hear his dying whine. Neither shall they. One of each will be enough, and one of each only shalt thou keep, while I take the other."

The lad's face blanched to the hue of death when he heard these words pronounced, and his somewhat slow understanding fully grasped their morning.

Too well he knew the threat was not a vain one.

He had already seen too many instances of the fiendish torture inflicted by the Normans on his fellow countrymen to doubt for a moment that his own hour of trial had come. Summoning, therefore his greatest resolution, he said with as firm a voice as he could command,

"If such be your judgment I know it would be vain for me to appeal against it. Still, I venture to humbly crave two favours."

"Well, by my soul thou art a brave lad, too, to bear it so well. I am almost sorry for thee that I have declared my judgment, which, once declared, is ever irrevocable. However, speak thy wishes, and if I can but grant them thou shalt have them."

There was a quiver in the lad's voice as he again essayed to speak. "Grant then, first my dog's life, and take my other ear instead."

"By my troth!" cried the prince, "the lad deserves the boon. Grant it him, de Langley."

"What, and let the spoiler of my lord the king's game go unscathed?" asked Langley. "That were not the way to teach these varlets to respect their masters' property. Nevertheless, as master and dog love each other, why, in the name of the foul fiend let us make them as like as possible. Instead, therefore, of taking the dog's life, we will take from him the same toll as we demand of his master, and with one eye and one ear each the less they will be less liable to look at what belongs not to them, and to listen to the voice of the tempter, and laughing at his own wit, Langley directed his follower to prepare for executing his wishes.

"No! oh, no!" cried the lad, when he comprehended what was now proposed to be done, "The rather kill him by an honest sword's thrust, and put him out of his pain at once."

"Now I have done with thee!" cried Langley, with pretended anger. "Thou art like a fickle maid who knoweth not her own mind for two minutes together. A moment since thou didst crave for thy dog's life, and now thou entreatest me to kill him! Thou see'st I have granted thy first request; what is thy second?"

The lad fixed his gaze undauntedly upon his persecutor's face, as though reading every line thereof, and then, in an unnaturally cold and quiet voice, he said:

"I would ask thee to let me know thy full name, that, while both my ears are left me I may drink into my memory through them the name, as I do now through my eyes the features of him who can be so cruel to my dog."

Notwithstanding his natural hardness of heart and fearless spirit – the one redeeming feature in his otherwise graceless nature – Langley felt a cold shudder pass over his frame as he heard this strange request. His usually ruddy features assumed a deathly pallor, and for a moment he could not control his voice sufficiently to reply. Then, passing it off with a forced laugh, he said:

"Well, that is indeed but a small boon to grant. It is not worthy to be called a boon at all. I give thee that as a free gift, and let thee ask another favour."

"Then art thou a better man than I took thee to be, and to show that I rightly value thy kindness, I ask the additional favour of being allowed to hold my dog while thy man goes through his task on both of us. It may help Crafanc, poor fellow, and I kuow 'twill help me to bear it."

"That shall you do, then, in God's name," said Langley, "and now, executioner, do thy duty," and he signed his follower to perform his allotted task.

The dog was now handed to his master, and lay quite still in his arms, ceasing even his snarling at the enemies who surrounded them at a single word of caution from the lad.

"And now thy name?" asked the boy again.

"Ah! Yes! I had forgotten," said Langley, with a repetition of the unpleasant sensation he had first experienced when the strange request was made. "I have never yet been ashamed of my name nor afraid to own it. Know then, boy, that I am called Sir Geoffrey de Langley, an humble knight, and follower of the good lord Alan de la Zouche, to whom only, under my lord the king, do I owe allegiance."

"Sheffri de Langli," said the lad, two or three times over, as though impressing the name on his memory, and then addressing his dog repeated, "Sheffri de Langli! Crafanc! Remember that name, good dog. Sheffri de Langli."

The dog, as though understanding his master's words showed his double row of gleaming teeth, as he turned with a deep growl towards de Langley. "And now, Crafanc, lad, let us not disgrace our Welsh blood by useless whining. Down, sir, down and be silent."

The intelligent animal crouched down at his master's command, and gave but one sharp cry as the keen blade of the man-at-arms severed his left ear. He, however, looked up in his master's face with a glance that seemed as though reproaching him for permitting this to be done.

Iin five minutes' time master and dog had been

served alike,* being each deprived of an eye and an ear.

The prince's party was not, however, destined to cross the ford without further interruption. Attracted by the piteous whining of the dog over his own and his master's loss, the little maiden who had so recently rejected the escort of Meredydd ab Ednyfed rushed into the midst of the astonished party, and throwing her little arms around the dog, caressed him, not perceiving at first the cruel affliction he had suffered. In a moment however, the strange appearance of her pet struck her, and her whole aspect changed: from a timid caressing child she was transformed into a perfect little fury, and a torrent of childish abuse was launched forth upon the strangers in whom even her childish intelligence recognised the perpetrators of this deed of cruelty upon her faithful friend and companion, Crafanc.

The prince could not forbear laughing at this display of childish anger, and turning round on his horse as he prepared to leave the glade, he called out:

"Thou hadst best bring the maiden with thee, de

---

* Lest it should be thought we are over-colouring the picture, especially as regards the consent of the chivalrous Prince Edward to so barbarous and uncalled for a punishment, we extract the following from a historical work treating on this period: – "The sanction which Prince Edward gave to the cruel exactions and insults of de Langley, and his scornful and heartless behaviour during this progress (through North Wales) such as causing a casual young wayfarer to have one far torn off and one eye plucked out, convinced the oppressed people that revolt remained the only remedy for their grievous wrongs (*History of Wales*, by Jane Williams, p. 353).
In the formal complaints sent to the King from Wales through the Archbishop of Canterbury we find the lords of Ystradalun complain that a dog having been found gnawing the hoof and leg bone of a deer, it was assumed by the Norman lord that the forest laws had been broken, and a fine was forthwith imposed upon the whole district.

Langley. She will serve at least as a hostage for her own future good behaviour – and possibly for that of her one-eared friends."

"Aye, my lord prince, you speak truly, and as owing to this delay, it is probable de Montfort will have reached the castle before us, some sort of a peace offering may be necessary. We may as well make this child our excuse, and say we sought for a companion for his daughter to cross the seas. That is now the only preparation we can hope to make for him."

The prince, deigning to reply by a simple gesture only, turned to depart, while the knight, commanding one of his men to take the child before him on his saddle, prepared to follow. Roughly seized by one of the soldiers, and lifted from the ground, the poor child's anger gave way to terror, and piercing scream after scream rent the air as she vainly struggled to free herself from the iron grasp which held her. With a deep imprecation, de Langley turned to his follower, crying:

"Clap thy hand over the child's mouth, or stuff her dress into it to stop this outcry. Her cries can be heard as far as the blast of a horn, and heaven knows how many of these wild Welshmen they may bring down upon us ere we reach the shelter of the castle."

Even as he spoke, the sound of bushes being roughly thrust aside, and of hurrying steps approaching, proved that the child's cries had already attracted the attention of others than those who formed the prince's party; the Prince, ready for every emergency of war, by a few short rapid orders, so arranged his men as best to meet any possible attack.

Chapter IV
Revelations

A vow, a vow – I have a vow in Heaven!
– SHAKESPEARE

The horseman whom we left at the close of a previous chapter had been meanwhile making his way up the steep path towards the home of Ednyfed. Though the shades of night were falling as he reached what he hoped might prove to be the end of his day's journey, there was sufficient light left to enable him to perceive the nature of the habitation at which he had arrived.

Compared with what the generality of farm buildings were even then in England, the present one would have been considered a miserable dwelling. And yet the practised eye of the traveller informed him at once that it was a house of more than ordinary pretensions for a Welsh peasant's home. It was a long, low, single-storied house, the walls composed entirely of wattle work, and, like the generality of buildings in the Principality at that period, such as could, it is true, be easily destroyed by the enemy, but which could, as well, be almost as easily re-erected by the owner once he found himself again at liberty to do so.

This peculiarity was undoubtedly one of the reasons which made the frequent ravaging incursions of the English and Normans over the borders so much less injurious to the inhabitants than the retaliatory visits which the Welsh seldom failed very honestly to pay proved to the English. The demolition of a wattle house,

Llywelyn

for the re-erection of which there was always at hand a never failing supply of osiers and mud, could by no means be so seriously felt as would have been the case had the house been built of wood, or, worse still, of stone, as were the houses of the English.

The present building only differed from the generality of Welsh farmhouses in being built on a somewhat larger scale, and in the fact that it provided more accommodation for animals than was generally the case.

As it were, gathering these facts at a single glance, the traveller advanced without drawing rein until near the door of the principal entrance, where his approach was heralded by the fierce barking of two or three dogs, which were, however, immediately quieted by a gruff voice within. Thus, by the time the stranger was ready to dismount, and without the necessity of, calling, he found two or three sturdy bare-legged men awaiting him.

According to the practise of the country, be merely signified his intention of remaining overnight, knowing that by the simple laws of open-handed hospitality, it would have been deemed as unnecessary on the host's part to offer it as it was on the guest's part to ask for shelter and food, and this though neither had ever seen the other before.

Throwing, therefore, the bridle of his jaded steed to one of the waiting men, he followed the one who was evidently the master into the house. Having claimed by his action the hospitality due to a peaceful traveller, he was now obliged to show reciprocal trust in his entertainers. Therefore, before seating himself in the wide chimney-corner, where place was made for him, he unbuckled the short sword which hung at his side and suspended it to a wooden peg on the wall of the large hall-like entry. Having thus divested himself of his arms, he took the seat offered him. As we have said, there had been no demand for hospitality on the one hand, and no verbal offer of it on the other. It had been taken by the one and given by the other quite as a matter of course. The reader may perhaps be led to believe by this that the arrival of the traveller was expected, and that previous arrangements had been made for his reception. But this was not so. Host and guest were utter strangers to each other, though probably well enough acquainted with each other's names had these been disclosed. To all intents and purposes the traveller was a perfect stranger to his host and his arrival was not only not expected, it was not even anticipated. Ednyfed had only shown to this wayfarer the ordinary every-day hospitality of the Weish farmer of the period.

The stranger having seated himself, one of the buxom waiting-girls brought in a wooden bucket a quantity of cold water, which she placed together with a rough towel, before him. With a simple acknowledgment of this attention he washed, first of all, face and hands, and then after divesting himself of his riding boots and hose, his feet as well. The latter action was an indication that he intended claiming a lodging as well as a supper there.

Dining the whole of this time nothing but the most ordinary topics of conversation had been introduced, none venturing to ask the stranger whence he came nor whither he intended wending his further journey. His ablutions, however, being over, and the table laid a freer conversation was indulged in on both sides. His host would have had the guest sup alone, while host and hostess waited upon him. This, however, though he knew it to be the custom of the country, the traveller would by no means allow, refusing to partake of any food unless in the company of Ednyfed and his wife.

The three accordingly eat together. Before each was laid a flat loaf, or cake of bread called bara llech,* on a wooden tray in the centre was placed a large piece of boiled beef. Platters of any sort there were none; the cake of bread, but little thicker than stout delf ware, served the purpose for which modern luxury demands a plate. Each one took his own knife, cut his slice from the common hunk of meat, and placed it on his bara llech, the stranger using for this purpose a small dirk of peculiar and exquisite workmanship, which he drew from his bosom. We need not follow the simple, homely meal in its detail, further than to state that the traveller did excellent justice to the meal provided him, washing it down with deep draughts from the drinking-horn handed him by the serving maid.

"And do all the men of Maesyfed wear their hair so long as that of Ednyfed ap Tewdwr?" asked the stranger, after some preliminary conversation.

"Thine own cropped head belies the peaceful character thou wouldst assume," replied Ednyfed, referring to the fashion in which the traveller wore his hair – a fashion which at a later period would have gained for him the title of Roundhead.

The other laughed. "I see that Ednyfed has not forgotten the time when he wore his own hair short."

"By St. David thou art right! And much I fear me the time will soon come when it may be necessary I should crop it again."

This was in allusion to the custom of the Welsh to wear their hair short during war time, so as not to

---

* This kind of bread is still in high favour throughout the rural districts, and goes, in various parts, under the names of "bara llech," "bara llechfaen," or "bara plank."

incommode them when travelling hastily through the dense forests which then covered so large a portion of the country.

"Say you so?" asked the visitor with unmistakeable interest. "I trust the rule of my Lord Mortimer at Cefnllys is not such as to make the people of Glan Ithon aweary."

"Whether it be the Lord Mortimer himself, or Lord Mortimer's seneschal Hywel ap Meurig, false Cymro that he is, or whether it be his followers or retainers, no man's life and no woman's honour is safe among us."

The countenance of his hearer darkened.

"And yet the men of Maesyfed make no complaint?"

"Make no complaint?" said the other, fiercely. "To whom shall such complaint be made? Tell me that."

"To the Lord Mortimer himself."

"To get thrown into one of his dungeons."

"To the nearest Welsh lord, then, who would represent their case better."

"Ay! To Gwenwynwyn's father's brother's son. Methinks every Cymro knows enough of that family to be aware that little sympathy can be hoped for there unless it be a personal gain to the family of Gwenwynwyn."

"Well, then, why not enter your complaint before the King himself?"

"And thus acknowledge ourselves his subjects? As well may we rank yourselves under Gwenwynwyn's or Mortimer's banner at once."

"In good sooth thou hast an answer to everything. But it strikes me there is yet another thou mightest complain to. They tell me that the lord of Snowdon lends a ready ear to complaints against the Norman knights and their English followers."

"Unless he be more than lord of Snowdon it is but

Llywelyn

little the men of Glan Ithon will be better of him."

"What would you have him be, then?" was the next question, in a tone of voice in which an observant hearer could have noticed more anxiety than had marked the stranger's previous utterances.

"What his grandfather was before him – Prince of Wales in name and deed, one under whose leadership every Cymro could fight, be he Gogleddwr or Deheuwr,(2) one to whose standard the men of Maesyfed, as well as of Gwent, Morganwg, Dyfed, and Arfon could alike flock and under whose reign rich and poor, noble and peasant, could have equal justice." And as Ednyfed spoke the farmer seemed to disappear, and the soldier and patriot gleamed from his eyes and breathed through his words.

The traveller seemed to be strongly moved by his host's remarks, and as though aspired with his spirit, sprang to his feet, and with distended nostrils and flashing eyes held out hand to the other, crying:

"Give me thine hand; for an honest Cymro as thou art. Had I but fifty such men as thou, Cefn Llys Castle, strong though it be, should not shelter a Norman or Englishman for another week."

"And had we but such a leader as thou seemest," said Ednyfed, returning his guest's hearty hand clasp, "the fifty men could soon be found."

"Aye, for here be five of them," a strange voice behind them, and turning in surprise they saw standing in the entry a group of fresh comers, whose entrance had been unperceived by either of them in the deep mutual interest they had felt in their late conversation.

"Ha! Rhydderch! Is it thou? And hast thou at last come to believe as I do?" asked Ednyfed of the stranger who had spoken, and who appeared as the leader of the party.

"Aye, have I, indeed, and full time is it that every other man who cares for kith or kin in this oppressed country should come to feel so, too," was the reply.

The speaker was a man in the prime of life, perhaps forty years of age, of strong build, and evidently, by his dress, belonging to the class of small farmers. On either side of him stood two others, who, though some half-century, if not more, separated them from each other, evidently standing the one at least twenty-five years older, and the other the same number of years younger than the last speaker, bore such a striking resemblance to him as to mark the three at once as representing the three generations of the same family. The fourth member of the party was none other than the lad who had suffered so cruelly at the hands of Geoffrey de Langley a few hours since.

The stranger, whose conversation with Ednyfed had been thus unceremoniously interrupted, scanned the new comers attentively, and with a critical gaze. A hale smile played abroad his lips as he noticed that the old man on the right of Rhydderch leant upon a stout ashen stave to support himself, while the lad on his left could not have seen at the most more than fifteen summers.

"You have heard the remarks of my friend Ednyfed and myself," he said, "and have offered yourselves for the service under one who is apt to be a hard master. The task we would set before us is not one suited to old age, or boyhood, or to the maimed," and he looked at the old man, at the boy, and the youth in turn.

"As to my age," said the old man promptly, "though nigh seventy winters have gone over my head, I can hold my own as many a younger man. And as we Welshmen say, 'Haws cofio na dysgu,' it is easier to remember than to learn, so can a man who followed Llywelyn ap Iorwerth into many a Norman castle do something to shake the walls of Cefn Llys."

"And thou?" said the stranger, turning to the boy. "Methinks thy boyhood hath more fitting occupation than engaging in the rough sport of men."

"An' it please you sir, said the boy, looking up boldly, I am some years older tonight than I was when this morning sun dawned upon me. Then I was a simple shepherd lad, looking for a missing lamb which I feared the wolves had taken away. Now I am a man who has a sister locked up in the castle of Cefn Llys, and I shall be none the less ready to dare the Norman wolves there than I was this morning to dare our native mountain wolves in search of my father's lamb."

"A sister, said'st thou?" asked Ednyfed, but the stranger, holding up his hand, proceeded with his interrogations.

"And thou? Dost thou think that one broken head is not enough that thou must needs seek for another?"

"There be some of my belongings in the Castle I would risk much to get back," said the youth, whose bandaged head had drawn forth the stranger's last query.

"And what may they be?"

"Oh, only an eye and an ear which one who called himself Sheffri de Langli took from my poor head at sunset," was the calm reply.

The stranger started at the name and his brow lowered.

"Thou hast in truth an excellent reason. But methinks, friend Rhydderch, thou saidst you were five. I see only four of you."

The youth with the broken head laughed.

"An' ye do not wish to count my Master Rhydderch for two, which ye can well venture to do, for I'll warrant him to do more than any two until little Gwen be found, why then, here be the fifth," and whistling for his dog, he pointed to the one-eyed, one-eared Crafanc, who now came into the circle of light showing himself a fellow-sufferer with his master.

The stranger gazed with more than ordinary interest upon the new recruit, and called the dog to him. The sagacious animal, to his master's surprise, immediately went up to the stranger, and placed his muzzle confidently in his hand.

"And even brute beasts must be made to suffer," murmured the stranger to himself. "Just Heaven will, of a certainty, aid me in that I have undertaken to do." Then in a louder voice, and addressing the wounded lad, he continued, "I accept this dog as one of the required party. He is truly a noble dog, and will, I doubt not, under thy direction, acquit himself worthily."

"He is come, indeed, of a kingly race," said the old man. "Llywelyn ab Iorwerth presented me a pup fathered by his own Gelert, and Crafanc descended from that pup."

"Say you so?" cried the stranger with re-awakened interest. "Indeed it must be so, for when I mark I see he bears some of the tokens of that truly kingly race of dogs. And wilt thou part with him?" he asked eagerly.

"He is not mine to give," said the old man. "'Twas Hywel who would have him as a pup, and who alone has now the right to say yea or nay."

"And what sayest thou, my brave lad?" asked the stranger of the wounded lad, "Wilt thou part with him?"

"That were scurvy treatment, Crafanc, for thy past faithful service. Tempt me not, stranger, for could'st thou give me Crafanc's weight in silver for him, I would not part with him. I have already paid an eye and an ear for him, and, in good sooth, as we have only a pair of eyes and a pair of ears between us, 'twould be a pity to part us," replied the lad, with grim mirth.

"So be it, then," said the stranger. "It shall not be said of me that I parted two such worthy friends, much as I should wish to own the dog. But I see that you have a story to tell. There is a reason for thy bound head, and for thy master's readiness to join in an attempt upon Cefn Llys."

The lad then, upon a sign from his master, gave a brief account of the occurrences we have already described as having taken place at the Ithon ford.

"Hardly," continued he, "had they got little Gwen in the saddle, and ready to start, than your brave boy Ednyfed, young Meredydd, rushed through the bushes, and without counting the odds against him, threw himself like a mountain cat upon the man who bore little Gwen before him. His childish efforts, of course, proved un-availing, and the party crossed the ford, carrying Gwen and Meredydd with them. Crafanc and I made our way to Lluest as soon and as best we could. My master, Rhydderch, and his father, and his son thought we should have sympathy and help from Ednyfed ap Tewdwr, and here we are, five ready to dare everything to get Gwen and Meredydd outside the castle walls again."

A deep silence, only interrupted occasionally by an exclamation of amazement or anger from the listening group, consisting now of the united families of Ednyfed and Rhydderch, had prevailed during this recital.

"I swear!" cried Ednyfed, now raising his right hand to heaven, "I swear that from this hour forth the sword shall never leave my side nor day nor night while a Norman claims tribute or fealty from me. Be they accursed of God and man. Let them learn that they have men to fight with, and not alone brute beasts, tender boys, and all but suckling babes."

"And I swear," echoed Rhydderch, with equal

fervour and solemnity, "that I bind myself with Ednyfed ap Tewdwr in the oath he hath taken, and swear undying fidelity to the cause we here adopt in life and in death."

"Now, Sir Stranger, it is thy turn to swear," said Ednyfed.

"But I am not going to swear," said the other with a smile.

"Ha! A traitor!" cried Ednyfed. "The curse of my country – her children fighting against each other, or selling each other's lives for gain. But as I have sworn my oath, so also I swear that thou shalt not quit this dwelling alive until thou satisfiest me of thy truth as an honest Cymro. Thou knowest too much to be allowed now to leave us. What say you, Llywarch?"

"I say, as my old leader Llywelyn ab Iorwerth would have said, 'Death to the traitor!' and do thou but give the word it shall be my hand that shall deal the blow," and the old man glared fiercely under his shaggy brows upon the stranger, who stood immovable, and apparently unmoved, under these threats.

He looked around him as though seeking for some means of escape.

Had such been his intention, one glance would have satisfied him that it was hopeless.

The whole group had gathered around him in a circle, with dark and lowering brows. On one side stood Rhydderch, backed up by his father, Llywarch, his son Eynon, and his servant Hywel. On the other stood grim and threatening Ednyfed ap Tewdwr, supported by his stalwart son Tewdwr, destined subsequently to play a not unimportant part in the stirring scenes which followed, and two or three others. Beyond these again stood the women-folk of Ednyfed's household, showing in their determined bearing that they would have to be reckoned with in any attempt he might make to escape.

There was only one member of the whole group who seemed to confide ill the stranger's honesty. This was none other than Crafanc, who now placed himself by the stranger's side, and with bristling hair and gleaming teeth seemed to resent even his master's bearing towards the stranger.

"See the dog!" cried Hywel. "Saw you ever the like? What can it mean?"

"What," said the stranger, calmly, "but that the dog's nature or instinct hath led him to divine what the intelligence of his masters has not enabled them to understand. And now, my masters," said he, drawing himself up to his full height, and looking proudly around him, "what would you have with me?"

Before his dignified bearing the group fell back, all save Ednyfed, who, undaunted by the almost threatening gesture of the stranger, boldly replied, "We would be satisfied that thou art one who may be safely trusted with the secret which thou hast heard among us this night."

"And if I refuse?"

"Then, by the heaven above me, I swear thou shalt never leave this house alive." The muttered support of the others of the party proved that Ednyfed's boldly spoken threat was approved by all.

A smile – more of satisfaction than of derision or contempt – crossed the expressive features of the stranger.

With a quick motion he gave a single step backward so as to allow the light to fall more fully upon him, threw open his doublet, and facing fully his threatening entertainer, asked,

"And what sayest thou now?" The aged Llywarch

seized a flaring torch from the fire-place and advanced eagerly to gaze.

On the stranger's left breast, beautifully worked in green and white silk, was the figure of a dragon, the royal emblem of Wales. (3)

With a loud cry, the old man threw the torch back to its place, and falling upon his knees, seized the stranger's hand in his own, and kissed it.

The astonishment of the others was hardly less profound. As the truth gradually dawned upon them their angry glances gave place to respect mingled with affection, and a glance satisfied the cause of this excitement that those who, a few moments ago, would have taken his life without compunction, were now as ready to risk their own to save his.

"Rise, my old friend, Llywarch, rise," said Llywelyn, for the reader will by this time have guessed his identity. "Rise, faithful follower of my grandfather. Llywelyn ab Iorwerth found in thee and thine strong arms and faithful hearts. Llywelyn ap Gruffydd is indeed blessed to find thy race to welcome him in Maesyfed."

"Let me greet thee, too," said Ednyfed, advancing with deep respect, not as a stranger, "not alone as lord of Snowdon, but as what thou art now in very deed, and what all shall yet acknowledge thee to be, Llywelyn, Prince of Wales," and he sank upon one knee.

Llywelyn gave him his hand, and, lifting him up, said:

"That may come in God's own time. Now we have other work in hand."

"Hush!" cried one of the women. "Someone comes!"

The noise of hurrying feet was heard outside, and the outer door was suddenly burst open.

Chapter V
A Brave Lad

For those that fly may fight again,
Which he can never do that's slain.
– HUDIBRAS

It seemed as if fate had ordained that the boy Meredydd ab Ednyfed should, on this eventful day, be the source of continued anxiety and alarm to others. In the first instance his conversation with Gruffydd ap Gwenwynwyn, and Gwen, the little daughter of Rhydderch ap Llywarch, had startled Llywelyn in the midst of his solitary meditations. As we have seen, his unexpected appearance a short while after disconcerted even the trained soldiers of Prince Edward. And now, for the third time, his unlooked-for advent caused confusion in his father's house and among his own friends.

It was, indeed, Meredydd whose hurrying steps and sudden bursting of the unfastened door of his father's house which had so startled the party there assembled, and doing homage to their native prince.

For a moment he stood panting in the entry. His torn clothing and limbs bleeding from many a bramble scratch testified to the roughness of his path, and to the haste with which he had travelled it.

"And thou art free of the Normans once more, lad?" said his father, glancing with mingled anxiety and pride upon his younger son, whose face and manner reflected the excitement he had undergone.

"Aye, father, I managed to give the wolves the slip, and came straight as the crow flies from Cefn Llys here."

"Straight as the crow flies, boy?" asked his brother Tewdwr. "That would mean down Craig Ithon and through Pwll Du. The first would require a sure foot and a clear eye by daylight and the latter would be deep enough to bury the tallest turret of Cefn Llys Castle out of sight in its dark waters."

"True," replied the boy with a laugh, "and yet that is the way I came. You will find a good piece of my cloak – good homespun though it be – hanging on the thorn bush halfway up Craig Ithon which saved me when I slipped and fell, and as to Pwll Du, why, here is a sample of its waters," and he shook himself like a snaggy dog sprinkling the floor with the water which weighted his garments.

"That was bravely done, lad," said Llywelyn, advancing and putting his hand on the boy's shoulder. "But thou must remember that over-recklessness is as much to be blamed as over-caution."

"'Twas no time to think of caution nor to choose my road with a score of howling Norman wolves at my heels," said the boy bluntly, and then, laughing again, he added, "They think my bones lie broken at the foot of Craig Ithon, or in Pwll Du, and that the carrion crow or the fishes will have a good feast in the morn, for they were near enough to see me stumble and fall in coming down the cliff, though they saw not that I hung for a time in the thorn bush, held up by the strength of the good cloth of my cloak."

"I have only to say again 'twas bravely done lad, and that thou hast the making of a man in thee. Wales needs such as thou art, and had I but five thousand such men as thou wilt be ten years hence, the Normans and English would have but a sorry time of it in wild Wales. But now, tell us plainly and clearly all that befell thee after crossing the ford, and describe what thou didst see or discover."

"If that can help to get little Gwen back again, I shall to my tale right readily, though in good sooth I would far rather be showing the way up Cefn Llys hill to those who would give these wolves the lesson they need than be wagging my tongue like a girl here."

"Nevertheless, it is necessary we should know how all things are," said Llywelyn, "so to thy tale. Be brief and clear."

The lad then related all that had occurred to him since being taken prisoner. It seemed that the cavalcade had wearily made its way up from the banks of the Ithon, in the direction of the castle, Meredydd and Gwen being securely held by those to whose care they had been entrusted. Having arrived near the castle, they found an encampment being hastily made to accommodate a strange noble and his retainer, who had only just arrived before them. Here the prince, after a short conversation with the knight who appeared to be in command of the strangers, and who seemed to be displeased at the prince's recital, commanded little Gwen's captor to hand her over to the care of a maiden who stood near, conversing with the knight and the prince. The two girls having disappeared inside a tent which had been hastily raised, the prince and his party approached the drawbridge to enter the castle. Here Meredydd saw that his only chance of escape lay. Once within the castle walls, freedom would be doubly difficulty of attainment. Slipping, therefore, suddenly from the arms of the man who held him and whose vigilance, when he found himself about to enter the castle, had relaxed, Meredydd dived under the horse's belly, and, before the soldiers had time to recover from their surprise, was clear of them and, running swift as a hare and straight as the flight of an arrow for the brink of Craig Ithon, where alone he would be safe from pursuit. Throwing himself down its steep path, be soon stumbled and fell, and, as he had already said, was only saved from a terrible death by the accidental catching of his cloak in a thorn bush, the stones which he had disturbed by stumbling – rolling with a clatter down the precipice – materially assisted in deceiving his pursuers, who immediately returned, well satisfied that the daring lad had met with his death. Having become satisfied that they had indeed left, Meredydd, by some exertion, freed himself from the captivity of the friendly bush, and continued his course, swimming the deep and dangerous Pwll Du, which washed the base of Craig Ithon, and which was the only possible outlet from the critical position in which his daring had placed him.

"And so," said be in concluding, "here I am, and I tell thee, Rhydderch, that thou hast twice the chance of recovering Gwen tonight, when she is outside the walls of Cefn Llys, than thou canst hope to have again when she is shut off from thee by bolt and bar and solid masonry."

"One moment," said Llywelyn. "Canst thou describe the knight in whose charge the child was left.?"

"No, that I cannot do. I only noticed that he was tall and strongly made, and as haughty as any noble among the Normans. I noticed that the maiden at his side was surpassing fair."

A slight increase of colour suffused the swarthy cheek of the prince, as he asked:

"And her name? Didst thou hear her called by any name?"

"If I mistake not, the knight called her Elen," replied the boy. "But what have names to do with us now? It is little Gwen's release we want, and not Norman nobles' names."

"Answer my questions," said Llywelyn sternly, in a voice which made Meredydd start and flush. "Didst thou hear the knight himself called by any name?"

A warning glance from his father assured the lad that his questioner was not to be trifled with, and he replied somewhat sullenly,

"Yes. I heard the prince address him by some Norman name or other."

"And dost thou not remember what?"

"No. My Welsh tongue is not fashioned for their Norman names."

"But try to remember. Did the name remind thee of anything?"

The lad's eyes sparkled. "Yes," he said eagerly, "it struck me at the time. Something about – yes, something about a mountain and a castle but, now I come to think, was it a castle or a river? It was one of the two, I well remember, because it struck me all the time as connected with the place, and you know there is a mountain and a castle and a river at Cefn Llys."

"Was it de Mont-ford?" asked Llywelyn.

"That was the name! I will swear to it!" cried Meredydd, eagerly.

"Good," said the prince with what sounded like a sigh of relief. Then, after a moment's deep thought, he turned to Rhydderch, saying:

"A word with thee, friend, apart," and leading him to the corner of the room, he conversed eagerly with him for a few moments, apparently endeavouring to persuade Rhydderch to adopt or consent to some proposed course.

"And you promise?" asked Rhydderch.

"I give thee my word as a prince that, unless I return ere dawn with thy child, she shall be cared for as I have said."

"So be it, then," said the other, with an effort, and the two rejoined the group which had, with native courtesy, withdrawn to, the part of the room furthest from that where the two men had been conversing.

"Ednyfed," said the prince, "who is there here that will lead me up to the castle?"

"Lead you, my lord, to Cefn Llys Castle, to the hands of your enemies?" cried Edynfed in surprise. "No one, thanks be God!"

"It must be done, Ednyfed, and at once. I run no risk, and the work I have to do must be done this night. When the dawn breaks in the morning 'twill be too late."

"Well, an' that be so, I will e'en lead you myself," said the farmer.

"Nay, father, I am younger and more nimble than thou art; I will go," said Tewdwr, the eldest son.

"I think, as it seems we are going to where my sister is confined, that it becomes me better," interposed Eynon ap Rhydderch.

"Nay, Eynon, lad," protested Hywel. "Thou knowest Crafanc and I have an eye and an ear each at the castle, and it is fitting we should see them ourselves," and the youth tried to laugh.

Llywelyn smiled at these various offers, and said, turning to Meredydd, "I think I must choose my own guide, and if thou art willing, brave lad, thou shalt be my guide this night to Cefn Llys Castle."

The lad responded eagerly:

"And shall we see Gwen?"

"Thou shalt see her, and speak with her," was the smiling reply. "And the sooner we go, the better."

"But, my lord," again protested Ednyfed, "'twere surely better that someone who can wield a sword should accompany you."

"It is not the service of a strong arm and sure sword

that is needed tonight," was the calm reply. "Collect as many them as you can by to-morrow night, when I shall need them. Now, all I require is a practised eye and a sure foot to leave me to the encampment of Simon de Montfort at Cefn Llys. Meredydd knows the exact position, and has proved that he fears nothing."

The lad's face glowed with pleasure at this praise.

"Before I go," said the Prince, turning again to a Ednyfed, "I should say, hasten thou and thy friends to summon such trusty aid as you may safely depend on. Get me but fifty strong men and bold ready at the ford an hour before midnight tomorrow, and I promise you the next morning's sun shall see a different sight on Cefn Llys from that his rays will show tomorrow."

"Not fifty, but a hundred, I trust," said Ednyfed.

"'Tis well," replied Llywelyn. "And thou, Rhydderch, be easy in thy mind. What I have promised I will do. Come, Meredydd, time flies, and we must go."

And having resumed the arms he had placed to hang in the entry on his arrival at Ednyfed's house, accompanied by Meredydd, Llywelyn started on a mission full of present danger, and pregnant of future events.

Chapter VI
The Alliance

Sweetheart, good bye! The fluttering sail
Is spread to waft thee far from me:
And soon before the fav'ring gale
Thy ship shall bound upon the sea.
Perchance all desolate and forlorn
These eyes shall miss thee many a year,
But unforgotten every charm –
Though lost to sight, to memory dear.
– RUTHVEN JENKYNS

Under Meredydd's experienced guidance – the lad knowing every foot of the way, and apparently as able to keep his course by night as by day – Llywelyn soon found himself within sound, and, though the night was dark, within sight of the Earl of Leicester's encampment. Sound and sight warned him at the same moment, for, as the echo of the patrol or sentry's steady tramp fell upon his practised ear, his watchful eye caught the white outlines of the tents showing vaguely against the darker background of the frowning castle walls behind them

"Now," said Meredydd, "I have performed my part of the engagement. There be the tents."

"Right, boy, and I suppose thou would now seek permission to return. Well, so be it. I shall doubtless find my way back alone."

"No, no!" was the eager reply. "I go not back till I see and speak to little Gwen."

"True it is I had promised thee, but I must admit the

promise was not now present in my memory. But art thou not afraid of venturing among these Norman wolves, as thou art fond of calling them?"

"Methinks," was the ready reply, "if there be no danger for you, my lord, who wear a sword at your side, certainly a harmless lad like me, who carries naught but this shepherd's staff, will not be interfered with. I have noticed that when one dog show his teeth, another snarls, and your sword, good sir, is much more likely to arouse the spirit of war among these men than my defenceless appearance. But how mean you to gain entry? They watch and guard those tents as though they contained a royal treasure."

"And so do they, boy. A royal treasure, indeed, any king might be proud to possess. But let us on. An' I mistake not, I have a charm wherewith to make our entrance possible. Follow me, and speak not a word as thou valuest thy life."

Advancing boldly, like a man having nothing to fear, he soon attracted the attention of the sentry who sternly bade him stop. A man came forward to meet him and demanded his business.

"My business is with thy master, the good Earl of Gloucester, the friend and defender of the people of England," was the reply. "I would have speech with him."

"So," replied the man with a laugh, "many a crying babe would have the moon when he sees it shine in the sky. And methinks he has as much chance of getting it as thou hast of gaining speech this night with my master, seeing he has retired to his tent."

"Take to him this guerdon," was the rejoinder, and taking a ring from his finger the prince handed it to the man, adding, "and tell him that he who wore it craves audience of him who gave it."

"And like enough have my trouble for my pains, and a saucy scolding from my lord's page," said the man.

"Better that than a scored back, which I promise thee thy master will direct thou shalt have as soon as he finds thou hast failed to carry him the ring with all due speed," replied Llywelyn, sternly. "I parley not further with thee. Take thou the ring as I direct thee, or I find other, and for thee less pleasant, means of having audience with thy lord."

There was that in the tone of these words which assured the man that here he had no ordinary man to deal with, and so, with a muttered remonstrance, he called another to remain with the stranger while he went, with some misgivings, to deliver the message with which he was charged.

He had been absent but a very short time, when he returned under altered mien, and, with a low obeisance, begged the Prince to follow him to his lord's presence. Accompanied, therefore, by Meredydd, who took good care to remain in close proximity to his father's guest, Llywelyn followed the soldier, and soon found himself at entrance to the principal tent.

Chapter VII
The Night Attack

They that fight for freedom undertake
The noblest cause mankind can have at stake:
Religion, virtue, truth, whate'er we call
A blessing, freedom is the badge of all.
  – COWPER

It wanted an hour of midnight. Strange sounds, though hushed, mingled with the rush and roar of the Ithon. The small glade near the ford, which had been the scene of de Langley's cruelty some thirty hours previously, was now almost filled by a dark mass of moving forms. The stealthy movement, the evident effort to make no unnecessary noise, proved that it was the wish of those gathered at the spot not to betray their presence to any watchful ears, or casual passer-by; while the occasional tinkle of metal, and now and again a faint ray of starlight reflected from a burnished surface here and there in the group, denoted the presence of armed men among them.

Suddenly a voice was heard saying, "He comes!"

A dead silence, broken only by the sound of the rushing river and the rustle of the wind in the bushes around, fell upon the group, as a small party of half-a-dozen men might be faintly seen advancing towards the centre of the glade.

A low murmur of welcome greeted them as they paused, and the larger body, who had occupied the glade before their arrival, now approached and closed around the small party of newcomers.

"My friends," said Ednyfed ap Tewdwr, in a clear, but low voice, "he whom I promised should lead you tonight is here. I know the welcome your hearts would give him, and that it would be a pleasure for all to shout that welcome aloud. Now, however, I have to ask you to keep that welcome unspoken in your hearts. It behoves us to keep our presence a secret, that we may have a better chance of taking our enemies unawares."

A low, hoarse murmur of approval was the only response. Then spoke another voice, whose tones made every heart present bound with long-unawakened feelings. Like Ednyfed, he spoke the home language of the people, though with an occasional difference of accent which denoted him to be more accustomed to. the vernacular of North than South Wales.

"Fellow countrymen," said he, "I would gladly talk to you for an hour, but we have met together to act and not to speak. My good friend Ednyfed just now asked you to keep your welcome for me unspoken in your hearts. I say no. Do not keep it unspoken in your hearts. Give free vent to it – but in deeds, and not in words. Every Norman and Saxon of the garrison who falls beneath a Welshman's blow this night will be a welcome for me warmer than your words. Every door you force open in our oppressor's stronghold above us will be a shout more acceptable to the ears of my soul than any cry of welcome could possibly be to my bodily ears. Show, then, your welcome in deeds this night. I had said that if Ednyfed found me but fifty men like himself, this eagle's nest from which has swooped down so often the destroyer of Welsh homes should no longer shelter the oppressor. I am told there are twice that number present now. That proves to me that the men of Maesyfed are twice as patriotic as I thought them, and makes our task doubly easy. We must remember, however, that it is by united and concerted and determined action only we can hope to prevail. Let each man, therefore, obey the orders given him by your self-elected leaders. Let each arm raised to strike be nerved by the thought that it strikes for freedom; that it revenges past wrongs, insults, and injuries. You know what you have suffered here: our oppressors take care to keep us well minded of this by renewing their deeds from time to time. Think tonight you are paying old debts for the time gone by, and securing freedom from similar wrongs in the future. Remember, too, that you strike for more than the people of Glan Ithon − you strike for the whole of Wales. You aim at securing freedom for the whole nation to which you belong. Remember, therefore, the time when Welshmen ruled and held the whole country. Remember what these Saxons and Normans have done for you and yours. And remember, too, that it rests with you, that it depends upon the blows you strike tonight whether our country is to remain any longer trodden under foot, or is to claim and hold its own once more."

Had there been sufficient light to see the faces of the listening group, the speaker would have found in each countenance a ready response. The set teeth, the lowering brow, the flashing eye, the nervous grasp of sword hilt, or axe, or fork, all testified to the workings of the heart within in thorough sympathy with the speaker. After a slight pause he resumed:

"Two things are necessary to enable us to recognise friend from foe. The ear and the eye should each be able to serve us. Has every man been supplied with the white badge on the left arm?"

"Yes, all have it," said Rhydderch ap Llywarch.

"Good. So much for the eye. Now for the ear. We must have a watchword, known to us but not to our enemies. Our word is 'Rhyddid'!" [*Freedom*]

A shout was with difficulty suppressed.

"Have all things been provided?"

"All," responded Tewdwr ab Ednyfed.

"Ladders for scaling the walls?"

"Six are ready," answered Tewdwr.

"The book there to secure, sharp and strong?"

"That will I answer for," said a hoarse voice from the front rank. "Never call me Smith again if one of them fails. My own hand forged them, and rang as merry a tune in doing so as my good old pledge hopes to do on many a Norman headpiece for an anvil this night!" and Siôn y Gof held out at the full length of his brawny arm a ponderous hammer, from which no headpiece, however well forged, would welcome a second blow.

"Good," briefly responded the leader. "And the faggots for the moat?"

"Fifty men have them in charge, while twenty others have planks to suit."

"That is well. It will now be our fault if tomorrow's sun should see a Norman banner wave above Cefn Llys. The nearer we approach the castle, the more wary must we be. Who leads the way up the path?

"Tewdwr ab Ednyfed."

"Good. Let each man try to keep the one before him in view, stop when he stops, and move when he moves. Now, Tewdwr, lead the way."

In deep silence the party left the glade, crossed the ford, and began mounting the steep hillside, each man carrying, in addition to his arms, some allotted portion of the materials provided for storming the castle.

More than two-thirds the distance had been covered and increased caution had become necessary, when Tewdwr suddenly paused. Turning to the Prince, who came next to him, he said:

"I fear me we are watched."

"What makes thee think so?"

"I have fancied more than once since we crossed the ford that I have seen some dark figure on the path before me, and just now I am certain I saw it clearly between me and that white stone to our left. Yes! There it is again!"

The prince looked in the direction indicated, and clearly saw some dark body intervene between them and the white stone Tewdwr had pointed out.

"He hath missed our following footstep, and hath returned to see where we are," said Tewdwr.

"That were folly if he be an enemy," said Llywelyn. "He would naturally hasten to inform the castle of our approach."

"Aye, unless that hath already been done, and a surprise awaiteth us. However, the matter shall soon be decided. You will remain here. Eynon, pass the word back for each man to lay his burden down and be ready to take to his arms in case of need."

The whole party as it had been previously arrayed had halted when the leaders stopped, and the word was now quickly passed. Tewdwr then threw himself on the ground, and by a silent and rapid movement managed to reach the stone from a different direction to that from which a watcher would naturally have expected him. Arrived here, he cautiously raised himself sufficiently to enable him to see any object which might be on the path between him and his friends. Nothing, however, was to be seen!

Tewdwr, brave though he was physical, was deeply imbued with the superstitious ideas native to the country, and now felt a cold, creeping sensation pervading his frame as the thought forced itself into his mind that he had cone thus alone to encounter a disembodied spirit.

A deep sigh near him, and his own name uttered in a hushed voice close to his ear, completed his discomfiture, and he was about to flee precipitately, when a hand laid upon his arm convinced him that he had something more substantial to deal with than the aerial being he had feared. This conviction brought back to him the physical courage which had fast been oozing out under the influence of a supposed unnatural presence.

Knowing that he had flesh and blood to contend with, he felt himself fully able to cope with it, whatever the odds against him. Turning, therefore, he saw at his side, dim and indistinct, but none the less unmistakable, a human form. Quick as thought his left hand grasped the stranger by the throat, while his right flashed his dagger out, and in a low, stern voice he said:

"Utter but a cry and it will be thy last!"

The prisoner made no effort to escape, but loosening somewhat the Welshman's hold upon his throat, he said:

"Tewdwr! Whom takest thou me to be?"

The voice was familiar and unmistakeable.

"Meredydd!" he exclaimed, almost forgetting his caution in his surprise.

"Aye, Meredydd, of course," replied the lad.

"And what brings thee hither? This is no place for thee. It is no child's play we are about to engage in. Get thee gone to thy hope and thy bed, and that as quickly as thou mayest."

"But, Tewdwr, listen!"

"Not a word! Get thee gone, I say! Thou presuming to come here among fighting men, and risking our discomfiture and defeat by thy childish folly. Get thee home, I say."

"Nay, but Tewdwr, indeed, listen. A thought struck me –"

"Unless thou takest thyself off something more serious than a thought shall strike thee," said his brother, raising his arm threateningly.

"Nay," said another voice, "let the lad say what he hath to say. It may be important."

It was Llywelyn, who, having seen the two figures between him and the stone, had approached unperceived during this parley.

"Speak, then, and delay us not," said Tewdwr somewhat ungraciously.

"The thought that struck me was this: I minded me that there is a small postern in the outer wall of the castle, opening on to a small footpath which bounds the moat, and which is used when there is no occasion for traversing the main entrance."

"And what of that?" said his brother. "A small door can be the better guarded by half-a-dozen than the large gates by a score."

"True, if it be guarded. What I thought was this: If one of us could get inside the walls un-perceived, he might have the chance of opening this postern for our friends' easy entrance."

"As well might't thou say, 'If one of us could fly over the castle wall,' for to get in un-perceived is as easy as flying."

"Nay, but listen. Thou knowest, Tewdwr, that the walls hanging over the Caig Ithon are unguarded, as no assault is likely ever to be made there. A dozen yards or less from this end of Craig Ithon the rock and wall become one, and one might manage to climb over. There be some bushes which might help."

Llywelyn turned to Tewdwr, asking, "Is the thing

practicable?"

"The risk would mean almost certain death by daylight, much more in the darkness," replied the youth. Still, the value of the plan Meredydd speaks of is so great that I think even this risk might be justified. In any case it need not mean the loss of more than one life. Thou hast done well in telling us of it, Meredydd. Now get thee gone."

"But who will make the trial, Tewdwr?" asked the lad.

"Who? Who but myself? I am as good a cragsman as any in Glyn Ithon, and if any man can do I can."

"Nay, but, Tewdwr, do let me try," urged the bold boy.

"Art thou mad?" asked his brother.

"No, but thou knowest I am as sure of foot and eye and lighter of body than thou. Last night I got safely down Craig Ithon in the darkness, which few would care to try in the light of day. And more than that, I am smaller than thou, and less likely to be seen by those within the castle."

The elder brother was silent. The younger, falling on his knee before the Prine, again pleaded:

"Oh, my lord, do let me do this this! I am too young and too weak to be of any use in the fighting. Even if I fall, in this thou wilt not have lost a man, while, if Tewdwr fell, the best fighter in thy troop would be lost to thee."

The agitation of the Prince was evident even in the obscurity of the night. He paused a moment before replying, in order to recover his composure. His voice even then betrayed the depth to which his feelings had been stirred.

"My brave boy," he said, "though the God who knoweth all things knoweth that I would far rather run the risk myself than endanger thy tender limbs, yet I see that thou hast a chance where others might fail. A tuft of grass which under thy brother's foot would give way may support thee; a twig by which thy light body may be held would snap in his grasp or mine. Of thy courage and daring, and of thy caution even beyond thy years, I already know; and so, subject to thy father's consent, thou shalt make the attempt. And may the angels guard thee!"

The three now returned to their friends. A short council of the leaders was held, and the new proposal discussed. The very boldness of the project approved it to these hardy mountaineers, and though at first some objection was made to entrusting so important and dangerous a duty to a child, the representations of the Prince and Tewdwr carried conviction that the lad would after all run less risk than any man in their small force. Ednyfed's consent was readily given, and after a further discussion for the perfection of the plan of assault under these changed conditions, the whole party again moved warily forward. Arrangements had, of course, to be made to meet the contingent possibility of Meredydd's brave attempt proving a failure, either through his falling over the precipice or by his being seen and prevented from fulfilling his self-appointed task.

So wary was the approach of the attacking party, and so secure did the garrison deem themselves, that the Welshmen crossed safely over the moat, and sheltered themselves under the castle walls, without a sign having been given that the garrison was aware of their presence.

Gathered together at the poster, anxiously waiting for Meredydd's services, were Llywelyn himself and the leaders, including Ednyfed, Rhydderch, and Tewdwr.

Suddenly the tramp of a heavy footstep was heard

approaching in the direction of the door inside the walls. Then it as suddenly paused, turned, and hastily returned the way it had come. Bolts were heard moving in their rusty sockets and the watching party, in momentary expectation of seeing the door opening grasped their arms ready to rush forward. The footstep first heard was now again heard approaching, but this time at a run, and a hoarse voice crying:

"Ho! There! Who art thou, and what art thou doing?"

Then the sounds of a struggle within, and Meredydd's boyish voice crying:

"Force it now, Tewdwr; there is only one bolt left!"

Meredydd, by a combination of luck, agility, and daring, had indeed gained entrance unperceived. Hastening towards the postern he heard the sounds of the approaching footsteps of an armed man. There being no place to afford him concealment if the knight who was approaching should once come near enough to him, Meredydd's ready wit found a means of turning the man's attention elsewhere. Seizing a loose pebble he had felt under his foot, he threw it so as to descend with a clatter upon the pavement behind the approaching knight. This unusual sound thus in the dead of night caused the stranger to pause, and finally to return the way he came, to investigate.

No sooner was the knight's back turned than Meredydd hastened to the postern and began hastily to withdraw the rusty bolts. Many of these were heavy and stiff from infrequent use, so that it required the utmost exertion of his childish strength to move them. His laborious task was not completed when, to his dismay, he heard steps returning in his direction. With trembling eagerness he hastened to remove the remaining bolts which made the postern an impassable barrier to his friends outside.

The noise he necessarily made in doing this caught the now suspicious ears of the knight, who, hastening forward at a run, shouted out:

"Ho! There! Who art thou, and what art thou doing?"

Meredydd, who was in the act of raising a ponderous bar which now formed the chief obstacle to the opening of the door by those outside, vouchsafed no reply.

The knight leaped towards him seizing him roughly. To the lad's glad surprise, the bar fell clear of its socket, leaving now only one slight bolt to hold the door. He cried out with all the might of his childish voice:

"Force it now, Tewdwr! There is only one bolt left!"

The knight seeded to grasp at once the situation and the terrible predicament in which the garrison had thus unexpectedly been placed, and throwing the lad from him with such force as hurled him against the wall, where he fell a huddled, insensible mass, leaped towards the postern to replace the bolts and bars, shouting in stentorian tones:

"Ho there! To the walls! The Welshmen are on us! A Mortimer! A Mortimer! To the walls!"

Chapter VIII
The Fall of Cefn Llys

They razed the castle to the ground.
It thus became the thing ye know
A ruin fair in sunset glow
A ruin fair as may be found.
– "DRYSLWYN CASTLE,"
JOHN JERVIS BERESFORD

There was a simultaneous rush for the postern from within and without. Within, the knight rushed to replace the protecting bars on which now practically rested the safety of the castle. Without, Llywelyn and his immediate followers rushed in a body against it to force open the only remaining bolt.

The bolt which now alone held the postern against the attacking party was near the top of the door, and the rush of the Welshmen showed the weakness of this frail defence, for the lower portion of the door was forced inwards some two inches. So tough, however, was the bolt, and so firmly fixed in its solid socket, that the united force of the half dozen leaders was insufficient to force it, while on the other hand the utmost efforts of the knight to replace any of the other bolts were equally unavailing. Still, the advantage lay evidently with the defender, for could the door be but held closed long enough to enable the garrison to turn out, most of the advantage gained by the surprise of this important post would be lost, inasmuch as a few determined men could defend the narrow entrance against a host.

It was, indeed, a critical moment.

"Try the ladders!" cried Llywelyn, and a dozen ready hands prepared to endeavour to fix them to the wall towering above them.

"I think I have the key that fits that lock!" cried a deep voice, and the sturdy smith, Siôn y Gof, advanced to the postern, bearing his ponderous hammer.

The knight within had not ceased his warning, and the flashing lights within, the clank of arms, and the hasty tread of hurrying footsteps all told the tale that his efforts to rouse the garrison had proved successful.

"Put the end of a stick from that faggot between the door and the post, Tewdwr," said Siôn. "It will keep the lower part open while I fix my master key to the other.

Tewdwr, understanding the smiths intention, placed a piece of wood from the nearest faggot to prevent the lower part of the door again closing, and thus rendering it impossible for those within to replace the bolts and bars which Meredydd's self-sacrifice had removed.

"Now clear all!" cried Siôn. "This is Llywelyn's welcome!"

The others stepped away, leaving the smith alone facing the postern. Rapidly his practised eye fixed the position of the only remaining obstruction to the opening of the door. Then, swinging the sledge with professional skill, he brought it down with terrific force upon the very spot behind which lay the bolt.

No second blow was needed. Tough though the iron bolt was, and well though it was secured, it offered but a comparatively feeble obstruction to this swinging blow delivered with all the nervous force of the smith's brawny arms. With a rattling clatter its fastenings fell on the pavement inside, and the door was now only held by the strength of one single man against a dozen.

The knight no sooner saw the bolt flying than he

placed his back against the door and held on with all his strength. The united rush of the attacking party, however, was now irresistible, and the door was immediately forced open, throwing the knight forward on his face, while the whole party of Welshmen rushed in, led by Llywelyn himself. The knight was about to raise himself when Llywelyn placed his foot upon him, saying:

"Yield thee, Sir Knight, ransom or no ransom! Thy word at once! I have no time to parley."

"I yield me, then," was the sulky answer.

The Prince, handing the discomfited knight over to the care of some of his followers, gave a few rapid orders, which were as rapidly put in execution, and soon the sounds of strife echoed throughout the castle. The impetuous rush of the Welshmen carried all before it. The garrison, for the most part aroused from their slumbers came unarmed, or only partially armed, and offered but a feeble resistance. Neither was there any concerted defence, all looking in vain for orders from the governor, who – perhaps fortunately for himself – had been the first made prisoner, he being, in fact, the knight whose unaided efforts at the postern had been so well-nigh successful.

Wherever a closed door met the rush of the storming party, there a blow from the smith's hammer gave a fresh "Welcome to Llewellyn!" as Siôn facetiously said, in reference to the Prince's remark in the early part of the night.

We need not linger longer over the details. Sufficient to say that in a short space the whole of the castle was in Llewellyn's hands, and the inmates, garrison, and household either slain or captive.

The prisoners were mustered together in the main hall by break of day. A youth, with bandaged head,

Llywelyn

followed by a strange-looking wolf-hound of ferocious appearance, walked among the prisoners, scanning every face eagerly, but with an appearance of deepening disappointment as he approached the end of his evidently futile search.

"He is not here, Crafanc!" he muttered between his set teeth. "We must search elsewhere. Mayhap he is already slain," and Hywel, the one-eyed and one-eared servant lad, followed by his similarly disfigured four-footed ally, went out to continue among the dead and wounded their vengeful quest for Sir Geoffrey de Langley.

"Hath anyone seen Meredydd?" asked Ednyfed, as the leaders of the party congregated in the main hall to determine their own future action and the fate of their prisoners. No one, however, had seen the boy. All had been too busily engaged since their entrance through the postern to think of aught but gaining full possession of the castle.

At this moment the governor, Hywel ap Meurig, accompanied by his wife and children, entered under the escort of a dozen of Llywelyn's followers.

"I think I have little need to ask thee for the keys of the castle," said Llywelyn grimly. "My sturdy friend, Siôn y Gof, hath all too well used his great master-key."

"I have to submit me to the fate of war, Sir Knight, for such I take thee to be, though thou art not armoured. May I ask who is my vanquisher?"

"*Needest* thou ask, false Welshman?" asked the Prince sternly. "Doth the shepherd's dog, who, false to his trust, consorts with the wolf in worrying the flock, ask his master when he seeth him who is he?"

The governor, now for the first time recognising the Prince, turned pale as death, and his limbs shook under him. His wife and children, in tears, regarded his agitation in terror.

At this moment Hywel the One-Eyed, as he was already dubbed, re-appeared on the scene, bearing in his arms the limp body of poor Meredydd, whom he had found lying where he had fallen, hurled by the governor's mighty arm.

"Here," said the youth, "here be another of the fruits of Welsh traitors conspiring with Norman tyrants."

Ednyfed rushed forward.

"My boy! My brave Meredydd! Light of my eye, and joy of my life! And art thou the first to be sacrificed?" and the tender-hearted father, whose sword had gleamed oftenest when the fight had raged fiercest, and even now dripped gore, leant over the pale body of his boy, and the tears welling up from the big manly heart within rained down his rugged cheeks, and dripped from his beard on the unconscious form of the brave but unfortunate boy.

"Oh! Father! It was I that did it!" cried Tewdwr in anguish, bending with his father over his brother's body.

"Thou didst it? What meanest thou?" asked Ednyfed, in dismay.

"I did it, inasmuch as I let him climb the rock and scale the wall to open the postern for us. It was my place, and he took it, and was killed!"

"Aye, but how! And by whom?" asked the one-eyed Hywel significantly. "Methinks a Welsh youth of thy nerve hath somewhat else to think of and to do for thy brother's memory than this."

Tewdwr seemed as though awakened from a trance. "Ha!" said he, after drawing a deep breath. "Right, Hywel, right! 'Twas at the postern thou didst find him?"

The other nodded.

"Ay! 'Twas there we heard the struggle. And none could have done the dastard deed save the knight we found there. Where is he?" and the youth gazed wildly around.

His glance fell upon the now quaking form of the governor. "Aye, craven hound! 'Twas thou!" cried the youth, now beside himself with grief and rage. "But thou shalt know what it is to murder children. See!" and leaping forward he seized a child, a flaxen-haired boy of eight or ten years, who stood proud, but trembling, at his father's side. Lifting his sword, which had already been deeply dyed, he made as though to cleave the boy's head. Sir Hywel ap Meurig's groan and his wife's heartrending shriek roused Llywelyn, whose gaze, fixed upon the inanimate form of his whilom boy guide, had made him so pre-occupied as to be practically unaware of what his follower was doing. Darting forward, he seized Tewdwr's descending arm in time.

"Would'st thou murder the child in cold blood?" be asked sternly.

"What did his father to my father's child?" asked the youth sullenly.

"Killed him doubtless to save the castle, when the lad was doing a man's work," said the Prince. "Sir Hywel ap Meurig hath many a deed to repent of, but he cannot be blamed that thy brother was the first to suffer in our attack upon the castle. I, thou, thy father would have done the like in like case. Loosen thy hold on the child."

The boy, who had stood, trembling, it is true, but boldly gazing in his captor's face, retreated slowly and proudly to his father's side as soon as he found himself once more free.

"Well, there! I have let the child free. 'Tis true he could not help what happened. But, my lord, I pray thee let my thirsty sword drink this craven traitor's blood. I do not mean to slay him in cold blood. Let him have his sword, and I mine, and here, in thy presence, let us fight it out, and God will teach my sword to avenge my brother's death."

"Tewdwr!" said his father. "This is unseemly on thy part. Be a man. 'Tis but the fate of war. Sooner or later thy brother would have fallen. Look at him."

The youth turned and looked. Was it fancy on his part, or was the boy's cheek indeed less pale than it had been? Was that a trembling of the eyelid, or was it only a passing flicker of light upon the countenance?

Tewdwr knelt; down and gazed and listened breathlessly. Then rising to his feet he said:

"He lives! Thank heaven, he lives!"

The words were no sooner uttered than the governor's wife approached, and with motherly tenderness examined the boy.

"I have some leech knowledge," said she. "Let me see what state he is in."

With rapid, skilful, and tender hands she felt him in every part, first laying her ear, then her hand, lightly on his heart. Then she looked up. "The boy lives and will live," she said. "'Tis but a broken arm and a stunned head, with a night in the cold mountain air to make the harm worse. See, the warmth of the room is already bringing the blood back to his face. In an hour he will be fit to be borne hence, but I will first set his poor broken arm, and then give him a good draught of a wonderful cordial of mine own make, if your rough followers, sir knight, have not broken my phials," she added with a smile, glancing at Llywelyn.

The arm was quickly and deftly set and bound, the wounded lad showing his consciousness by a groan of pain as the bone was set in its place. By the time she had finished her work of mercy Meredydd had opened his eyes, and gazed around in wonder.

Llywelyn

Fortunately she found her phials untouched, and gave him a draught. Then turning to Tewdwr, she handed him the bottle, saying:

"There, take that with thee, and give thy brother the same quantity as I now gave him at sunset and sunrise for three days. Then get him each morning, fresh from the spring, three times that quantity of water from the Blessed Well[*] on the Common beyond Cwm Brith, and in a week's time he will be as well as ever save that his arm will need care."

Tewdwr seized her hand and kissed it respectfully, saying:

"The life your husband all but took you have saved, and my debt to you is as great as I felt it to be to him."

"Then," she said, with a smile, "ask his life of your leader."

Little was any such intercession needed. The chivalrous Welsh chieftain had no intention of harming his prisoners. They were all allowed to depart on their simple promise not to aid in garrisoning a Welsh castle, and not to bear arms against the Welsh, under any circumstances, for five years.

Sir Hywel ap Meurig's youthful son, whose quick perception had enabled him to gather who his father's vanquisher was, approached the Prince, and kneeling, took his hand and kissed it with deep respect, saying:

"My father hath sworn not to fight against you for five years. I swear to fight for you forever as soon as I am able to bear arms."

"Brave boy," said the Prince, with deep emotion. "So will the son repair the father's wrong. May the

---

[*] The now famous Old Pump House Well, Llandrindod, whose medicinal virtues, attributed at the time to miraculous causes, seem even then to have been known in the neighbourhood.

saints have thee in their keeping!"

While the garrison were taking their departure, and Tewdwr was preparing a rough litter to carry his brother home to Lluest, Llywelyn's followers were busy divesting the castle of all that could be of use or value to them. By Llywelyn's advice a number of them, aided by scores of others whom the news of the fall of the castle had brought from all the surrounding districts, undermined all the principal walls, reducing the whole structure to such a tottering state that the first storm would bring the whole mass to the earth. That night an enormous fire was lit in the centre of the keep, and the forked flames, leaping skyward, proclaimed far and near that Mortimer's stronghold at Cefn Llys had fallen.

Chapter IX
Historical

*Blest is that ground where, o'er the spring
Of history, glory claps her wings,
Fame sheds the exulting tear.*
          – WORDSWORTH

*I can esteem none as well-informed to whom matters pertaining
to their own country remain unknown.*
          – CICERO

Llywelyn having, by this signal victory, roused the slumbering patriotism and spirit of the men of Maesyfed, and shown them that the length of their bondage under Saxon or Norman yoke depended entirely upon themselves, hastened on his journey northwards, leaving Ednyfed ap Tewdwr in charge of his interests in Glyn Ithon.

The forecast of good Dame Gwenllian, Sir Hywel ap Meurig's wife, as to Meredydd s progress to recovery, proved a correct one. Whether it was her wonderful cordial, or the miraculous waters of the Blessed Well, or his own robust constitution which brought round, it is true that in a short time Meredydd ab Ednyfed was as blithe and active and daring as ever, though his broken arm kept him for a time under some restraint.

Lord Mortimer's anger when the news reached him of the fall of his Castle of Cefn Llys was unbounded. Calling for the assistance of his friend, Humphrey de Bohun, with his retainers, Roger de Mortimer set out at the head of a strong band to reoccupy the castle.

Ednyfed, acting on Llywelyn's instructions delivered before he went to North Wales, offered no opposition, and advised all who had taken part in the recent outbreak to remain quiet. Roger de Mortimer and Humphrey de Bohun erected tents inside the bare walls of Cefn Llys, but they ill protected from the biting winter's blasts, while their men tried to prop the tottering walls, which each night threatened to bury all beneath their ruins.

To make their predicament still worse, Llywelyn, advised by Tewdwr ab Ednyfed in person of the state of affairs, suddenly reappeared on the scene, with a large army, considerably strengthened by recruits from all parts of Radnorshire, and invested Cefn Llys hill, practically catching Mortimer and Bohun in a trap he had laid for them.

Frantic as were the efforts made by these two renowned warriors and hitherto dreaded Lord Marchers to break through the cordon of enemies who surrounded them, they all proved unavailing. The straits to which they were reduced may be guessed from the fact that they lost five hundred men in futile sallies, and that the survivors were on the verge of famine. Every messenger who attempted to leave the castle was invariably taken, and sent back to the castle, with his despatches endorsed by Llywelyn's scrawling signature, as a token alike of their weakness and his power. The only couriers, too, who entered Cefn Llys with news from the outside world were such as carried news of Llywelyn's successes elsewhere. When the information arrived of the fall of four of the Norman castles one after the other before detachments of Llywelyn's victorious army, Mortimer and de Bohun began to seriously fear for their own future. When finally, on the Christmas eve, there arrived at the castle the late governor of Mortimer's castle of Cnwcglas (Knucklas) bearing the ill news that that stronghold, hitherto deemed practically impregnable, had fallen into Llywelyn's hands four days previously, the proud spirit of the Lord Marcbers was completely broken and Mortimer was compelled to appeal to his kinship with Llywelyn as a plea for considerate treatment.

With that high chivalry which marked this period of his history, Llywelyn informed his cousin that he and the garrison of Cefn Llys ruins were at liberty to march whenever and wherever they chose, and, ere the new year dawned, Roger de Mortimer and Humphrey de Bohun, with a few disheartened, weakened, and half-starved followers, marched sadly down the hill and across the ford of the Ithon, under the galling sense that they owed their lives to the generosity of a hitherto despised foe.

Llywelyn followed up these successes so energetically as to strike terror throughout the marches generally. The Bishop of Hereford, in a letter to King Henry, still extant, says that the country was plundered and burnt near Webyl, [*Weobley*] and Eardisley, and Wigmore; that all the folk in his diocese had betaken themselves to the churches, and hardly felt safe even there; that many knights had held "Parliaments," had sold their corn and store, and alienated their lands even; whilst others had left the country entirely under the effects of the prevailing panic.

Success followed success, and the Norman castles fell quickly one after the other into the hands of the Welsh. The secret alliance made between Llywelyn and Simon de Montfort outside the walls of Cefn Llys Castle, and ratified the following day at Abbey Cwm Hir, was made public in the early part of 1263, and the armed forces of the great English leader and of the great

Welsh leader were united to the great discomfiture of the royal forces. The timid bishop of Hereford found his worst fears realised, for he fell a prisoner into Llywelyn's hands, and was placed in forced retirement in Eardisley Castle.

Peter de Montfort, who a few months previously had so stubbornly opposed the Welsh in their attempted passage of the fords of the Usk, near Abergavenny, now threw in his influence with his father's ally, Llywelyn, and others following his example, the alliance between de Montfort and the Prince of Wales bade fair to result in the complete overthrow of the Norman power in England. In acknowledgment of the assistance de Montfort had given him in Wales, Llywelyn sent a strong body of his own men under Tewdwr ab Ednyfed, to follow and aid the fortunes of the great Earl of Leicester, and right manfully did they play their part on the fateful field of Lewes, where Henry fell a prisoner into de Montfort's hands.

Llywelyn, however, experienced a terrible loss following the defeat and fall of de Montfort at Evesham in 1265. Notwithstanding this, he continued to hold out so bravely for years, that Henry and Edward, after several futile attempts to overcome him, felt compelled to consent to terms of peace, and under a treaty, bearing the double date of Shrewsbury, September 29th 1267, and Montgomery, September 29th, 1267, what may be deemed honourable and favourable terms were granted Llywelyn, and it is especially stipulated that the lordship of Maelienydd, in which Cefn Llys was situated, should be left subject to adjudication between Llywelyn and Roger de Mortimer.

Chapter X
Old Acquaintances

Kindness fadeth away, but vengeance endureth.
– SCOTT

We take up the threads of our story again on an autumn day, but time and scene are changed. Eight years have elapsed since the fall of Cefn Llys Castle, and instead of the bleak mountainside, which was the scene of action in previous chapters, we find ourselves among more beautiful even if somewhat less romantic scenery.

Reclining on the velvety turf beside a rough bridle-path, leading through a deep wood, a few miles from Caerphilly Castle, were two youths, engaged in earnest conversation.

Both were strongly built, and evidently well accustomed to bearing arms. The younger of the two, possibly seventeen or eighteen years of age, had a peculiarly frank, open, and pleasing countenance, presenting in this respect a marked contrast to his companion, the unpleasant effect of whose dark and sullen looking face upon an ordinary beholder was still further increased by the absence of one of the eyes. The contraction of the lids falling into the depths of the socket showed that the eyeball was altogether wanting and gave a decidedly repulsive case to features which would not probably have been deemed charming at the best. The missing light of this eye might, however, almost be imagined to have been added to the remaining orb, so fiery were the quick, restless, suspicious glances it threw in every direction.

Reclining at the feet of these youths was a noble wolfhound, which lay with head resting on its extended paws, facing the elder of the friends. The most casual observer would have been struck with a peculiarity in the appearance of this animal, for one of the ears was missing; a second glance would have shown that this was not the only organ of which it had been deprived, for, like its master, one of his eyes was also completely wanting from the socket.

"I tell thee, Meredydd," said the elder of the two, "I like not this journey. Thou knowest I am ever ready to take my part in any fighting that may be going on, and have had my share of blows as well as any other man. But something tells me there may lie much more behind this invitation to our good prince than appears on the surface."

"It may be so, Hywel," replied the other somewhat carelessly, "but thou art aye suspicious when we have anything to do with Normans."

"And good cause have I to be. Since they have one of my eyes and one of my ears in their keeping, it is all the more necessary I should make a good use of the only one of each pair that I have left. And thou, Crafanc, thinkest the same, dost thou not?" and the speaker placed his hand caressingly on the dog's head.

"Thou speakest the truth, Hywel. God knows we have all good cause to disdoubt these Normans, but thou more than many of us. But still this conference, to which Prince Dafydd hath been sent on behalf of his brother, may lead to good results."

"Mayhap," returned the other doubtfully. "Yet I must say Llywelyn is stronger in battle than in council. The only comfort I draw from this journey is that it must draw the brothers nigher each other, and this is a time when we can ill afford having any division among us.

"True. And for the same reason am I glad that mine old friend Gruffydd ap Gwenwynwyn is in Prince Dafydd's train. His family hath never been of the most faithful, and it was wise on Llywelyn's part to place him in a prominent place in this business, young though he is."

"The conference or council, or whatever name thou givest it, is to take place, thou sayest, at noon tomorrow?"

"Aye, an hour's march from this place."

"And what certainty is there that there is no treachery meant us?"

"None that I know of but the knightly faith of de Clare on the one hand, and our good swords and battle axes on the other," was the light response.

"The first we cannot depend on for he is a Norman. The second is well enough had we more of the same sort. But – well, what is it, Crafanc?"

The dog had raised its head and sniffed the air, and then uttered a low growl.

"Someone cometh. It will be wiser we should not be seen so far from our camp."

"They may be our own men," said he who had been called Meredydd. "They come from that direction."

"Yes, but Crafanc would not be bristling up as he does now in that case," was the reply. "Come; we must shelter ourselves. Even if they prove to be friends, we shall be none the worse of seeing them before they see us."

The two men, with the dog, immediately left the path, and hid themselves in the underwood which bordered upon it. In another minute two horsemen were seen approaching. As they came in sight, Meredydd was startled by a sudden movement and exclamation from his companion. Turning in surprise, he saw the dog standing up facing the coming strangers, with every appearance of fury, while his master Hywel's face wore an aspect of deep malignity Meredydd had never before seen.

"Down, Crafanc! Down! We must not warn him or we lose all!"

The obedient animal crouched, while his master whispered in Meredydd's ear: "It is Sheffri de Langli!"

Chapter XI
English Guile

It required the exertion of the utmost self-restraint on the part of Hywel, and all the influence of his master's authority on Crafanc, to prevent them betraying their presence to the common enemy to whom both owed so much. Meredydd, looking at them, saw that master and dog alike trembled with suppressed rage as de Langley rode past almost within reach of a blow, and each moment feared that feeling would get the better of reason in the man and of obedience in the dog, and that thus an encounter would become inevitable.

The two knights were, however, too deeply engaged in earnest conversation to be suspicious of their surroundings, though, when Meredydd saw them draw rein within less than a dozen yards of his place of concealment, he involuntarily felt for the hilt of his sword, as though fancying that the time for action had arrived.

Where the two knights had paused, the road, or rather bridle-path, branched in two, and it soon became evident either that the horsemen were undecided which of the two paths to follow, or that they were about to separate. The listeners were not long left in doubt as to the intentions of the newcomers, for they were sufficiently near to hear and understand the whole conversation which passed between the two.

"Well, Sir Patrick, and what reply am I to receive?" Sir Geoffrey de Langley was heard to say.

"Thou knowest, Sir Geoffrey, that I am always as

ready as thou art to strike a blow at these proud Welshmen in open, honest warfare, but I must say that I like not the plan thou proposest. It savoureth too much of dishonour to accord with my views."

"Is it dishonour to carry out the wishes of your sovereign, Sir Patrick?" asked de Langley somewhat sternly. "Do you consider rightly what it is I propose you should do?"

"I think I do," was the reply, somewhat uneasily given. "You would have me play a treacherous part with these Welsh ambassadors. They come here in all good faith, under arrangements entered into with our lord the King's sanction and approval, to decide upon terms of peace. They come in peace and with peaceable intentions, trusting to our knightly faith. And you would have me betray this faith, and, instead of meeting them in amity, would have me attack them unawares, take them under a disadvantage, and – "

"And rid the country of some of its pests, you would say?" asked de Langley, with a laugh. "Why, the principles which these Welshmen themselves teach and advocate justifies you."

"How so?"

"It is one of their axioms that it is no treachery to betray a traitor, and methinks this Prince Dafydd, as he calls himself, is a double-dyed traitor, whose past treachery alike to our king and to his brother put him beyond the pale of knightly consideration."

The other remained silent while de Langley proceeded:

"But of a truth, Sir Patrick, you put too strong a colour upon it. You speak as though I advised you to fall treacherously upon quiet and inoffensive people. I do nothing of the kind."

The other again shook his head.

Llywelyn

"Nay, but listen," urged de Langley. "I only ask you to take reasonable precautions. These Welshmen come to-morrow to meet you in friendly council. Their numbers, though not great, are fully equal to yours. They are hot-headed, and a council commenced in peace and harmony may terminate in high words and hard blows. Now, should that be the case, you might be worsted. To prevent any such danger, I ask you to authorise me to demand of the governor of this castle of Caerphilly a sufficient number of men whom I can place in ambush near the spot, and who can, when the quarrel breaks out, as assuredly it will, suffice to exterminate the whole of this band of 'traitors'."

"But you propose giving them just ground for offence, and making it impossible for them to do otherwise than come to blows?" urged Sir Patrick.

"And what hath that to do with you?" asked de Langley. "Lay that sin, if sin it be, to my account. I will be answerable for it, so that it need not trouble your over-tender conscience."

Sir Patrick still remained silent and evidently undecided. De Langley's impatience now seemed to gain the mastery over him, and he said brusquely:

"Well, then, Sir Patrick, I will be plain with you. If you refuse to do this, if you seize not the opportunity I shall place in your hand of removing from the king's path so many of his enemies, I must lay my plaint before him against you as one who careth more for a Welshman's life than for the King's honour. He cannot regard as well-affected towards him a knight who wilfully refuseth to reach out his hand to strike the king's deadly enemies when just cause and reasonable opportunity is afforded him. I ask not that you should raise a finger or utter a word yourself to betray your knightly faith. I have said that I will myself give these

Welshmen such cause of offence as will compel them to unsheath their swords. When that happens, as most certainly happen it will, I tell you plainly that if you be after this warning unprepared, I shall declare you a traitor to our lord the king. Could I proceed on this matter myself alone, I would gladly do so. But I must have your written demand for these soldiers from Caerphilly before I can expect the governor to hand them over to my authority. Give me this authority, and I save you and your men from almost certain death, and the king's honour from being trodden under foot. Refuse this, and I still say the occasion shall arise as though you were well prepared – but let the consequences fall, in that case, on your head and not on mine."

Sir Patrick, either convinced by the other's reasoning, or overpowered by de Langley's superior force of will, submitted.

"So be it then," said he. "You leave me no choice but to comply. I wash my hands, however, of all complicity further than that of taking due care to protect myself and men. If you will come with me to my camp I will give you there the necessary order on the governor of Caerphilly Castle."

"Let us on, then, in the devil's name," said de Langley, putting spurs to his steed, and dashing along the path which branched to the left, followed at an equally rapid pace by Sir Patrick.

"Aye, in the devil's name, indeed!" said Meredydd, drawing a deep breath. "Saw any man ever such deeply-dyed devilish treachery?"

"What else can you expect where Sheffri de Langli is engaged?" asked Hywel, while the fierce gleam from his eyes showed the depth to which his feelings had been stirred. "The whole affair is evidently a deep-laid plan.

Here have they proposed to our Prince Llywelyn a peaceful conference to adjust differences, and at the same time they make arrangements to induce us to quarrel with them, and then take precautions which will ensure our being outnumbered two to one!"

"Aye. Just so. And doubtless they hoped Llywelyn would himself be present, and that thus at one fell blow they would again bring our country on her knees. But what meanest thou to do, Meredydd?"

"De Langley hath shown me what to do!" said Meredydd bitterly. "Did he not say, 'Nid brad bradychu bradwr,' – it is no treachery to betray a traitor. Let us arrange that he fall into the pit he hath dug for us."

"But how?"

"That will I explain as we go along. Come, it is time we should be moving!"

Chapter XII
Retributive Justice

*Neither the fields nor the woods gave safety to the foe.
When the shout of the Britons came
Like a wave raging against the shore."*
– TALIESIN

The next morning dawned brightly on the woods around Caerphilly, and little could anyone have dreamed, when gazing upon the peaceful scene, that these same quiet woods would, ere the shadows of night again fell on them, witness the deeds of treachery, of bloodshed, and of retribution they were fated to conceal.

As mid-day approached, Prince Dafydd, Llywelyn's brother, accompanied by a number of other nobles, and followed by a goodly array of some two hundred well-armed men, set forth gaily to meet the king's envoy, Sir Patrick de Canton. All unsuspicious of the treacherous intentions of their would-be hosts, the Welsh leaders and their men marched as it were blindfolded into the trap so artfully laid for them. There was no one there to whisper in their ears that the bare two hundred Norman and English knights and retainers who met them showed less than half the actual force at Sir Patrick's command; there was no friendly genius near to draw aside the leafy veil which concealed nearly three hundred men from the neighbouring garrison of Caerphilly, whom de Langley's treacherous foresight had so skilfully hidden within ready call to do these unsuspecting Welshmen to death. None of them guessed the deadly purpose hidden behind the false smile of welcome with which de Langley greeted the Welsh ambassadors, and introduced them to Sir Patrick de Canton and his fellow commissioners.

The formal greetings having been gone through, the business which had brought together was mooted.

De Langley, impatient to glut his passions with bloodshed, took care to give even the opening of the negotiations a tone of unfriendliness, which the Welsh, confident in their superior numbers, disdained to notice until what was evident to all was intended as a deliberate insult was offered to the fiery Prince Dafydd by de Langley himself. The Prince, carried away by his passions, drew his sword, exclaiming:

"Out upon thee, base knight! Thinkest thou I have come hither to brook thy insults?"

This was the throwing of a brand into the dry glass, and in a moment conflagration of passions broke out, and all was tumult. Swords flashed and daggers gleamed on each side, while de Langley called out in stentorian tones:

"What ho, there! Treachery! Treachery! Down with the traitor Welsh!"

The partisans of both sides naturally joined in with their leaders, and the contest became general. At this moment, however, there rushed upon the scene the reserve forces so skilfully hidden by de Langley.

The Welsh, who had been carrying all before them, were no little dismayed at this unexpected increase in the number of their enemies. Prince Dafydd, whatever might have been his faults, could certainly not be charged with cowardice. Too late he saw the trap which had been laid for him, and into which he had so blindly fallen. Instead, however, of being totally totally disheartened by the appearance of this reinforcement to the English, the Welsh leaders seemed spurred thereby to greater effort.

Calling his men together, he hastily formed them to the best advantage to meet this unexpected onslaught, and, being ably seconded by his companions and followers, presented a bold and threatening front to the overwhelming forces of the enemy. Bold, however, as was their front, determined as was the opposition they presented to the onslaught upon them, it was all too plainly evident that the courageous band of Welshmen was foredoomed to practical annihilation, and that de Langley's deep-laid plan of treachery was about to be crowned with success.

But in the height of their exultation the Normans were in this instance fated to as great and unexpected a surprise as that they had prepared for the Welshmen.

Meredydd and Hywel had not been idle, but during the hours of evening, night, and morning intervening between their overhearing de Langley's plans and his putting them in operation, they had given information to a strong body of Welshman encamped a dozen miles away, of whose presence they had become aware during a hunting expedition that day. The action taken was as prompt as it was sagacious. Instead of joining these new forces openly with those of Prince Dafydd and thus overawing the Normans, they followed de Langley's tactics and hid these reinforcements within suitable distance of the place of meeting. A forced night's march, and the experience these hardy mountaineers had of rapid transit through a difficult country, accomplished what, under ordinary circumstances would have been an impossibility, and ere the morning sun dawned on Dafydd's camp there lay on the hillside within ten minutes rush of the place fixed by de Langley for the scene of this treachery some three hundred men eager for the fray.

Llywelyn

Thus it happened that at the very moment the Normans, exulting in the victory which they seemed to have within their grasp, were preparing to make a united rush upon the little band of doomed Welshmen, they found themselves in turn utterly taken by surprise, and not only bereft of all the advantages they had secured by their ambush, but placed under the very disadvantage to which they had hoped to subject the Welsh.

With wild shouts the reinforcements secured by Meredydd and Hywel threw themselves upon the flank and rear of Sir Patrick's paralysed forces, while Dafydd's band, infuriated at the treachery done them and encouraged by this unexpected aid, made as vigorous an onslaught in front.

Attacked thus on all sides, the Norman forces became immediately demoralised, and what would, under ordinary circumstances have been a fight, stern and perhaps indecisive, degenerated into a rout and a massacre. Poor Sir Patrick le Canton, fortunately for himself, did not survive this disgrace.[*] He felt his courage dimmed and his arm enfeebled by the consciousness of the treachery to which he had somewhat unwillingly committed. Among other noble knights who ingloriously fell indirect victims of de Langley's treachery were Sir Walter Malefiant and Sir Hugo de Vynes.

De Langley's experiences of warfare had satisfied him almost on the first appearance of the Welsh

---

[*] To be strictly accurate as to facts, and to enable the reader to distinguish between fact and fiction, it would be well to state here that the incident here located in the neighbourhood of Caerphilly actually occurred at Cilgerran, September 3rd, 1268. The incidents as given in the story are otherwise historically correct. The fall of Caerphilly Castle actually took place October 13th, 1270.

reinforcements that nothing but a miracle could now save his friends from complete annihilation. He therefore immediately cast about him for means to secure his own safety.

Sir Geoffrey, like many other knights on each side, had, at the commencement of hostilities, mounted their charges the better to enable them to play the part expected of them in the contest. Seeing now the utter helplessness of his cause, he extricated himself from the melee and spurred in the direction of Caerphilly with the double purpose of securing his own safety and warning the feeble garrison which remained there.

He was not, however, destined to get off so easily. His mad career was as suddenly as it was unexpectedly stopped. Dashing at full speed along the narrow path which led to safety, he saw what seemed like a beast of prey bound with a fierce growl straight for his horse's head, and, seizing it by the nose, brought it to his knees with a stumble. At the same moment a blow on the head from and unseen hand completed his discomfiture and laid him senseless beside his struggling steed.

When he came to himself a few minutes later, he found himself bound hand and foot with withes, which, try as he would, he could not loosen in the least degree. Groaning in deep anguish, he tried to turn, but found that this also he was prevented from doing by the manner in which he had been bound.

But now he heard approaching footsteps – oh, welcome sound!

"Hi!" he called. "Whoever thou art that approaches, draw near and cut loose these bonds, and as I am a Christian knight I will amply repay thee."

In another moment he saw the figure of a man approaching. His impatience, however, would not permit him to wait.

"Haste thee! Haste!" he cried. "The withes cut into my flesh and gall me. Haste, say, or by the rood I will chastise thee when I am free."

The newcomer laughed.

"An' that be thy greeting," he said, "I may as well go back the way I came, and so I shall bid thee good e'en," and he made as though to depart a second time.

"No! Oh, no! For the sake of heaven quit me not, forsake me not bound thus! I did not mean what I said. But cut me, I pray thee, these cursed bonds, and I will amply reward thee."

"And how am I to know that thou meanest that which thou dost promise more than thou meanest that which thou did'st but just now threaten?"

"Thou canst know, I mean, what I now say. Come, good friend, do me this favour, I pray thee, forthwith. Then will I, on the word of a Christian knight, settle fairly with thee, and give thee whatsoever thou dost see fit to ask."

"Ah, that reminds me," said the other in a changed tone of voice, "I too have somewhat to settle with thee."

"Thou! To settle with me? That cannot be, for I never saw thee before."

"Art certain?" asked the other, and pushing his head-dress back, he leaned forward over the prostrate knight, displaying features on every line of which deep malignity and undying hatred were stamped.

"Knowest thou me not?" he asked again. "If that be so I can aid thy memory. Here, Crafanc, good dog, here. Show thou thy features too, and see if he to whom we owe so much can recognise thee!"

At these words the large wolfhound approached, and, at a sign from his master, laid his immense forepaws on the knight's chest, and stretched forth his head until the muzzle almost touched the knight's face.

De Langley, looking from man to dog and from dog to man, felt as though under the influence of some terrible nightmare. The two faces seemed to be mixed up in a strange and grotesque manner, as though the man's body had a dog's face and the dog's body bore a man's features. There was some grotesque and yet terrible similarity between the biped and quadruped which brough up a train of recollections to de Langley's memory, and cause a tremor of apprehension to pervade his whole body.

"Did I not tell thee, Sheffri di Langli, that I and Crafanc would bear thee in memory? And thou dost, I am sure, well remember that day on the banks of the Ithon at Cefn Llys, when thou didst, by taking an eye and an ear each from Crafanc and myself, make us warmer friends than we had ever been. 'Twere a thousand pities thou should'st thus have forgotten us, but methinks thou wilt remember us both after this day. What say'st thou, Crafanc?"

The sagacious animal, as though understanding the appeal, showed his teeth in a threatening manner, which made the tortured knight shudder.

"If thou holdest me to ransom," said he, trying to summon his self-command, "thou wilt be duly paid."

"Of that I have no fear. But as it happens, I intend demanding payment ere thou goest;" and Hywel the one-eyed laughed.

"Take care what thou art about to do," said Sir Geoffrey. "As a knight who submits himself a prisoner, I demand treatment worthy of my knighthood."

"Thou shalt have treatment worthy of thyself and thy past doings," said Hywel sternly. "As thou hast done, so shall it be done unto thee. Thou didst take away an eye and an ear of mine; I will do the same with thee, and – "

"Avaunt!" cried de Langley in deep dismay. "Darest thou threaten me thus, man or devil, whatever thou art?"

"I dare more than threaten, as thou shalt see to thy cost," was the reply. "But let me finish my tale. Thou didst deprive my dog Crafanc also of his eye and ear, and he demands the same of thee. I will, however, be more merciful than thou. I will leave thee an eye to see where thou goest to, and Crafanc must e'en be satisfied with thy ear only. But bear this in mind, Sheffri de Langli. I leave thee thy life and one eye, that thou mayest know what I have suffered. But as I live, the day we meet again thy life shall pay the forfeit."

Heedless alike of the imprecations, threats and entreaties of the prisoner, Hywel performed upon de Langley the terrible triple operation he had threatened. Then, having deprived the knight of both ears and one of his eyes, the one-eyed Welshman cut the bonds of de Langley, and whistling to his dog, disappeared in the depths of the forest, leaving Sir Geoffrey at liberty indeed, but almost regretting already that his captor had not taken his life instead of leaving him thus deformed.

The little army of Prince Dafydd had, meanwhile, not only almost exterminated the band of Englishmen in the forest, but following up their success, attacked Caerphilly Castle, and ere night fell this great stronghold of de Clare, which had so long overawed the Welsh of the surrounding districts, fell into the Welshmen's hands, and acknowledged Llywelyn as its master.(4)

Chapter XIII
Eleanor and Gwen

A gentle-maid in secret sighed
"Come back, my only love, to me!"
Proud suitors sought her for their bride
With vows of truth and constancy;
But still the maid for ever sighed,
"My love, I live or die for thee!"
— Walter Maynard

The events which followed the fall of Caerphilly Castle are matters of history.

The Welsh left such tokens of their occupation of this stronghold on its walls that, when they left it, Gloucester began to think of restoring it and thus making it again capable of defence. This did not accord with Llywelyn's views. He was naturally averse to replacing in the hands of his enemies the means of oppression he had at such cost wrested from them. He therefore sent Gilbert de Clare a peremptory demand to discontinue the proposed restoration, to make the Prince full compensation for the injury already done to his subjects in and around Caerphilly, and to give a sufficient guarantee that he would not again proceed to strengthen the defences of the Castle. This demand was accompanied by a threat that unless the replies proved satisfactory to Llywelyn, he would, within three days, again invest the place and reduce it to complete ruin.

So successful had Llywelyn been of late, so powerful and dreaded had he become, that the great Earl was filled with alarm. While his haughty nature would hardly permit him to make the humiliating concessions demanded by Llywelyn, the certainty that the prince would be inclined and probably able to carry out his threat led him to seek for some way out of the difficulty in which he was placed. He therefore formally handed over the castle incompletely restored to the bishops of Worcester, Coventry, and Lichfield, to be held by them in the king's name until the matters in dispute between the earl and the prince could be settled by arbitration.

To this arrangement Llywelyn somewhat unwillingly consented. His previous experience of English good faith had not been of a very reassuring character, and it was therefore with grave doubts as to the wisdom of the step he was taking that he consented reluctantly to the arrangement. Nor were his fears unfounded. On one pretext or another the meeting of arbitrators was postponed on the side of the English from July, 1272, the date first agreed upon, to another, before the arrival of which it was deferred again, and then again to the end of March, 1273. The prince was in the meantime over and over again reminded that his own word of honour prevented his taking any warlike steps in connection with this matter until the decision of the arbitrators was given!

In November of 1272 King Henry died. Edward, his son and successor, was at the time absent in the Holy Land, and did not return to England for nearly two years afterwards. In the, meanwhile, though Llywelyn did more than hold his own, he suffered much from death and defections among his adherents. A number of his firmest friends and supporters died; others, including his fickle brother Dafydd, either publicly or secretly attached themselves to the fortunes of the new King of England. Notwithstanding these heavy losses, the cause of Llywelyn had so prospered by the early part of 1276 that he felt himself in a position to claim his long-betrothed bride. Preparations were therefore made for sending am ambassadors to the court of France demanding the hand of Eleanor de Montfort.

It was about the time that preliminary preparations for sending a suitable embassy were being made at Llywelyn's court that we again take up the broken thread of our narrative.

*   *   *

The Castle of Montargis, in France, had been for years the centre of attraction for most of the chivalry of France, who gathered there to gaze upon the charms of the beautiful orphaned daughter of the great Simon de Montfort, Earl of Leicester.

Many and noble were the suitors for her hand, frequent and earnest were the courses run on her behalf at the tournaments, in which the chivalry of the age and the country delighted, and numerous and amorous were the outpourings of the troubadours' art and heart beneath her lattice.

But vain alike had the trance of love, the valour of knighthood, and the charms of poetry proved to move the heart of Eleanor de Montfort from its unswerving allegiance to the princely lover of her childhood's days. Her warm imagination kept forever present to her mental gaze the figure of the lover who had parted from her with such reluctance in the tent under the walls of Cefn Llys Castle, and her formal betrothal to whom had received the blessings of parents and of Church at Cwm Hir Abbey the following day. Thus, though she had never set eyes on him for so many years, be was ever present in her thoughts and affections, and thus her heart was steeled against the approaches of her numerous ardent admirers. Seated at her open window, one fine evening in the spring of 1276, attended only by her tiring maid, the conversation of both turned naturally, as it had many a time and oft, on the distant homes and friends of both.

"And thou, too, lookest forward, Gwen, to the time when we shall be summoned back to our country."

"Sweet lady, thou knowest my home is as absent from my thoughts as the person of thy princely lover is from thine."

"Then is it seldom indeed, Gwen. And yet I feel me that the prince hath not for me that feeling I would wish, else had he not left me these long years without one visit."

"He hath been wisely employed and all too hardly pressed during most of the time, as we well know," was Gwen's reply.

"Yes, and notwithstanding treachery from friends and guile from enemies, he hath nobly held his own," said Eleanor proudly. "Who but he could so well and so long have withstood all the power of the proud Henry and of his still more able son?"

So intent had both been on their conversation that neither had noticed the stealthy approach of two persons, evidently bent on reaching unseen a favourable position underneath the window at which the maidens were seated. Ignorant, therefore, that their conversation would now be overheard – though the listeners had until now been too distant to catch the sense of what had been previously said – Eleanor de Montford, changing the subject, remarked:

"It grieves me much, Gwen, that my cousin the King should have placed upon me the burdensome honour of being Queen of the Lists tomorrow."

"And why so, my lady?"

"Need'st thou ask why? Because I shall of necessity be called upon to award the prize to some knight or other when I would willingly give it to one who must needs be absent, and who though absent is so much worthier than any who will enter these lists tomorrow."

At these words one of the listeners gave such a start,, whether of gratification or dismay, as had nearly betrayed their presence. His companion placed a warning hand on his arm, and both again listened.

"'T'will not be the first time you have done so," was the reply of the maid.

"For the first time I have grieved to be obliged to do so," was the ready response. "As for thee, Gwen, I suppose thou wouldst also gladly welcome back the gay Welsh gallant Gruffydd ap Gwenwynwyn, who paid thee such marked attention when he last bore me letters from the Prince."

It was now the turn of the second of the two listeners to start and be warned by his companion.

"I daresay me he will return in good time. Did I not tell you he hinted he would possibly again visit as shortly on an embassy of importance from the Prince?"

"Aye, thou remindest me that he did so. And thou wilt, I suppose, welcome his reappearance?"

"Aye, gladly." (Here the listener who had last shown such signs of agitation was again on the verge of betraying his presence, either through joy or anger.) "As gladly as I would welcome any other man from my dear country, who could bring me news of homeland friends, and father."

"Would that my Prince were to bring me a message himself, instead of contenting himself, as he always doth, with sending others in his stead. But I am getting melancholy with brooding over his long-continued absence. Reach me my lute, Gwen, and let me see if the spirit of music can banish the spirit of regret."

The handmaiden handed her mistress the instrument, and the lady, after a little preliminary tuning, and allowing her hands to wander over the strings as though to seek inspiration from the sweet chords she evoked, broke out in the following song, which she delivered in a sweet soprano voice of unusual power and charm, accompanying herself the meanwhile with a practised hand on her instrument.

ELLEN'S SONG

Though, darkened now the heavens above me,
  Though fate upon me frown to-day,
There still is left me one to love me,
  Who bids my aching heart be gay.
Then now away each foolish tear!
  Away! Away! Let all doubts flee
For if alive, I need not fear,
  Llywelyn will come back to me.

What though for him I'm made a stranger,
  What though the sword in battle wave?
I know of one who fears no danger,
  And who'll be faithful to his grave!
So strong his arm, his smile so pleasant,
  And in his bosom I yet shall be,
My heart it sings in strains incessant,
  'Llywelyn will come back to me!'*

---

* We append a free translation of this song as it appears in the author's Drama-Cantata *Llywelyn Ein Llyw Olaf.*

CÂN ELEN
Os tywyll imi ydyw'r wybren,
  Os gwgu arnaf y mae ffawd,

The listeners had remained entranced by the singer's delivery of these, her heart's most secret thoughts, and feared to move lest the spell should be broken. The lady, as though wishing that the sweet thoughts to which she had just given utterance should be her only companion for the night, handed the instrument to her maid, and without uttering a word dismissed Gwen for the night. The maid, having fastened the windows, made her obeisance, and leaving her mistress to her slumbers and thoughts of love, sought her own more lowly but not less welcome couch.

The listeners outside remained until satisfied they had no hope of any repetition of the treats they had just been favoured with, and then departed as stealthily as they approached, unseen, and unsuspected.

> Daw eto'n well, fe wena'r Heulwen,
>   A chyfyd calon Elen dlawd,
> Ni rhaid im' grio chwaith na becso,
>   Nac i wylo dagrau ffôl,
> Os byw yw ef, os rhwydd-deb gaffo,
>   Fe ddaw Llywelyn eto'n ôl.
>
> Beth os lluosog ydyw'r Saeson
>   Ac os creulon ydyw'r cledd,
> Mi wn am un sy'n ddewr ei galon
>   Ac a fydd ffydlon hyd ei fedd,
> Ei fraich sydd gref, ei wên sydd lawen,
>   A llechu eto gaf yn ei gol,
> Tra bydd hi byw, fe greda Elen
>   Y daw Llywelyn eto'n ôl!

These words, with the remainder of the songs in this historical play, have been set to music by Alaw Ddu. (5)

Chapter XIV
The Nameless Knight

'Know'st thou me not?' his actions said,
'Thou priestess of my highest shrine,
Where worshipped the Leucadian maid,
Where love and glory mingling twine!'
 – The Fountain of Love

The mid-day sun of the following day shone down on a gay and gallant scene at Montargis. Gallant knights, fair ladies, and eager spectators made the jousts at Montargis a scene long looked forward to and long remembered.

A few preliminary courses of lesser importance had been run, but the great event of the day was yet to come off. The King of France, attended by the principal nobles of his court, was present, and, seated by the side of the queen of the sports on a raised platform overlooking the Lists, had for some time been disappointed at the little response to his gay sallies or well-turned compliments which Eleanor de Montfort vouchsafed him.

"I see how it is," he said at length; "you, fair cousin, are looking forward all too anxiously to the running of the one great course on which the thoughts of our chivalry are fixed. They look forward to the coveted award from your fair hand, and you, doubtless, are anxious to see the face of him who will have a claim to your smiles for the rest of the day."

"Believe me, my liege – " began Eleanor, in some confusion.

"That you wish the order given for the grand course to be run?" asked Philip, wilfully interrupting and and misunderstanding her. "So be it. Let the heralds proclaim." And before Eleanor could interpose the order was given that that preparation should be made at once for the great event of the day.

The proclamation was accordingly made. By the terms of the joust the lists would be held by a knight of noble birth, who would challenge all comers. Should he maintain his self-chosen position, and vanquish the opponents who might venture into the lists against him, he would be publicly rewarded by the Queen of the Lists, and be appointed her especial esquire for the remainder of the day, having a right to a seat by her side at the banquet which was to follow, and a claim to the enviable position of opening the evening dancing with her as his partner.

Scarcely had the proclamation been made than there entered the lists a tall knight mounted on a powerful black horse. This knight had made himself conspicuous during the earlier part of the day by his assiduous attentions to the Queen of the Lists, though it must be confessed he could not flatter himself on having received any encouragement. Indeed, the repulse he had met with had been so decided as to arouse all the hot blood, if not the evil passions, of his nature, and Henri de Marle was not one to be trifled with in such a mood.

"I fear me," said the King to Eleanor, "that my hot-headed cousin de Marle will spoil our sport, and that we shall have none to enter the lists against him."

The knight thus referred to had won for himself the reputation of being practically invincible, for his muscular development, coupled with a thorough training in the art of tilting, had enabled him hitherto to overcome in every joust in which he had been opposed.

So high, indeed, was his reputation, and so severe – in some cases, fatal – were the falls his ponderous strength had given to those who had met him in other lists, that few cared to encounter him.

"I cannot think so lightly of the chivalry of France," said the queen of the day, somewhat uneasily, in reply to the remark of Philip. Of all the knights who had paid her attentions, de Marle had been the most persistent and the least welcome, and the prospect of being practically at his mercy for the rest of the day was, to say the least, unpalatable.

In giving utterance to these words she had looked around her, her gaze resting for a moment. unconsciously, perhaps, on a youthful knight who stood near enough to overhear her words. It had seemed, indeed, as though the king's forecast would prove to be correct, for no one had shown any wish to run the risk of almost certain overthrow, although the prize for the fortunate winner was so coveted a one.

Scarcely, however, had the words fallen from Eleanor's lips than she regretted them, for the young knight referred to, and who happened to be an especial favourite with her, sprang to his feet, and hastened away with a flush on his youthful brow.

"That madcap Duchatel cannot mean to meet de Marle!" cried the King in dismay, as he saw the young knight hasten away. "Do you follow him, Amaury, and tell him that I require his immediate presence."

As though fearing he might meet with some opposition in his foolhardy enterprise, Duchatel had lost no time in giving instructions to his squire and herald, and even as Amaury de Montfort, Eleanor's brother, found him, his herald was sounding his reply to de Marle s haughty challenge. It was now too late to interfere. Had the youthful combatant been the King's son instead of only the son of his friend, the monarch would not have ventured to interfere until at least one course had been run after the challenge had been publicly answered. When the youthful champion shortly appeared in the lists, the contrast between him and his burly opponent was as great as it was unfortunate. Of a more than usually slight, if graceful build, Duchatel, however well fitted to grace a gay court or a merry dance, was hardly adapted for the rough play of the tilting lists, and certainly not to meet such an opponent as de Marle, who was fully twice his weight and strength.

A murmur of mingled pity and admiration passed among the spectators as the young knight caracoled on his steed around the lists to take his position at the opposite end of the lists from where stood de Marle.

The signal was given and the knights met in mid-career.

Duchatel fared better than he had a right to expect. Whether it was that de Marle disdained to put forth all his strength against so comparatively puny an opponent, or that he really felt some pity for the courageous lad – for he was little better than a boy – he contented himself with unhorsing his youthful opponent as lightly as possible.

The courageous entrance into the lists of Duchatel had, however, broken the charm which seemed to have hitherto withheld the elder knights from contending with one of the renowned prowess of de Marle, and scarcely was the vanquished knight removed from the lists than another took his place.

This knight, Fulk Trisold, was an opponent far worthier of the late victor's steel than Duchatel. Of an acknowledged prowess scarcely, if any, inferior to that of de Marle, he was, indeed, the only one of all the knights present who could have the least chance of running a successful course against the renowned knight who had first occupied the lists. His discomfiture, however, proved as complete and almost as speedy as that of his more youthful predecessor, for though his own spear shivered right doughtily against the shield of de Marle, that of the latter caught him fairly on the helmet, and after a vain attempt to recover himself, Trisold fell heavily to the earth, where he lay partially stunned, while his adversary continued his victorious career round the lists.

No other knight ventured to take up the challenge after this signal discomfiture of so renowned a cavalier as Fulk Trisold. The heralds having thrice repeated de Marle's proud challenge, the king reluctantly declared him the winner, and Eleanor de Montfort was, much against her will, perforce obliged to award the prize – a silken scarf she had worn throughout the morning around her own fair neck – to one whom she so much disliked as de Marle.

The glance which the victor threw upon her as she somewhat disdainfully threw the scarf over his shoulder as he knelt in mock humility before her assured her that he would demand the full quota of personal favours from her, to which his victory gave him a right for the rest of the day.

Having received the coveted prize, he secured it as a pennon to his spear, and lightly vaulting on the back of his charger again careered around the lists. Then halting, he directed his herald to sound a final challenge to any knight who might be present to redeem the lady's guerdon from bis possession by force of arms.

To the surprise of all hardly was the challenge given than a solitary blast from the outskirts of the crowd of spectators showed that the challenge was accepted. All eyes were strained to endeavour to make out who the bold knight might be who thus ventured to risk his life in redeeming the prize so well earned, for it was well-known that a course run under such circumstances would be a much more serious matter than one simple run to gain the prize before he had been awarded. The shame of defeat to the victor, after once having had the prize in his possession, would have been deemed so much the greater, that everyone knew de Marle would not be inclined to show much consideration for anyone who had the hardihood to dispute its possession with him.

Nothing, however, could be gathered from the device of the herald, who now made his way slowly through the crowd towards the king's dais on behalf of the bold knight whom he represented.

"Sir Herald," said Philip, "do we understand that there is here a knight who is inclined to do battle with Sir Henri de Marle on this occasion?"

"Sir King," replied the herald, "the knight on whose behalf I appear is prepared to do battle with Sir Henri de Marle, or any other knight whatsoever in this assembly who holdeth or may hold any favour or gaze of the fair queen of these lists."

"Say you so?" said the king, well pleased that anyone was bold enough to challenge de Marle's supremacy. "And what may be the brave knight's name and qualification, for I see no device by which he may be known."

"Sir King," replied the herald, "the knight desires not to be known in person. He is under a solemn vow neither to make his name or rank known, nor to show his face, nor even to speak a single word except alone in private converse, until he hath been received and acknowledged by his lady fair, from whom the Fates have long estranged him."

This was no unusual thing in those days, the vows taken by the chivalry of the age being frequently of the most eccentric nature. The king, therefore, consented to the contest being fought on this understanding.

Chapter XV
The Combat

No sooner had the king's consent been formally given than the knight who had so boldly accepted the challenge of de Marle rode slowly into the lists. Halting when once inside the barriers, while the final arrangements were being made, he naturally found himself the object of earnest attention on all hands. And well he bore the scrutiny in more senses than one. His vizor being lowered, his countenance of course could not be seen, but the easy and unaffected grace with which he sat his steed showed that he was used to such scenes as that in which he had elected to play so important a part, and that he was totally free from all embarrassment in the prominent position in which his audacity had placed him. Equally well did he bear careful and critical scrutiny in other respects. True that compared with the brilliant, almost gaudy armour in which de Marle dazzled the eyes of the spectators, that of the Nameless Knight appeared plain even to bareness, its rigidly uniform plainness being unrelieved by any ornamentation, chasing, or even device. Unfavourably as he thus compared with his opponent to a casual observer, the practised eyes of the knights and squires who subjected his appearance to severe criticism saw that nothing serviceable had been lost in the total absence of ornamentation, and that the simple armour worn by the stranger was, to say the least of it, quite as capable of standing the rough usage or the tilting lists as the gayer trappings of the French knight. The ease and grace with which he sat his horse bespoke his acquaintance with the work he had before him, while the development of bone and muscle evident in the muscular limbs and massive trunk proved that – though not of such ponderous make as de Marle – that knight would meet in him an opponent at least as dangerous as Fulk Trisold.

Now, however, an unforeseen difficulty arose. De Marle, standing on his rights, declined to accept combat with the stranger until satisfied that he was of equal rank with himself. As he had a perfect right to demand that he should not be called upon to meet any person whom it might be derogatory to his character to encounter, de Marle seemed to be on the point of being able to retain his well-earned prize undisputed. The king could not interfere, and unless the Nameless Knight should make himself known de Marle's objection would be sustained and his victory confirmed. At a sign from the stranger, the herald who had already approached the king on his behalf again approached the royal dais before which de Marle now stood with raised vizor and lowering brow.

"Sir King," said the strange herald, "the Nameless Knight acknowledges that Sir Henri de Marle hath a perfect right under the laws of chivalry to demand that he be satisfied of the noble birth and knightly standing of his opponent. At the same time, the vow of the Knight of Silence forbids him making himself known in the ordinary way. If, then, Sir Henri de Marle refuseth to meet him in friendly joust, I claim on behalf of the nameless knight the exercise of his privilege."

"And what may that be?" asked Philip, with some display of eagerness.

"He claims that either Sir Henri de Marle shall return without reserve to the fair Queen of the Lists the gage he hath won; or, if he refuseth, he challengeth him, through me, not to a friendly joust, but to mortal combat. Should Sir Henri de Marle refuse this also, then do I, sir King, as a royal herald, demand of you that you do proclaim Sir Henri de Marle a craven knight, unworthy of the order of true chivalry, and as such that his spurs be struck off ere he quits these lists."

As the herald uttered this bold speech the features of de Marle became absolutely convulsed with rage. Clenching his mailed hand, he shouted:

"Satisfy me that I can meet him without affecting mine honour, and I shall far more gladly accept his challenge to mortal combat than see him accept mine to a friendly tilt."

"That is he prepared to do, sir knight," replied the herald. "He will attend you in your own tent, and will there unvizor himself and declare to you his name and rank. That, however, being done, the terms of his vow require that only one of you can then quit these lists alive."

"So be it!" cried de Marle. "Gracious sire, grant me this permission."

"No, no, de Marle!" replied Philip. "That we cannot do. We would not have our sports thus ended."

"Sire," said de Marle, "If ever aught I have done gives me a claim to demand a favour of you, I demand that favour now. Do me not the dishonour of knowing that I have been obliged to suffer such an insult as hath here been publicly given me."

Philip reflected. "So be it, then," he said at last, "We declare that Sir Henri de Marle and the nameless knight do meet in these lists and combat *à outrance*."

Attended by their respective esquires, the two knights rode to the entrance of one of the tents, which marked the extreme limit of the lists, and there, leaving their horses in the charge of the esquires, together entered the tent, and disappeared from view. The interest in the approaching contest was naturally doubled by the strange events which thus preceded it.

The sudden appearance of the Nameless Knight, and his eccentric refusal to divulge his identity, accorded well with the romantic feeling of the day, and heightened their interest in him, while the far more serious aspect which the contest was now to assume, of course, added to the zest of the enjoyment to which most of the spectators looked forward.

The reappearance of the two knights was thus eagerly and impatiently awaited, and when they finally emerged from the tent they were greeted with loud cheers. Mounting their horses, they rode slowly side by side until they once more approached the royal dais, where they again dismounted.

It was noticed that de Marle's face was pale and stern set, and those who knew his nature boded no good therefrom for the stranger knight who had thus boldly challenged him.

"Art thou satisfied, de Marle, of the rank and station of the Knight Without a Name?" asked the King.

"Perfectly, sire," replied de Marle; "and I here publicly declare that should I fall, I shall have the satisfaction of knowing that I have done so before a knight who hath no superior in Christendom."

This declaration heightened still more the interest felt in the stranger, were that possible. Both knights now approached the place where sat Eleanor de Montfort, and together knelt before her.

"Fair lady," said de Marle, "grant me, I pray, you some fresh token of your favour, and give me your good wishes in the course I am about to run on your behalf."

The lady looked at both the supplicants. The silent knight was debarred by the terms of his vow from uttering the prayer which doubtless his heart also felt. His eyes, glowing like coals of fire behind his vizor, spoke, however, as eloquently as words could have done. Under their burning gaze the eyes of the Lady Eleanor fell abashed.

"Sir Henri de Marle," she said, "you already hold one token of my favour, which you have honourably won in fair combat. If you deserve it, you will be able to keep it. If otherwise, no additional favour of mine and no good wish of mine could aid you. And you, Sir Silent Knight, who appear to offer a similar prayer, to you also I reply that it would ill beseem me to show any favour to either of you before the other. My favour must go with my gaze, and my prayer is that the best knight may win it. Therefore if you, Sir Henri de Marle, desire to retain my favour, you must retain my gage which floats as your pennon; and you, Sir Stranger, if you wish to gain my favour, must win it from the keeping of your opponent. I wish neither of you ill, but may God favour the knight who deserves best of Heaven and of me."

The knights now rose to their feet, and having again bowed, retreated to where their squires held their horses.

The Nameless Knight was the first to mount. Placing his hand on the pommel of his saddle, he leaped lightly on his steed's back, and the next moment was caracoling lightly around the lists, displaying as he went the paces of his horse and such feats of horsemanship as the knights of that day delighted in.

Sir Henri de Marle followed more slowly, along the opposite side of the lists. Having made the rounds, the combatants placed themselves one at each end, and prepared for the deadly course they were to run. The French knight, neglecting no precaution, and fearing his spear might have been weakened by the two shocks it had already withstood, changed it for another, removing Eleanor's scarf to the new weapon. His vizor had of course been lowered and fastened by his esquire, and both knights shortly gave the requisite signs that they were ready.

Then came the signal, and like the bolts discharged from the catapult, the horses darted forward to meet in mid career the deadly spears couched.

De Marle received his opponent's spear full and fair upon his shield, the stout ashen stave being shivered into a thousand pieces by the shock. By a mixture of skill and strength the Nameless Knight caused the other's spear to glance harmlessly aside, and no sooner felt his own spear shiver, than, ere de Marle could well recover the shock, he seized that knight's spear and wrested it from his grasp, continuing his onward course holding proudly aloft the prize scarf the winning of which had been the cause of the present contest.

Almost beside himself with rage, de Marle only waited to procure another spear and then prepared to run the second course, determined that it should be the last if skill and prowess on his part could compel fortune to smile upon him.

Again the knights met with a thundering crash, a moment it appeared doubtful with whom the advantage lay, as both horses had been forced backward upon their haunches. But it was only for a moment that any doubt prevailed. A second glance showed that while the Nameless Knight had received the spear of his enemy on his breastplate with such force as had caused him to reel in his saddle, his own, with truer aim, had struck the other in the slit of the vizor, and pierced the brain.

The brave and hitherto unconquered de Marle fell from, his horse, expiring without a groan.

The ashen stave broke short off in the socket of the

iron head, leaving the Lady Eleanor's silken scarf still affixed to the part which the Nameless Knight still held in his hand. Taking it reverentially off, he folded it carefully, and then, dismounting, presented it on bent knee to the fair lady on whose behalf he had run the fatal course, and thus returned her the liberty of which de Marle's first victories had deprived her.

Having thus signified that it was not his intention to take part in the gay proceedings of the rest of the day, he remounted his steed, and soon again disappeared among the crowd which had hidden him during the earlier part of the day.

Chapter XVI
The Serenader

It was late that evening when the festivities were well over, and the Castle of Montargis had been left once more to the quiet which usually surrounded it, that the Lady Eleanor and Gwen, her tiring maid, might again be seen sitting at the open lattice. The events of the day formed naturally enough the topic of their conversation, and of these the appearance and actions of the Nameless Knight, of course, formed the most prominent feature.

"'Twas nobly done, Gwen, 'twas nobly done," said the lady, "that he, a strange knight, should thus risk himself on my behalf."

"And wherefore should he not, my lady?" asked Gwen. "I trow he is not the first who has done so, and I will dare swear he is not the last who will be led by your charms to venture quite as madly, if less fortunately."

"Nay, Gwen, nay, there though doest this good knight grievous wrong. It could not have been any attraction in me, but rather the generous impulse of his own heart which led him to this, else had he been all too glad of the opportunity his victory gave him to remain at my side for the remainder of the day. He hath doubtless a fairer lady elsewhere on whom his heart and thoughts are fixed."

"Nay, lady, as to that I must doubt you. Mayhap his vow prevented his remaining with you as it prevented him revealing himself to others. And as for there being any other fairer lady to occupy his mind and thoughts, that I am ready to swear there is not."

"Why thinkest thou so, Gwen?"

"Why, for the simple fact that the face of the earth bears no fairer a one than my own dear lady."

"Tush, Gwen, that is thine own partial favour for me. But did'st thou see or learn aught of this strange knight?"

"He took good care that we should see as little as might be of him, but yet I saw his heart."

"His heart? Where? How?"

"In his eyes when kneeling before thee both before and after his combat. I have never read man's eyes if I read not heart's love for you, lady mine, in his eyes, carefully though he screened himself behind his vizor."

"Thinkest thou so?"

"I am certain of it, and I must say, my lady, that you treated him all too coldly. You could have given him far greater favour than you did."

"But Gwen, do thou remember that I am the betrothed of another, and that Llywelyn hath the only claim upon me?"

"Llywelyn indeed! A warm lover forsooth, who leaveth thee all these years to pine in solitude or love another as thou listest without ever paying thee a visit! I warrant me this Nameless Knight, silent though he was perforce compelled to be, would not have so left his lady-love."

"Now Gwen, there thou exceedest the bounds I can permit thee to take. Not a word will I hear against Llywelyn. And as to this strange knight, said he not that he also had been parted long years from his lady-love?"

"Aye, of a truth, now I remember me so did he."

"Yes, and therein sympathised I with him until my heart warmed more towards him than it hath to anyone since I last saw the brave Prince of Wales. And that reminds me, where didst thou place the scarf he returned me? Fetch it me."

Gwen thereupon handed it to her mistress, saying as she did so:

"Methinks, sweet mistress, that the good knight must have placed the key of his secret within the scarf. It feels somewhat heavy, and I fancy somewhat hard as well."

"So doth it indeed, Gwen," and the lady, lifting the scarf up by one corner, unrolled it on to her lap. An exclamation of surprise escaped her as there fell from it something on to her dress. Taking it in her hand, she held it up, exclaiming:

"A leek, Gwen! A leek, as I live!" (6)

"A leek, my lady? Then must the knight be a Welshman?"

"A Welshman? Of a surety, yes! What if after all it should prove to be *him* – but oh, my foolish heart would have told me!"

"And did it not? Said you not you felt warmer to him than you had done since you last saw our good Prince?"

"Ay? So did I! And it may well be that Llywelyn himself wished thus to see me unknown to all. But hush! I hear footsteps – yes, and on my life a guitar. A guitar? No! It is the harp. Can it be the brave knight come to serenade me?"

The two women leaned out through the window, and saw two men standing in the shadow of the wall close under their window. One of them held a harp, whose strings he now touched with a practised hand, singing in a powerful tenor voice the following:

THE KNIGHT'S SERENADE
Some love the world, its joys, and sports,
Its palaces rich-laden,
The knight he loves his war steed swift,
But oh! Give me my maiden!

The bees they love the flowers sweet,
　The bard his harp – no dumb one,
The sailor loves the billowy sea,
　And I – well, I love someone!
The bard with ear to nature tuned,
　Her music aye adoring,
Loves forest harps, and zephyrs mild,
　And tempest's loudest roaring.
And wavelets patter, one by one,
　Birds' song, or when bees hum one;
But oh! My heart it finds sweeter far,
　The clear loved voice of someone!*

---

* These verses have lost somewhat of their force in translating. We subjoin the original, as they appear in the Drama-Cantata *Llywelyn Ein Llyw Olaf*.

CÂN LLYWELYN

Mae'n dda gan rai am wychder byd,
　Anedd-dy clyd a chysur:
Y marchog fyn ryfelfarch chwim
　Ond rhoddwch i'm fy meinir.
Fe gara'r gwenyn flodau hardd
　Fe gara'r bardd ei delyn
Fe gara'r morwr tonnog li,
　Mi garaf finnau - rhywun!
I glustiau'r bardd peroriaeth yw
　Y miwsig gana Anian,
Telynau'r wig, yr awel gref,
　Ac uchel lef y daran.
A churiad ysgafn ton ar don,
　A chaniad llon aderyn
Melysach, mwynach imi'n wir
　Llais clir soniarus – rhywun!

YMDDIDDAN ELEN A LLYWELYN

Elen: Pwy yma sydd yn eofn ei lais
　Pa gais sydd gennyt grythwr,

"Gwen!" whispered Eleanor excitedly, "It is he! I will swear it is he! It can be no other! Reach me my guitar! Quick, lass! Quick! How slow and lingering are thy footsteps!" And snatching the instrument from the girl's hand, she ran her fingers quickly over the chords, and then sang, to the same metre as the other had sung:

> *Who art thou, stranger, bold of voice?*
> *What seek'st thou, harper, singing?*
> *What brings thee 'neath strong castle walls,*
> *Thy lays to maidens bringing?*

With equal readiness the harper replied:

> *Though strong this castle, stronger far*
> *My heart with love o'erladen,*
> *And though an earl this castle owns,*
> *I know who owns the maiden!*

When singing this the musician had approached the open window, and now found himself, though on a

---

> Dy fod fel hyn yn dod yn hyf,
>   At gastell cryf bonheddwr?
> *Llywelyn:* Os cryf ydyw, cryfach yw
>   Y cariad byw'n fy nghalon
> Os eiddo'r Iarll yw'r castell hwn,
>   Mi wn pwy bia'r Fanon!
> O tyred mwy yn eiddo imi,
>   Tydi yn wir rwy'n garu!
> Cei goron Cymru ar dy ben
>   A Gwalia Wen i'th foli
> *Elen:* Nis dof er mwyn coronau heirdd,
>   Na molawd beirdd yn gytun,
> Nid ydyw gwychder imi'n swyn –
>   – oni dof er mwyn Llywelyn!

somewhat lower level than the lady, yet almost face to face with her. Turning, therefore, his eyes full of the light of love upon her, he continued:

> *Oh! Come then, come, and be my own!*
> *From love-sick depths oh raise me!*
> *And Cymru's crown thy head shall grace,*
> *And Gwalia's bards shall praise thee!*

At this warm appeal the lady turned coldly away, singing:

> *I will not come for crown nor bard,*
> *From Snowdon to Helvellyn!*
> *I love not pomp, nor gaiety,*
> *But thee I love - Llywelyn!*

And at the last line she turned towards him with a countenance beaming and joyous as his own.

The Prince – for of course it was he – needed no second invitation, but leaped lightly through the open window, and the next moment held her clasped in his arms.

Chapter XVII
The Prophecy

Lengthened and sweet was the converse between the lovers, who had been so long and so unhappily parted, and many and bright the views of their happy future which their imaginations pictured for them. Each had much to tell the other of the past, with its trials, disappointments, and deferred hopes of the present, with its unalloyed pleasure and unbounded love of the future, with its plans for the consummation of the happiness for which each had longed for years.

Llywelyn, the natural warmth of whose affections had been necessarily placed under enforced and unnatural restraint, now for the first time for many years gave free expression to the passions which had been so long pent up, and while he revelled himself in the joys of communion with the object of his love, drew forth at the same time a fuller expression of the Lady Eleanor's affection for himself than under other circumstances would have been elicited. There was no affectation of maiden coyness on her part, no restraint placed upon the outpouring of heart's deepest feelings on his. It was as though the floodgates of all the pent-up affection of years were now opened, and the stream of love allowed to pour forth, bearing the happy couple with it to utter forgetfulness of all around them.

Hardly less sweet was the converse of Meredydd and Gwen, though here there was wanting to a great extent that knowledge of a previously felt and a previously expressed mutual love which added so much to the tenderness of the meeting between the Prince and his lady. But the germs were there, though the full-grown plant was not developed. The chivalrous respect of Meredydd's childhood for his whilom playmate had not been forgotten; and though it had not been fed by that personal intercourse which would have ripened it into ardent love, it had, to say the least, been preserved from decay and death by a naturally warm imagination. In many a dream – both day and night – had he pictured to himself what the little Gwen, on whose behalf he had so bravely though so unavailingly bearded de Langley, could have grown to be. On her part, too, young though she was at the time of her capture by the Normans, she had not been too young to be deeply impressed with the bravery of her boyish cavalier, and the recollection of that eventful night had been ever kept alive by many an evening's conversation with her mistress. Though too young at the time to fully realize the true chivalry of Meredydd's boyish attempt at rescue, all her afterlife at the court of France and among its chivalry had opened her eyes more and more to its value, so that her imagination had in the end endowed her child knight with all the virtues of a Paladin, and when Meredydd, who followed Llywelyn into the apartment, made himself known, he met with such a welcome as he had never allowed himself to hope for.

The hours passed quickly for both the young couples. The gossip which Meredydd had to give of all the small details of her humble home, her parents, and her playmates proved of quite as great an interest to Gwen as the more weighty details of policy and of state which Llywelyn had to communicate to Eleanor did to her mistress.

The result of these long hours of sweet converse, which passed all too quickly for each member of the quartet, was that the Prince found himself more hopelessly enslaved than ever; that his esquire was in no little danger of falling into a position hardly less dangerous than his master's; that Eleanor de Montfort found her high ideal of her prince and future lord more than realised and that Gwen, though she was obliged to confess to herself that her ideal spiritualised Paladin was somewhat different from the actual squire in physical form, was also fain to admit that there was an undefined something about this same Meredydd which was very pleasant to think about and remember when he was gone.

"And you consent then, fair Eleanor, to acquiesce when my ambassadors arrive at the court of your cousin, the King of France, to demand you in my name?" asked Llywelyn, as the earliest tints of the eastern horizon warned them that the approach of dawn would soon make it necessary for him to leave the precincts of the castle in order to preserve his incognito.

"Yes," was the ready reply. "I have given you my word. I can but leave all arrangements in your hands, good my lord. Whenever you see right to claim the fulfilment of the promise made in my father's name and presence, and of my own free will and consent, then I shall be ready."

His response to this reply was of that nature which lovers of all ages seem to be equally well conversant with, and which, therefore, needs no further demonstration.

"Hush said she; methinks I heard a step."

Llywelyn's hand involuntarily sought for his weapon, but the twanging of a musical instrument soon assured him that there would be no immediate necessity at least for resorting to arms.

"What?" said be, turning gaily to his betrothed, "have we here another serenader? And will it be your good pleasure to accord him an equally pleasant welcome to that you have given the previous troubadour?"

Playfully shaking her head negatively, she placed her finger on his lips in token of silence, and the four listened.

The instrument, which was for a time unaccompanied by any voice, gave forth strains of melody too mournful and touching to be mistaken for the serenade of a love-sick knight; and the curiosity of the listeners was raised in proportion to the unexpectedness of the music to which they were treated. After a few moments' rendering of a wailing air, indescribably sad and touching in its effect, a voice, somewhat weak and broken, but still evidently a practised one, joined in with the following music:

THE CURSE

Oh! Happy homes of pious joy!
Where worship true without alloy
Was offered to the Christian's God!
Where heavenly grace bedewed the sod!
Where peace, and love, and faith combined
To make each human heart refined
Where now are ye, oh homes of grace
What sorrows do my spirit face?

Oh Ask the tyrant Norman lord *
Who aye Waldensian faith abhorred!
Ask of the wolves what of their prey
The Albigenses' homes – all they
Before de Montfort's fury fell!
He, cursed by heaven and helped by hell,

---

* Simon de Montfort, the grandfather of Eleanor and father of the great Earl of Leicester, was one of the chief leaders in the persecution of the Albigenses, or Waldensians. The cruelties perpetrated by this knightly upholder of the Church of Rome are matters of history. He was killed in battle in France. (7)

> *Hath broken heavenly altars all!*
> *The curse of heaven upon him fall!*
>
> *The curse it came! The curse it comes!*
> *By sword he fell, by sword his sons*
> *And on the daughter of his son*
> *The curse must rest ere it be done*
> *Oh, woe to him who shall thee wed!*
> *My father's curse falls on his head!*
> *His love, proud lady, blind for thee,*
> *Shall cost his country's liberty.*
>
> *Thou Prince so brave, of distant clime,*
> *Be warned by past, be warned in time!*
> *Pray to thy God who rules the wave*
> *That in the sea she find her grave,*
> *Or through her heart let thy sword be*
> *Now, saviour of Welsh liberty!*
> *Even better this than she should prove*
> *To thee, brave Prince, a fatal love!*
>
> *Before she weds thee thou wilt give*
> *All that for which thou thought to live!*
> *And when she dies, her spirit dark*
> *Will leave on thee its fatal mark.*
> *Lose warrior's fame, lose princely pride,*
> *'Twill lead thee midst the woods to hide,*
> *Bring thee through loss, and grief, and woe,*
> *To fall unknown to worthless foe!*

The surprise of the four listeners at the unexpected nature of the song they had thus been made unwilling listeners to was so great that neither of them had thought of interrupting the unwelcome musician, whose song, therefore, came to an end without any effort being made to discover him.

Llywelyn, in whose bosom anger was now the dominant passion, recalled to himself by the somewhat abrupt ending of the song, was about to leap out through the window to take summary vengeance upon the bold intruder, when be felt his betrothed slipping from his grasp.

Eleanor had fainted. The effect of this weird prophecy, coming so unexpectedly as an interruption to the welcome pleasures of love, had been too much for her, and a merciful unconsciousness drew for a time at least a veil between her and the terrible picture the musician had painted before her mental vision.

Hastily summoning Gwen to the assistance of her mistress, and satisfied that the tiring maid could do more for her than he could, no sooner had he, by the girl's assistance, placed the Lady Eleanor on a couch in the apartment than, drawing his sword, he leaped out through the window in search of him who had brought the love scene to so abrupt and unpleasant a termination.

Meredydd, who feared nothing human, followed the Prince with alacrity. But though the two made a thorough search of the vicinity, no trace of the intruder could be discovered. He had disappeared as completely as though the earth had swallowed him. Though, as we have said, Meredydd feared nothing human, yet he was subject to all the superstitious fears native to his country, and the mysterious disappearance of the musician impressed him deeply with the conviction that he had to deal with the inhabitants of another world.

It was, therefore, with a white and scared look on his face that he followed Llywelyn on his return to the room where they had left the ladies. Here they were fated to meet with a still greater surprise.

Chapter XVIII
Love's Trial

When Llywelyn and his followers re-entered the apartment, they found Gwen still bending over the inanimate form of her mistress, endeavouring to restore her to consciousness. Standing behind Gwen, gazing over her shoulder at the reclining figure of Eleanor de Montfort, and evidently unperceived by the maid, was a tall draped figure, whose outline, in the dim light of the early dawn, appeared blurred, shadowy, and undefined, causing the two Welshmen to doubt whether what they saw was a human being or a disembodied spirit.

Even Llywelyn's stout heart, filled as it was with a burning desire to punish the bold intruder on his privacy, quailed somewhat as the strange figure turned towards them, displaying gaunt features of a deadly white. Gliding rather than walking towards them, the strange apparition, holding up a warning finger, to Llywelyn, passed between the Prince and Meredydd and disappeared through the still open window, the rustle of its garments alone betraying its presence to the ear.

Both men, brave warriors though they were, were too much overcome by superstitious dread to think of following the apparently ghostly visitor, and piously crossing themselves, approached the place where the Prince's betrothed still lay. As though with the departure of her unseen visitor the chain which held her senses captive also disappeared, Eleanor opened her eyes and looked wildly around.

Her first glance fell upon Llywelyn, who bent

tenderly over her. With a happy cry she threw her arms around his neck and sobbed in mingled dread and happiness on his breast. Then suddenly withdrawing herself bashfully from his embrace, she said:

"Pardon, I pray you, my simple, foolish fears. Methought I heard some strange words of dread import, which must have been a foolish dream," and she looked up wistfully in the countenance which beamed naught but warm admiration and tender affection upon her.

"But no!" she cried again, "It was no dream! Now I remember me! It was a voice I heard singing."

"Hush, lady, and fear thee not. Naught shall befall thee while I am with thee," pleaded Llywelyn, who was himself almost overcome at the sight of the state of extreme nervous prostration to which his betrothed had been reduced, and with soothing words and tender actions he endeavoured to restore her again to the self-command she once more appeared in danger of utterly losing.

With a mighty effort she at length controlled herself sufficiently to stand without assistance. Turning to Llywelyn, she said, in tones which still betrayed symptoms of her late agitation, "It is time we should now part. Go thou now, Sir Prince, and may God speed thee, and His saints have thee in their holy keeping."

"And you will remember, fair lady, your promise to me?"

"My promise?"

"Yes. That when my ambassadors arrive to claim you of your good cousin the king, you will offer no opposition."

"Sir Prince," said she, still with a slight tremor in her voice, "it were better by far that we should part now and here to meet no more."

The Prince gazed upon her in well-warranted surprise.

Llywelyn

"To meet no more?" he cried at length. "Wherein have I merited your anger? Is it that I did not slay that bold intruder with his vile jingle who hath so upset you? An' that be so, I will yet hunt him out if he be a dweller on the face of the earth, and put an everlasting stop on his folly."

"Nay," said she, with a shudder. "Shed no man's blood for me. Too much of that hath already been done for my peace in time to come. Harm him not. Methinks I now remember me of the voice as that of a man who suffered much and heavily at my grandsire's hands. I heard he had lately been seen wandering about half crazed. Harm him not, for my sake."

"For thy sake, then, shall he go scatheless of me," said Llywelyn.

"But, by my soul," whispered Meredydd, aside, "an' he be a living man, and not what I feared, a dweller of Annwn: for thy sake and Gwen's shall he not go scatheless or my sword shall have lost its temper and my hand its cunning." (8)

"And now, sweet love, must I bid thee farewell, and hasten back to Wales to make preparations to give thee a reception worthy of thee, and of the fair land and brave people over whom thou wilt henceforth rule."

"Nay," she replied again, "that must not be."

Seeing Llywelyn again about to interrupt her, she held up her hand and continued, uttering her words rapidly, as though she feared her courage would fail her ere she could reach the end of what she had to say. "Nay, it must not. The curse which must fall shall fall upon me and mine only. Thou shalt be no partaker of it. Think not it is lack of love for thee which bids me do this. Though it be unmaidenly to say it," – and here she blushed somewhat confusedly – "I love thee better than I do my life; and it is my love for thee which helps me now to bid thee go and never see my face again."

"Thou thinkest but lightly of my love and of my knightly faith if thou deemest it possible I could thus leave thee and give up all hope of having thee for my bride. Betrothed to me at God's own altar, by his priest, and in thy father's presence and with his sanction, thinkest thou I would let any power to part us now? Think no more of this foolish prophecy of an erring human being, whom thou sayest is already half-crazed. Even were the fates against us, my love shall conquer fate, and in my love shalt thou be safe, and in thine shall I be happy," and without listening to the further remonstrances she would have uttered, be clasped her in his arms, and pressed his kisses upon her lips.

Then tearing himself away, after having succeeded in restoring perfect tranquillity to the agitated bosom of his betrothed, and secured a renewal of her promise to accede to his wishes, the Prince at length took his departure, and, accompanied by Meredydd, managed to leave the castle and its neighbourhood unsuspected of all.

Chapter XIX
English Gold and Welsh Treachery

Brave and gay was the party of Welsh knights which formed Llywelyn's embassy to the Court of France, and hearty and cordial was the reception accorded to them. Llywelyn's letter[*] had been graciously received and readily responded to by Philip, who also acquiesced in the Prince's wish that the King's ward, the Lady Eleanor de Montfort, should be forthwith sent, under due and proper escort, to Wales.

Among the Welsh nobles who formed this embassy was Gruffydd ap Gwenwynwyn, who, finding Gwen had developed into a lady of more than customary attractions, renewed with her the acquaintance of their childhood, and paid assiduous court to her.

---

[*] This historical document, the original of which is still preserved in the archives of France, runs thus:

"To His Most Excellent Lord, Philip, by God's grace the illustrious King of France, his faithful Llywelyn, Prince of North Wales, sends health, and true and reverent service, as devoted as due. What return shall I make to your excellent nobility for the singular honour and inestimable gift wherewith you, the King of the Franks, yea, the prince of the kings of the earth, have assigned to me your knight, in testimony of the league between the Kingdom of the Franks and the Principality of North Wales; your letters, bearing the golden seal, not less magnificently than munificently anticipating me, your faithful servant? These letters I have caused to be preserved in the treasure-house of the Church, like consecrated relics, that they may be a perpetual memorial and an incontrovertible proof that I and my heirs, inseparably adhering to you and yours,

Being himself possessed of an attractive appearance, a ready and plausible tongue, acquired wit and courtly graces, it is not to be wondered at that he soon succeeded in ingratiating himself with Gwen, who had now been elevated from the humble position of maid to the more honoured one of companion, and on whom some portion, at least, of the greater importance with which the approaching marriage of the Lady Eleanor had invested de Montfort's daughter was reflected. These things directly tended to endow Gwen's position with increased dignity, so much so, indeed, that it would not have been considered

---

will be friends to your friends and enemies to your foes. That too I humbly ask and crave of your kingly dignity to be by all means royally observed towards me and my friends, and that it may be inviolably observed, having assembled a council of my nobles, and by the common consent of all the princes of Wales, all of whom I have bound together in friendship to you and this league, by the witness of my seal I promise that I will be loyal to you for ever; and, as I promise faithfully, more faithfully will perform. Moreover, from the time that I received your sublimity's letters, I have held neither truce, nor peace, nor parley with the English. But, by the grace of God, I and all the princes of Wales, unanimously confederate, have manfully resisted our – yea, *your* enemies, and by the aid of the Lord have, by force of arms, recovered from the yoke of their tyranny a great part of the land and the strongest castles which they by fraud and treachery had gotten. In the name of God we hold them thus recovered; wherefore we, the princes of Wales, earnestly beg that without us you will make neither truce nor peace with the English, being assured that we, on no account, nor for any gain, will be yoked with them in any league or peace, unless in consonance with your fore-ascertained goodwill."

This letter seems to have been accompanied by another message containing a formal demand for the transference of the prince's betrothed bride to his principality, a demand which Phllip readily complied with.

derogatory to the well-known pride of ap Gwenwynwyn to unite his somewhat uncertain fortunes with the more substantial and stable ones of his whilom playmate.

Had poor Meredydd ab Ednyfed seen some of the passages, sometimes lively, sometimes tender, which took place between these young people, it is probable his anxious waiting for the arrival of the Princess and her suite in Wales would have been made even greater than it was. As it happened, he was, for a time at least, spared this cause of disquietude.

No sooner had the exact date of the departure of the bride from the French shores been decided upon than Gruffydd ap Gwenwynwyn absented himself for a day from the court. Had he been followed and watched, he would have been discovered to have mounted his horse and ridden a distance of some leagues from the city to a place where his arrival was evidently expected; for scarcely had he dismounted at a low hostel in the village than the host led him to an apartment at the rear of the house, where sat a man who no sooner saw who his visitor was than he leaped to his feet and welcomed him effusively.

The appearance of the stranger was peculiar, having lost an eye, possibly in some hard-fought fight, or mayhap in a tavern brawl. On his head he wore a cap which came down over his ears, giving his head a peculiar bullet appearance, somewhat similar to that presented by the Roundheads of a later period.

After calling for a flagon of wine, and having carefully closed the door aft, the host, who had himself served them, the stranger turned to Gruffydd, and with ill-concealed impatience said:

"And hast thou succeeded? Canst tell me the very day of sailing?"

"Aye, in good sooth, that can I," was the reply. "But

it is dry work talking after my long and dusty ride. Help thyself, then, and wash the dust down. But tell me, tell me, man, when is it to be?"

"Softly, softly, good sir. I part not with my wares but for full payment at the tune of delivery."

"Malison on thy doubts," said the other, drawing from a cupboard at his side a small, sealed bag. "Thou seest I trust thee better than thou dost me. There is thy money, a goodly five hundred marks."

"But methought it was to be thrice five hundred?" said the Welshman.

"And so it is, man, so it is. But thou dost not think me fool enough to give thee all before I have any value from thee therefore? The other thousand will be as readily forthcoming as this the day I have the Lady Eleanor safe on board my ship."

"But suppose you should miss us? Am I to have all my trouble for nought?"

"For nought? Is there not there a good five hundred marks for thy hungry pocket? And see thou that I miss not the ship. Else may'st thou sig in vain for the fair companions of that bag," and the man laughed at his own wit.

"But come," he continued, "we do but waste time. Thou hast enough in thy hand now to make thee long for more. So tell me what is the day of sail and port of departure."

"Well then, the day is this day sennight, and the port Nantes."

"Then have I no time to spare. My ship shall cruise around the Scillys. Do thou, shouldst the captain of the ship incline to take a good sea berth, make some pretext for getting within view of the Scillys. And as the bag thou hast is only a foretaste of better to come, so shalt thou consider the fifteen hundred but a token of King

Edward's future favour. Thy future lies in thine own hand."

"I have done what I could," said the other somewhat sullenly.

"So thou hast, man, so thou hast. Do but what thou canst again in the same spirit, and, as I have said, thy future is certain. Two thousand more the day Prince Dafydd quarrels again with his brother; and the lordship of Machenydd the day Llywelyn falls into our hands, dead or alive."

The other flushed with gratification.

"The first is almost assured," he said. "I took good care to have Llywelyn refuse his brother's claim to lead this embassy, and Dafydd's proud spirit ill brooks a slight. I have little doubt but that I shall soon have him ready again to do as he hath been used to do in the past."

"Good. See thou now to thy part in the present bargain being duly and honestly performed. But now I think of it, I will change the word. 'Honestly' fits thee not. Let us say, then, duly and well performed. Then thy reward is secured."

The other bent his brows at the ill-disguised contempt of the other Englishman, and replied somewhat brusquely:

"I hope I shall keep my ears in any case, Sir Geoffrey."

It was now de Langley's turn to wince, for it was indeed he whom King Edward had entrusted to carry through this unworthy plot to seize Eleanor de Montfort on her way to Wales for her bridal.

"Come, come," he said, "we are too good friends to quarrel. Help me finish this flagon to our mutual success, and then we will each our way and to our work."

And the flagon having been finished, the pair of worthies separated, Gruffydd to return to lead poor Eleanor into the trap which de Langley hastened away to prepare for her at King Edward's instigation.

Chapter XX
An Unknightly Attack

It was a gay party which witnessed the embarkation of the fair Lady Eleanor de Montfort, when on her way to consummate at last the long delayed marriage with the Prince of Wales; and it was with a bright and hopeful heart for the future she was going to meet, though not without a pang of regret for the past she was leaving, that Llywelyn's betrothed bade adieu to the friends and companions with whom she had mixed for so many years.

Her brother, the Father Amaury, attended her for the double purpose of acting as her escort and of performing the ceremony which would unite the two loving hearts so long divided. There being no open war between England and France, and the relation between the former country and the principality of Wales being less openly hostile than had been the case for some years past, it was not deemed advisable to burden the expedition nor hamper its movements by needlessly adding to the number who formed it. For this reason Philip of France, on his side, had not deemed it necessary to send any but a mere guard of honour to accompany the bride on her wedding journey, and the Welsh ambassadors, not a little influenced by the representation of Gruffydd ap Gwenwynwyn, forbore to ask for any addition thereto. The natural consequence was that Eleanor's escort, however well fitted to grace a court, was, neither in point of numbers nor in the quality of its individual parts, suited to act as an efficient protection in case of need.

But there was, or there was supposed to be, no prospect of any such need arising, and it was with thoughts of meeting pleasure rather than danger that the members, both male and female, who composed Eleanor's party, set on their voyage for the land of the Welsh – a land which to many of them was essentially a land of romance, a sort of enchanted country in which experiences ever strange and new might be met with.

Gruffydd ap Gwenwynwyn was a born diplomat. He knew – none better – that if a doubtful deed was to be done, it were better that he should by whatever means induce some other hand to do that deed than that his own should appear prominent in it. When conveying any message, or making any statement, the wisdom or policy of which might be doubted, he by preference ascribed the words to others rather than laid claim to the questionable honour of authorship of them for himself.

By a carefully planned course of conversation he managed to raise Eleanor de Montfort's desire to see her future home to the highest pitch, and then, by a natural and easy gradation, made her feel sick of the endless expanse of sea and air, and almost morbidly anxious to get a glimpse of any land ahead.

As was often the case in those days, the real commander of the ship was a knight who had no practical knowledge of seamanship, and yet under whose orders the whole of the working crew, as well as the fighting crew, were placed. The sailing master, who was the practical sailor, was only a subordinate officer under the command of the knightly captain, and as such subject to his orders in all things.

Having raised Eleanor's feelings to the point we have described, it needed but little further effort to lead the lady to express her feelings to the captain in such a way as to induce him to issue orders that the head of the ship should be turned in the direction where land might first be seen.

It was some hours before sundown that a group of persons were gathered together on the small raised deck of the ship, gazing at the first land sighted – the rocky islets of the Scillys.

"There, fair lady," said ap Gwenwynwyn, with a courtly bow, "there before you lies the first strip of land which connects you with your future home."

"But methought these isles owned the sway of my uncle, the King of England," said Eleanor; "and if so, they can have but little interest for me, whose future lot is laid in Wales."

A smile of doubtful meaning crossed ap Gwenwynwyn's countenance as he replied:

"True, fair lady; and still it is a sure token that your home lies beyond."

"Aye, you say true, so does it in very deed!" she replied in a blither tone of voice, "My home, and that of the brave people among whom I go to live, lie beyond the barren rock we now see."

At this moment the sailing master came up, saying to the captain:

"An' it please you, the man at the watch telleth me that he hath just seen three or four ships put out from the shelter of the islands, as though to make out to meet us."

"Well, and what of that?" asked the captain.

"I wished to know what might be your pleasure. Shall we put about and sail more to the westward?"

"And what purpose shall we answer thereby?"

"Why, we shall then see if these ships are bent upon following us or not, and if they be, we can put back towards France."

Llywelyn

"Is it not more probable," suggested Gruffydd, "that these ships may turn out to be friends sent out by our good Prince Llywelyn to meet and welcome his bride?"

Eleanor's face flushed with gratification, and the captain seized the idea eagerly.

"It must be so," he said. "Make therefore a course straight for Wales, and let these friends of ours, for friends they doubtless are, bear us company."

"An' should they turn out to be English?" asked the sailor again.

"What a croaking raven art thou!" said the captain angrily. "Wouldst thou fill the heart of the Lady Eleanor with apprehension? Even if they turn out to be English, which seemeth not probable, they can have nought to do with us. Make thy course as I have bid thee."

The sailor turned away to give the necessary orders, muttering as he did so:

"Fill her heart with apprehension. 'Twere better so than let her fall into the hands of our foes. However, my hands are clean of it. Nevertheless, though I must perforce obey the captain's orders, and mayhap run into the lion's jaw, yet will I take good care that my men are ready so far as our numbers can avail, in case of need."

Less than an hour sufficed to bring the ship which bore Eleanor into close proximity to four other ships, which appeared, indeed, to be prepared to act as a guard of honour, as they separated, two and two, permitting the other ship to pass between them, and then drawing gradually closer as would have beseemed a naval escort.

In a short time the largest of the strange ships was within hailing distance, and, almost before the French vessel was aware of it had closed up with her, and fastened herself by grapnels to bar. The deck of the stranger was seen to be crowded with armed men, a number of whom rushed upon the other as soon as the two vessels were found sufficiently close together to admit of such an action.

"How now! What meaneth this?" cried the captain of the royal ship to the Knight, who, clothed in complete armour, led the boarding party.

"It meaneth that I, as representing his most noble majesty, the King of England, do demand of thee the persons of the Lady Eleanor de Montfort, of her brother the priest Amaury, and of such Welshmen as may be on board thy vessel."

"Knowest thou that thou art trespassing on the claims and rights of my master, the King, Philip of France?"

"I neither know nor care," replied the other grimly. "All that I know is that the lady and the priest are wards of my lord the King."

"'Tis a most unknightly deed!" cried the French captain. "Would thy master so far demean himself as to strike at the noble Llywelyn through his betrothed bride? Doth he acknowledge that, having failed to conquer him by force of arms, he must now do so through detaining his promised bride?"

"Know you not that she is his ward, the daughter of his sister, and that he claims the right of wardship over her, and the disposal of her hand in marriage?" asked the English Knight.[*]

"I know nothing but that she hath been entrusted to my care, and that with my life I will answer for her safe delivery to the hands of her betrothed husband, the noble Prince Llywelyn," replied the other.

---

[*] This was, indeed, the shallow pretence put forward by Edward as an excuse for one of the most dastardly and disgraceful deeds which dishonoured a reign noted for its high chivalry in many other respects.

"I am loth to do you harm," again replied the English knight. "To oppose us now would be an act of folly and of madness. See you not these four ships of mine, each with twice the men you have on board, and all sworn to the capture of the King's ward?"

"I care not," replied the French captain, "and should care not had you twice the number you boast of. Get you gone to your own ship without more ado. What ho! There! Sailing master! Cast off the grapnels and set us free."

At this the English knight gave the order for attack, and, ably seconded by his men, soon beat down the opposition of the escort, ill-fitted and worse prepared as they were for repulsing such an attack. The French captain paid with his life for the want of foresight which had led him into this strait, falling before the English knight's blow, and, in his fall, discomfiting his followers.

The ship was not, however, to be so easily won as appeared probable. The sailing-master had armed himself and his men; and, taking advantage of the bold stand made for a few moments by the escort, had managed to cast the ship loose so as to separate the boarders from their companions on the other ship. This having been done, he led his men forward in a fierce attack upon the rear of the English so sudden, furious, and unexpected, as seemed for a moment to promise success.

But it was only for a short time. The ill-armed and armourless sailors had little chance against the half-dozen knights in their coats of mail, and their men-at-arms in their breast-plates and strong buff jerkins, and one by one the sailors either gave way or fell before the boarders. The English captain was about to congratulate himself on the complete success of his attack, and the utter defeat and subjugation of his enemies, when a new and unexpected foe appeared.

Crawling with some difficulty on to the deck was an old and toothless hound, whose fighting instincts, as he lay below the decks, had been stirred by the sounds of the combat and the scent of blood. The animal's appearance was strange, not alone on account of its evident great and enfeebled age, but also from the fact that an ear and an eye were missing. As the animal reached the deck the voice of the English captain issuing an order seemed to affect it. It paused with one forefoot lifted up, and its solitary ear as though strained to listen. Then its hair was seen to bristle, and with a deep growl, rising in power and culminating in a furious bark, it leaped forward with a strength and agility to which it had evidently been for some time a stranger.

The beast made straight for the English captain, and, with the instinct of its race, leaped at his throat, seizing him in its toothless gums, and almost overthrowing him by the force, suddenness, and ferocity of its attack. Well was it for the knight that this new opponent was indeed devoid of the fangs which had been wont to let out the life blood of many a wolf and many a stag; had it been otherwise, de Langley's life would have fallen there to Crafanc's vengeful attack.

De Langley, for the English commander was none but be, endeavoured to beat off the animal, which held on with savage pertinacity by its toothless gums to the throat of its old enemy, but in vain. A cruel cut from the sword of one of the men-at-arms, however, brought the poor animal down, and de Langley, with a furious kick at the fallen beast's body, from the deep cut in which the life blood was rapidly oozing, vented some of the vengeful feelings which filled his heart.

As he did so, a sailor, who had been prominent in the recent fight, broke away from the two or three whose opposition had hitherto prevented him, but whose attention, like that of all others on board, had been engrossed by the strange conduct of the dog, rushed forward, and dealing a mighty blow at de Langley, knocked the helmet off his head, exposing to the view of all the knight's own deformity. Even at that moment the onlookers were struck by the fact that knight, and sailor, and dog all bore the same peculiarity, each possessing but one eye and one ear.

"Have at thee, thou born of the Evil One!" cried Hywel of the One Eye. "Warned I thee not that when next we met thy life should pay the forfeit?" and he threw himself with renewed ferocity upon the surprised knight, overthrowing him on the deck, already wet and slippery with blood. The dying hound, roused by its master's voice, seemed to revive and repossess himself of some portion of his old fire and energy, and again fastened himself upon de Langley.

Over and over they turned and twisted, and tumbled, Knight, Sailor, and dog, in inextricable confusion, and then a shout of horror went up as the trio, striking against the bulwark, fell over into the sea.

The weight of the knight's armour was of course so great that he sank at once, and so bent were Hywel and Crafanc upon satisfying their vengeance on their old oppressor, that neither would let go its hold, and the three disappeared for ever beneath the waves already reddened with their blood!

Chapter XXI
In England

To be wise, and love,
Exceeds man's might; that dwells with gods above.
– SHAKESPEARE

The tragic end of Sir Geoffrey de Langley and of Hywel, the one-eyed Welshman, brought the combat to a close, as the Englishmen had by this time, through their overpowering numbers, subdued all opposition. The captured ship was furnished with a fresh crew, and the little fleet made rapid way up the channel, bound for the Thames and London.

During the voyage Gruffydd ap Gwenwynwyn was unceasing in his attentions to the Lady Eleanor, and unremitting in the paying of his court to Gwen. So deeply did he appear to sympathise with the unfortunate bride, and so warmly did he evidently admire her Welsh companion, that no suspicion of his treachery crossed the mind of either. So thoroughly, indeed, had he ingratiated himself in their good graces, that it was with a feeling almost akin to dismay they contemplated the prospect of being deprived of his presence and assistance once they arrived at the English court.

It is almost needless to say that ap Gwenwynwyn was far-seeing enough to understand that it might yet be greatly to his advantage to continue, not alone, in the good graces of Eleanor, but of Llywelyn also; and that the surest way to the latter was through the former. As has already been seen, Edward aimed at the complete subjugation of Wales, and would not hesitate to use any means, however unworthy, for attaining that end. In the capture and possession of Llywelyn's promised bride, the English Sovereign possessed a most efficient aid to his projected scheme; he knew that Llywelyn's devotion to Eleanor exceeded the bounds of wisdom, and he trusted much to that devotion to induce the Welsh Prince to submit to the terms which might be dictated as the condition of Eleanor's release. Still he knew that there must be unknown factors in the problem he had determined to solve, and that the effects of some unknown influences on Llywelyn's mind might possibly lead him to make still greater efforts to withstand English aggression. Edward, therefore, did not trust entirely to the capture of his niece for subduing the fiery Welsh Prince, but determined, as has already been hinted, to endeavour to weaken Llywelyn's power in the principality by widening the breach between him and his brother Dafydd. Indeed, unless de Langley had done his sovereign wrong, Edward seriously contemplated a deed of still blacker treachery, and aimed directly at the assassination of his rival.

Of all these projects Gruffydd ap Gwenwynwyn had been made acquainted, and had been very properly deemed to be the most suitable instrument for carrying them into execution. The reward which was placed before him as a lure was more than sufficient to induce so thoroughly unprincipled a man to fall in with the views of the English sovereign. It will, therefore, be seen how very much to the interest of Gruffydd ap Gwenwynwyn it was that neither Llywelyn nor Eleanor should suspect his fidelity in the slightest degree. How well he had succeeded with the lady we have already shown. How well or ill he succeeded with the Prince succeeding chapters in our story will explain. Suffice it now to say that by the exercise of a little diplomacy on his part he received from the Lady Eleanor before they arrived in London an autograph letter to the Prince, in which the self-sacrificing fidelity of Gruffydd ap Gwenwynwyn was lauded, and he himself most warmly commended to the good graces of his native prince.

Thus blindly did Eleanor assist in weaving the fatal web intended for her betrothed's destruction. Had she but been able to see to what end her action tended, she would have been led to believe more firmly than ever in the divine inspiration of the prophet of evil who had visited her on the eve of Llywelvn's departure from France, and had fore-doomed to misery whoever might be connected with her.

This knowledge was, at least for a time, mercifully withheld from her, and it was with a comparatively light heart that she wished him God speed, when, apparently, at her intercession, he was permitted to depart from the English Court on his mission to Wales. On this mission he was the bearer of triple despatches. The letter from Eleanor to Llywelyn has already been referred to. The second was from Edward to Llywelyn proposing terms of peace, to which we shall again have to refer later on. The third consisted of letters to several disaffected Welsh chieftains, in which they were urged to co-operate with Gruffydd ap Gwenwynwyn in whatever plans he might resolve upon. He had also all but received Gwen's plighted troth to him, and so with love and fortune smiling upon him, he departed on his mission of treachery.

Chapter XXII
In Wales

Who strikes at sov'reign power had need strike home;
For storms that fail to blow the cedar down,
May tear the branches, but they fix the roots.
     – JEFFREY

Gruffydd ap Gwenwynwyn had not allowed any time to be wasted on his journey to Wales. He did not, however, make his way direct to Llywelyn's abode in North Wales, where preparations had been made on an extensive scale to welcome the bride to her adopted country. The traitor wanted to have the meshes of his net complete before he found himself face to face with his prey, and for this reason once he found himself in Wales, took a circuitous route which enabled him to visit three or four of the chieftains on whose help he chiefly depended to obtain possession of Llywelyn's person.

While these events were taking place, the Prince had become anxious and alarmed at the non-arrival of his promised bride. A day or even two beyond the stipulated time was not considered of so much account, as the arrival of a vessel from France could not be precisely timed in the then imperfect state of the science of navigation. When, however, a week elapsed, and still no signs were visible of the approach of the expected party, Llywelyn's alarm became so great that he could no longer remain idly expectant.

"Meredydd," said he to the son of Ednyfed, who had now become his chief confidant, "I cannot bear this suspense anymore; I must set out myself in search of Eleanor."

"Nay, that will not do," replied Meredydd. "You must on no account leave Aber at present." (9)

"On no account!" cried the Prince, angrily. "Tell me not so. Who is there to prevent my going?"

"If there be no other, then will I prevent your going myself," was the blunt reply.

Llywelyn laughed half threateningly. "Methinks thou presumest too much on my friendship, Meredydd," said he. "It beseemeth not that a subject should tell his sovereign that he should not do that which he hath made up his mind to do."

"I know it beseemeth a subject to strike for his sovereign in any case of need, and methinks that in that I have ever done what was beseeming. But I know too that it beseemeth anyone who wishes thee well to prevent thee doing a foolish action."

"What meanest thou?"

"Why, this. Thinkest thou that the sea is nought but a garden path, so that if the Lady Eleanor start from one end, and thou from the other, you must needs meet? Almost as well might one bird flying hither from Glyn Ithon depend upon meeting another flying from Aber thither? No, no! To go thyself now in search of the Lady Eleanor might result in thy finding thyself in France to learn that she had reached here with none to welcome her. An' if she be, as seemeth probable, as foolish as thou, she might again start back to hunt for thee, and the saints only could tell when you would meet!"

The Prince laughed at the ridiculous light in which Meredydd painted him, and said:

"What then doth thy wisdom advise?"

"I should advise thy sending someone in whom thou canst rely to undertake this expedition in thy place."

"And where shall I find such a one?" asked Llywelyn

with a twinkle in his eyes.

"Well, failing anyone else, I am willing to undertake the journey myself," replied Meredydd demurely.

"On the chance that thou wouldst meet Gwen a few days sooner?" asked the Prince, laughing at having turned the tables upon his friend. "But, seriously," he continued, "I can think of none better than thou, none whom I can so well trust, none in whom the Lady Eleanor could have more faith. Thou knowest, too, the country and the language of France, and will be able to make the greater speed. So, as I see the wisdom of my remaining here, as well as the need of obtaining early and certain information respecting the Lady Eleanor, I would have thee prepare to start without delay."

This was accordingly decided upon, and in an hour's time Meredydd up Ednyfed was on the sea in quest of his Prince's missing bride, and the object of his own affections.

Little, however, did he imagine in starting on this voyage how it would end, and the succession of surprises in store for him.

*   *   *

Meanwhile Gruffydd ap Gwenwynwyn's private mission was flourishing all too well. He had succeeded in getting a number of the disaffected chiefs to promise to visit Llywelyn on a fixed date, under the guise of a visit of homage, and then, when located with their followers in his castle, to make an attack upon him in the night, and either to slay or take him prisoner. In this foul plot the fickle Prince Dafydd was involved, and he had himself undertaken to be present at Aber on the day fixed upon, to direct the operations of the conspirators, and seize immediately upon the authority which would naturally fall into his hands at his brother's death.

Chapter XXIII
The Sea Gives Up its Dead

With mournful look the seaman eyed the strand,
Where death's inexorable jaws expand.
   – FALCONER, *The Shipwreck*

It was not with an altogether light heart, nor, indeed, with very joyful anticipations, that Meredydd ab Ednyfed started on his quest. His heart had been filled with forebodings from the day that Gruffydd ap Gwenwynwyn had been appointed to so important a post on the embassy to France. These forebodings, it is true, had little to do with the future Princess of Wales, but it is no reflection on Meredydd's loyalty to state that since his last visit to France his personal interest in Gwen had become greater than in her mistress. He could not conceal from himself that Gruffydd ap Gwenwynwyn was eminently fitted in many ways to make himself an acceptable companion to one of Gwen's lively temperament; neither could he forget that his boyhood's rival must occupy in Gwen's remembrance a place of honour second only to his own. It was, therefore, with no little dismay that he had first heard of ap Gwenwynwyn's appointment and it was with considerable anxiety indeed that he had looked forward to the arrival of the bridal party, which he hoped would give him an opportunity of counteracting the influence of his rival.

How well-founded were these forebodings of evil previous chapters have shown. Meredydd's fears had, however, been confined to anxiety on account of

Gruffydd's influence on Gwen's mind and affections rather than for her personal safety, or that of her mistress. Still, the inexplicable delay in the expected arrival of the party from France had filled his mind with sore misgivings and apprehension, feelings which he had had the greatest difficulty in concealing from Llywelyn. His nervous eagerness to obtain some news of the missing ones had led him to give secret orders for fitting out a suitable vessel, to be held in readiness to sail at a moment's notice. Thus was he enabled to set off on his quest within a very short time of receiving the sanction of the Prince to do so. It will readily be believed that Llywelyn could have secured no more fitting messenger for the important service Meredydd had undertaken.

Neither sail nor oar was spared, and through their combined assistance, and the influence of Meredydd's personal energy on the crew, the gallant little vessel made rapid progress.

Indeed, so great were the exertions of the rowers, and so well did the wind favour them, that Meredydd entertained high hopes of reaching his destination in an unusually short period, and his spirits naturally rose in proportion. These hopes were, however, not fated to be fulfilled. The evening of the second day out was so dark and lowering that, notwithstanding Meredydd's eagerness to hasten forward at all hazards, even he did not feel himself justified in preventing the taking in of the sails, which the sailing-master deemed necessary to ensure the safety of his vessel.

The threatening aspect of the evening was fully justified in the storm which followed in the dark hours of the night, and, tossed hither and thither by the winds and the waves, the poor lover's vessel was only saved from foundering by the unremitting exertions of her crew. The grey light of the morning found her so much disabled that the captain declared it to be impossible to continue the voyage without first executing some repairs. Meredydd swallowed his disappointment as best he could, and found some outlet for his restlessness m assisting the crew in rowing the almost water-logged vessel towards the land, which they discerned not far from them on their lee. Here they were fortunate enough in finding a sheltered nook, where the sailors lost no time in commencing the necessary repairs.

Finding he could render no further assistance, Meredydd, unable to remain an idle spectator, started on a tour around the rocky coast of the little islet on which he found himself thus unexpectedly placed. His mind was too much occupied with the object of his voyage to notice whither he went, or what he saw; he wandered aimlessly forward intent only upon doing something to occupy the time which must intervene before the vessel would be again ready to proceed.

Suddenly he stumbled, and almost fell, his foot having struck against some obstacle on the beach. Casting only what was intended to be a passing glance upon the object, and noticing it was the body of a dog, he was about to pass forward, vaguely picturing to himself how the poor animal could have reached this solitary and desolate spot, when his eye fell upon the beast's head, and even his preoccupied mind was struck by something unusual in its appearance. Bending down with some curiosity, he noticed that the animal possessed only one ear, the other having been shorn off close to the head.

"Poor beast," said Meredydd, half aloud. "And so elsewhere than in Wales do men vent their cruelty on the brutes My old friend Crafanc would find in thee a sympathetic companion. I wonder if thy eye hath suffered too? A further examination satisfied him that this was so, and that this poor animal had at one time suffered the same punishment as had been inflicted upon poor Crafanc in Glyn Ithon. The coincidence could not but strike him as being remarkable, and examining the body of the dog more closely, the conviction gradually forced itself upon him that the animal before him was none other than the companion of his childhoods days, the playfellow of Gwen in many a romp on the banks of the Ithon.

Then, like a flash, came the thought: "Where is Hywel? Master and dog have never been separated! And Hywel? Yes; Hywel was specially appointed one of the crew of the royal vessel which was to bring the Lady Eleanor and Gwen to Wales!"

Almost overpowered by the fear which now, as it were, took actual form in his imagination, he sank down upon a rock at hand, and pressed his hand over his brow.

"Had Hywel lived," he thought, "he would not have left Crafanc unburied, to be food for the fowls of the air. Master and dog must have perished together. But where, and how? Has the vessel been wrecked? He sprang to his feet and gazed anxiously around for some tokens of a wreck, but there were none in view. Returning once more to where the dog's body lay, his attention was attracted by a rag fluttering in the breeze beyond the rock on which he had first seated himself. Hastening thither, he found his worst fears realized.

There lay a dead body, whose single eye and shorn ear sufficiently marked its identity. It was the body of Hywel, the one-eyed Welshman.

"Alas!" cried Meredydd, "the storm of last night, which nearly cost us our ship and lives, hath proved the death of Hywel, and those that were with him! And Gwen too! Thus perish my hopes. And, ah me! How shall I convey this news to the Prince?"

Then came another consideration. Was it his duty to return at once, to Aber, to break the sad intelligence of the wreck to Llywelyn, or should he first of all visit the French court to discover what had caused the delay which had proved so fatal? Then again, was it certain that the vessel had been wrecked at all? And, if so, was it certain the disaster was so recent as he had at first supposed?

To satisfy himself upon this point, he made a more careful examination of the bodies than he had at first done. A very superficial inspection proved that death must have occurred some days previously. The bodies themselves bore unmistakeable evidence of this.

Then, had they been wrecked, or had their death been caused by any other means? Two things soon satisfied Meredydd that their death was to be attributed to other causes than a shipwreck. The deep wound inflicted by Sir Geoffrey de Langley on the dog, coupled with the fact that Hywel still held his drawn dagger in his right hand, while his left grasped in its dying clutch some grey hairs, with even a portion of human skin attached, showed plainly enough that dog and man had fallen in some terrible contest.

Now came the question, where and with whom had the fight taken place? To this, however, there was no reply. Nothing in the appearance of the bodies could afford any clue to this, and the tongues, for evermore mute, could not be unloosened to tell the secret tale.

For Meredydd there was even some consolation in this uncertainty. Had Hywel been wrecked, the fate of Gwen would have been, naturally enough, the same, and little or no hopes could have been entertained of finding her yet alive. The fact that Hywel had evidently fallen in some fight pointed to at least the possibility of Gwen and her mistress having been saved. This, however, only made it the more necessary that Meredydd should continue his voyage of inquiry without delay.

He therefore hastened to find his companions, and to his unbounded satisfaction was informed that the vessel would be in a fit state to sail at the full tide, in an hour's time. Before leaving the island, however, he had a sacred duty to perform – the burying of the bodies of his old friends Hywel and Crafanc. This having been properly done, with the aid of some of the crew, Meredydd returned to the vessel more eager than ever to continue his voyage. The wind and tide favouring them, he once more set out to pursue the quest, little thinking how very greatly would this flying visit to, and consequent detention at, the island affect the results of that quest, as well as his own whole future.

Chapter XXIV
The Awakening

When anger rushes unrestrained to action,
Like a hot steed, it stumbles in its way.
– SIR T. SAVAGE

By one of those strange sarcasms of Fate which most of us have now and again to endure, hardly had Gruffydd ap Gwenwynwyn safely departed from the English court, bearing with him the letter in which Eleanor commended him most warmly to her future husband's consideration on account of the valuable service he had rendered her, than she became aware how very erroneous was her impression of his fidelity, and what a terrible weapon for harm she had unwittingly placed in the traitor's hands.

It is not necessary we should here give the details of how she arrived at this knowledge, further than to state simply that an attaché of the court, whose personal obligations to the late Earl of Leicester led him to take especial interest in de Montfort's daughter, in the first instance warned her against trusting too implicitly to the plausible Welsh chief. Her indignant remonstrance against any aspersion being thrown on ap Gwenwynwyn's fidelity opened the eyes of her father's friend to the greatness of the danger in which the Lady Eleanor and her betrothed husband were placed. Without hesitation, therefore, he unmasked the villain, and filled the unfortunate Lady Eleanor's heart with dismay when he produced undeniable proof of the treachery of which ap Gwenwynwyn had been guilty.

He showed her that beyond a doubt Gruffydd had played the part of traitor from the commencement of his embassy, and that it was owing to information directly derived from him that the English king had been able to make the necessary arrangements for intercepting the ship when on her way to Wales.

Though neither she nor her informant knew anything of the object of the traitor's present visit to Wales, enough was known of his previous deeds to fill her tender breast with alarm for Llywelyn's safety.

"Alas!" she cried, wringing her hands in despair. "To think that I have thus blindly trusted in him, and given him a key which will open for him the inmost secrets of the Prince's breast!"

"What mean you by that, lady?" asked the other.

"Why," she said, "it was but a few days since that I gave him a letter, addressed to Llywelyn, and written by my own hand, in which I commended him most warmly to the Prince's care, gratitude, and confidence."

The other looked grave.

"That is, indeed, a misfortune," he said, "and the man who could have betrayed you as ap Gwenwynwyn hath done will, of course, not hesitate to make use of the letter you have given him to further the treacherous designs he doubtless hath in view."

"Oh, woe's me! What can be done?" and the lady wrung her hands despairingly.

The other considered for a moment.

"There appears to me to be but one course open to you," he said.

"And that?"

"And that is that you should send a messenger without delay to inform the Prince of the treachery you have discovered."

"And where shall I find such a messenger?" she

asked hopelessly. "I have no one in whom I can trust – no living soul in the retinue the king allows me to whom I could venture to trust so important a message as that you advise."

"Think again, lady. Surely there must be someone in whose fidelity you can implicitly trust."

She considered again, and then again shook her head. "No," she said, "there is only one in whom I could trust, and that one I cannot send."

"And that one is?"

"My tiring maid, Gwen, who hath been with me from her childhood upwards."

"And is she not a Welshwoman?"

"Yes."

"And known to the Prince?"

"Yes."

"Then, if she hath any spirit left in her, let her be sent. Being personally known to the Prince, she will need no letter, and so, even if taken and examined by any of the King's officers, can fear nothing, as she will have naught with her to betray her. If she consents to go, I will arrange the means whereby she may be safely conveyed to the western shores of Wales in a vessel which is shortly about to sail. Speak over the matter with her and let me know again tonight. Meanwhile, on the chance that she may consent, or that you may think of another messenger, I will make the necessary arrangements to secure her passage in the ship."

The Lady Eleanor lost no time in summoning Gwen, and in telling her of the straits in which ap Gwenwynwyn's treachery had placed them.

Gwen was even more incredulous than her mistress had been of ap Gwenwynwyn's treachery. To her simple heart it seemed indeed impossible that any man should prove himself so double-dyed a traitor as must her quondom lover have been if the charge now preferred against him proved to be true.

The proofs of his double dealing were, however, too strong and convincing to permit of her remaining long in doubt. Her indignation more than equalled that of the Lady Eleanor when she finally satisfied herself of the treachery of the man who had all but won her troth. No persuasion was needed to induce her to undertake this journey to prevent the traitor benefitting by the trust reposed in him.

The same evening, dressed in a page's suit – more for her own safety among the sailors than from fear of recognition by others – Gwen was conducted on board a small ship lying ready for railing, and having received from the friendly knight, in the hearing of the crew, some parting injunctions and messages to be conveyed by the page to his master, found herself once more on her way to her native land.

It seemed, however, as though the fates were not only unpropitious, but malignant, and that while everything seemed to co-operate to favour Llywelyn's enemies in their machinations, even the elements warred against his friends. The vessel which conveyed the warning messenger from Eleanor to her betrothed met the full force of the gale which had so nearly proved fatal to Meredydd. Whether it was that the ship which bore Gwen was less fitted to withstand the storm, or that her crew proved less vigilant than did those under Meredydd's orders, it soon became apparent that the vessel was in imminent peril.

The crew, heedless of all but their own safety, lowered their only boat and crowded into it, deaf to the appeals of Gwen to be taken with them. With a sinking heart, she saw the boat disappear in the gathering gloom of night, and found herself alone on the dismasted and evidently foundering vessel. It required more than ordinary energy and effort on the part of a weak woman to rouse herself from the state of abject terror and helplessness into which it was natural that she should fall. The recollection of the vast interests at stake, of all that depended upon her being able to reach Llywelyn's home – and possibly some remembrance, too, of her personal indebtedness to the traitor chief – served to stimulate her to make some effort to secure her own safety.

Mechanically she managed to secure herself to a broken spar, as a sort of forlorn hope of safety. Hardly, however, had she done so than the ship, with a final plunge, disappeared under the waves, and poor Gwen's last despairing and solitary cry ascended to heaven as she found herself drawn into the vortex caused by the sinking ship.

Then the waves closed over her, and with her over the knowledge of ap Gwenwynwyn's treachery – that knowledge so necessary to the safety of Llywelyn.

Chapter XXV
To Be, or Not to Be

What man so wise, what earthly wit so rare,
As to descry the crafty, cunning train
By which Deceit doth mask in vizor fair,
And seem like Truth, whose shape she well can fein?
  – SPENSER

It is said to be an ill wind that blows no one good. The storm which so delayed Meredydd ab Ednyfed's quest, and resulted in such disastrous consequences to the faithful Gwen, made its effects felt elsewhere, and, to some extent at least made up to Llywelyn for the harm caused him by it.

Gruffydd ap Gwenwynwyn, as has already been stated, had arranged with his fellow-conspirators to meet him at Aber, the palatial North Walian home of the Prince. Among those who had undertaken to be present, and to take part in the night attack upon Llywelyn in his own home, and while enjoying his hospitality, was Prince Dafydd, who expected to be the chief gainer by his brother's downfall.

Gruffydd arrived at Aber on the morning of the storm, that is, on the day following the departure of Meredydd for France.

With much display of grief and sympathy he gave the Prince an account of what had befallen the bridal party on its way from France; how the perfidious Edward, jealous of his rival's growing power and prospect of immediate happiness, had, contrary to all the laws of chivalry and honour, attacked the vessel bearing the bride to her Welsh home; how, notwithstanding the devoted stand made by ap Gwenwynwyn and the remainder of the escort, they had been over-powered by force of numbers and how the Lady Eleanor was now detained a prisoner at the English Court.

Having allowed Llywelyn's first passionate burst of grief and anger to wear itself out, Gruffydd then handed him the note entrusted him by the Prince's betrothed.

Llywelyn's gratitude for the services reported by the Lady Eleanor to have been rendered her by ap Gwenwynwyn was so great, and so warmly expressed, that the traitor, hardened villain as he was, began to feel some compunction for the evil he was about to do him. For the first time he regretted the action he had already taken, and the arrangements he had already made to assassinate the Prince – for this was really the object he and the more advanced section of the conspirators had in view.

And it was not conscience alone which induced him to reconsider his position. Selfishness had much to do with it. Llywelyn's promises of patronage, advancement, and grants of land were so generous that if the traitor could only venture to accept them, he would find himself in a far better position than he could expect to secure at the English court as the wages of his perfidy.

Was there, then, a way out of the dilemma in which he was placed? Could anything be done to ward off the catastrophe he had himself arranged?

He feared not. Every moment he expected to hear in the courtyard the hoofs of the horses of those who had sworn to him and with him to secure the downfall of his host. Once they arrived it would be too late to retreat, and every succeeding moment of delay added to the danger of revealing the plot.

Thus, after weighing matters over very carefully, he

Llywelyn

decided upon letting things take their course, though it was not without a pang that he thus gave up, as it seemed to him for ever, the hopes of enjoying the lordship of Mailenydd, and the possession of Glyn Ithon and neighbouring districts already promised him by the Prince.

There were, however, other forces at work on which ap Gwenwynwyn had not calculated. The heavy fall of rain which preceded in the afternoon the terrible storm of the evening had so flooded the rivers that the fords became impassable, and the forces of Dafydd and the other conspirators on their way to Aber were effectually prevented from continuing their onward progress. Thus it happened that the shades of night fell, finding Gruffydd ap Gwenwynwyn the only one of the half-a-dozen leading conspirators inside the walls of Aber.

Well has it been said that a guilty conscience makes cowards of us all. So was it in ap Gwenwynwyn's case. The consciousness of his own guilt led him to fear the worst, and to doubt the fidelity of the restless spirits with whom he had joined himself. Illustrating the truth of the old Welsh proverb of measuring others by his own yardstick, and remembering his own inclination in the afternoon to confess all to the Prince, he now feared that others might have forestalled him; and even if they had not already divulged the secret of the conspiracy, it was evident enough that they fully intended doing so: for how else could he account for their non-arrival at the rendezvous agreed upon?

Was he, after all, to fall into the trap laid for others? Was the betrayer to be betrayed, and to be made the scapegoat of others' sins as well as his own?

Filled with these misgivings, his mind again reverted to the advisability of making some capital out of the failure of the conspiracy – for that the conspiracy had failed appeared to him to be now beyond a doubt.

Might he not, not only secure safety and indemnity for himself, but actually make the occasion serve another purpose, and really secure once for all the substantial benefits which Llywelyn's first warm impulses of gratitude had offered him? Filled with these thoughts, he determined to seek the presence of the Prince, and there divulge such portions of the conspiracy as might to him appear most suitable.

Chapter XXVI
An Unexpected Revelation

Uncertainty!
Fell demon of our fears! The human soul
That can support despair, supports not thee.
– MALLET

Meredydd ab Ednyfed re-commenced his voyage with a heavy heart. What he had already learnt did not tend to reassure him respecting that which was yet hidden from him in the future. It is true that the discovery that Hywel had met with his death in some sore conflict went to prove that the chances were in favour of Gwen and her mistress being yet alive. Still, that such a fate had overtaken him proved that some mischance must have happened to the ship in which the ladies were to sail.

A calm had succeeded the storm of the previous night, and the sails flapped idly against the mast, as though mocking his impatience to proceed. The crew, too, wearied with their exertions during the storm and the labour of refitting, were neither in the humour nor condition to toil at the oar. After lying for some hours thus idly on the waves, which yet heaved as mementoes of the storm which had passed away, it was with unbounded satisfaction that Meredydd at length saw signs indicating that the dead calm was about to end. By the time the wind had reached the ship, and the sails were beginning to fill out, the crew, refreshed by a long sleep, were ready to make every effort to avail themselves of the wind which had thus at last favoured them.

Like a thing of life the little vessel bounded forward, as though as eager as the sailors or their commander to make up for the time already lost. It seemed, however, as though the fates must have formed a conspiracy against Meredydd on this voyage, for while the ship was joyously proceeding at such speed as promised, if maintained, to bring the voyage to an early conclusion, Meredydd was approached by the sailing master.

"We are making good way," said Meredydd, glancing over the ship's side at the water, over which, rather than through, the ship appeared to be rushing. "If we can keep up this rate we shall yet reach France in fair time."

"Yes," replied the sailor, "but I fear me we shall have to stop, and e'n to beat back for a while."

"What meanest thou, fellow? The wind seemeth fair enough."

"Yes, so it doth."

"Then have we sprung another leak?"

"The saints be praised, we are as water-tight as when we first started."

"Well, why, then, in the devil's name dost thou speak of stopping and beating back?"

"An' you had better let me go on with my story in my own way I should have finished it ere now. But you are aye hotheaded."

"I will make thee sure headed an' thou dost not at once explain thyself," cried Meredydd irritably. "Come, speak out."

"That I gladly do did you grant me the opportunity," said the sailor with the same imperturbable deliberateness as at first

Meredydd bit his tongue to keep it silent, knowing by previous experience that the only way to get the sailor to finish his tale was to let him say say it in his own way, and at his own time.

"The man at the look-out saith he hath seen signs of a foundered vessel away yonder, and he thinks that what appears to be a body is to be seen on a piece of the wreck."

"And what dost thou propose doing?" asked Meredydd.

"As a sailor who am myself subject at any time to shipwreck, and who may at any time be beholden to the kindness of others for assistance, in sore need, I never pass by such signs as these without seeing if, by any chance, some unfortunate being may not be in need of such help as one sailor can and should render to another."

"What, then, must be done?"

"As to what *must* be done, it is for you to decide, not me. The ship is under your command. But as to what *ought* to be done, that I can readily answer. We should beat back to the neighbourhood of the place where this wreck seemeth to have occurred, and there let down our boat to see if haply some poor survivor may not yet be saved."

Meredydd paused and considered for a moment. Then, looking up, he said with decision:

"I had sworn to strain every nerve to reach the end of my journey as soon as wind and weather would permit me, and now the wind is in our favour, and to beat back to where thou sayest will mean the loss of some valuable hours. Yet, though I would give all I have to hasten forward, God forbid I should pursue my own selfish course if there may be any hapless fellow creature needing my help by the way. Therefore have the ship put about at once, and pray God I may not be a loser in my own quest by this," and poor Meredydd, as though unable to bear the sight of the ship's head being turned away from the place which he was straining every nerve to reach, left the deck for the only little cabin the vessel could boast of.

Though he had been brave enough to subordinate his own wishes to his ideas of duty, and permitted the departure from their course on their errand of mercy, he was too heart-sick to take any active part himself in the search now being made by the crew. The wind was so much against them that it took some considerable time to enable them to reach the wreckage which the look-out had discovered.

Meredydd, in his cabin, was able to distinguish by the sounds what was being done. He could hear the orders given as to the trimming of the sails when tacking, then the preparations for leaving to, and finally heard the boat being lowered, evidently either to make a thorough search, or else because some unfortunate one had been discovered. Even this, however could not arouse him from the strange and unexplainable lethargy which had overcome him. There he sat, listless and solitary, almost heedless of all that was going on.

He heard the boat return, and could understand that someone was being lifted on board. Then, in a short time, the door of the cabin was opened, and the sailing master appeared.

"We have found one poor lad," he said, "but I am afraid it is all over, and that we came, after all, too late. Will you come up and see him?"

Meredydd leaped to his feet.

"Now then," said he, "we can proceed. Let all sail be made to continue our journey."

The sailor scratched his head.

"Well?" cried Meredydd impatiently.

"Well," replied the other, "the wind hath turned since we hove to, and is now as favourable to returning to Wales as it was two hours since to take us to France!"

Meredydd rushed on deck. It was indeed even so. By one of those sudden changes the wind had veered completely round, and was now, as the sailor had said, a fair wind for Wales, but one it would be almost hopeless to beat against for France.

His heart was filled with bitterness as he turned to re-enter the cabin. The sailor, however, touched his arm.

"Take a look at him," he said, "poor boy! Someone will mourn for him."

Meredydd approached where lay the still body of a lad evidently fifteen or sixteen years of age, whose gay page's clothes were forever spoiled by the salt water. The sailors had found him fastened to a piece of wreck, and had cut him loose and brought him to the ship hoping some signs of life might be found still remaining.

Meredydd gazed upon the lad's corpse-like countenance, beautiful even in death. Something in the lad's appearance made him bend down with more eagerness than he had yet displayed.

"My God!" he cried. "How like! Had poor Gwen a brother, I could have sworn it was he. Is the poor lad dead?" and he undid the vest to place his hand upon the heart.

As he turned back the flap of the vest to do so, be saw the full, rounded breast of a woman!

Then the truth flashed upon him.

"My God! It is Gwen!" he cried, and passionately clasped the inanimate body in his arms.

Chapter XXVII
Another

The devil can cite Scripture for his purposes –
O, what a godly outside falsehood hath.
  – SHAKESPEARE *(The Merchant of Venice)*

When Gruffydd ap Gwenwynwyn finally made up his mind to betray to Llywelyn such particulars of the conspiracy as seemed to him most meet, he did not lose more time than was absolutely necessary in doing so. He understood that giving the information at as early a moment as possible would necessarily add to its value in the eyes of Llywelyn, and that every moment he delayed only increased his own danger by making it possible for others to forestall him.

Hastening therefore to the Prince's presence, he begged the favour of a private interview, a request which Llywelyn, with some surprise, granted.

Gruffydd was cautious enough, as well as wise enough, to gloss over his own share in the conspiracy and to state his story in such a way as to leave Llywelyn finally in doubt whether ap Gwenynwyn had been made a tool of by Prince Dafydd, or had consented to pretend to co-operate with the conspirators with the sole object of becoming more fully informed of their intention, that he might the better place his Prince upon his guard.

It would be difficult to say whether it was grief, surprise, or indignation which predominated in Llywelyn's breast when this astonishing revelation was made to him of a conspiracy the existence of which he had not even suspected.

Llywelyn

That Dafydd, his brother, who had been already more than once pardoned, and that against the advice of these very chiefs whom Gwenwynwyn's report now showed to be disaffected, should have forgotten again, not only the relationship of blood, but the more tender one of friendship and deep personal obligations, was indeed a bitter thought, which for the moment seemed to un-nerve Llywelyn.

"Oh, ap Gwenwynwyn!" he said, "Tell me it is not true! Tell me that thou hast thyself made up this story in order to frighten me, and I will forgive thee freely and readily – nay, I will reward thee, too. I cannot bear the thought that Dafydd, whom I have so trusted, for whom I had done so much and contemplated doing more, that he should attempt my life! Thou hast surely dreamt this, ap Gwenwynwyn?"

"My lord," replied the traitor with pretended feeling, "would that I could indeed say 'Yes, it is a dream!' But, hard though the duty is, I feel it is my duty. And though nought could pleasure me more than to pleasure thee, still, I remember that my first duty is to protect my prince – my second to please him. All that I have told thee is, alas, only too true!"

"Then may God forgive them that first moved in this matter, and led my brother and the other chiefs once more astray, to forget their duty to Wales and to me! I say may God forgive them, for I feel I cannot. Methinks I have been too lenient in the past. My kindness hath been misplaced, my clemency abused. Had I but meted out to Dafydd and to other traitors the justice they deserved for former treasons, this would not now have happened. My pardon hath ever begot treason."

"Oh, my lord, say not so," cried Gruffydd, throwing himself at Llywelyn's feet. "Say not so. It hath not ever begot treason. In one case, at least, it hath the rather begot such fidelity, such affection, as I believe no man ever before felt!" and with well-assumed emotion he covered his face with his hands.

Llywelyn was deeply moved. "Rise, ap Gwenwynwyn," said he kindly. "Rise! I would not do thee wrong. Nobly hast thou redeemed thy past errors. The service thou hast now done me only justifies the confidence the Lady Eleanor bade me bestow in thee. Deep as will be my vengeance on those who have hatched this treason, higher in comparison, far higher, will be the honour I will place upon thee. Wales shall see that Llywelyn knows how to punish his enemies and how to reward his friends. Now go. I would be alone."

With a heart full of joy and elation Gruffydd ap Gwenwynwyn left the presence of the Prince, well satisfied with the results of his double treachery, and congratulating himself on the wisdom of the course he had pursued.

Chapter XXVIII
A Confession

'Tis not my talent to conceal my thoughts.
– ADDISON

Gwen was not dead. A naturally robust constitution brought her through a trial which would have proved fatal to a more delicate organism. Even as it was she had only been rescued in time. A very little longer exposure would have sufficed to place her far enough beyond the aid of even such tender and untiring care as Meredydd devoted to her restoration. Indeed, it was to this care alone that she was indebted for her recovery, an indebtedness of which she became fully conscious before the arrival of the vessel at Aber.

Meredydd had, of course, directed all sail to be made for home as soon as he had recognised one of the objects of his search in the apparent page who had been so providentially rescued, after having, of course, fully satisfied himself that there was no other unfortunate on the wide waste of waters near them. Now it was that he acknowledged the merciful wisdom of the over-ruling Providence which, under seemingly adverse trials, had in reality aided him in the object of his search. I shall not attempt to describe the horror and anger which possessed him when he was informed by Gwen of ap Gwenwynwyn's treachery.

"Treachery was born in him," he said, "and will never leave him while he liveth! But that shall not be for long. Let me but get him once more within reach of my good sword, and were he defended by all the imps of

Annwn, I will place him beyond the means of doing further harm."

"No, Meredydd, no," said Gwen, placing her hand on his arm. "For my sake you must not do this. If we find, as I hope we may, that he hath not done our Prince any personal harm, let us forgive him the past, were it only as an acknowledgment to heaven for having spared me."

"So be it then," said Meredydd, sullenly. "For thy sweet sake, Gwen, and in recognition of Heaven's mercy in leading me to thee in time, will I forego once more the pleasure of ridding my country of such a traitor. But let him beware! For, as there is a God in heaven, if he again crosses my path he shall die."

Poor Meredydd had not, even yet, mustered up sufficient courage to plead his cause with Gwen. That he was deeper than ever in love with her was as evident to her as to him, but a feeling of natural delicacy, perhaps, prevented his pressing his suit now lest he should appear to be taking advantage of her sense of obligation to him. Thus it happened that they arrived at Aber without his having ventured to put to her the important question.

As we have said, Gwen was by no means ignorant of his feelings. Maidens then were as keen of perception in this matter as they are in the more enlightened and civilised nineteenth century. No modern ball-room belle or unsophisticated rustic coquette of today could have been more certain of the hidden thoughts of the lovesick swain at her side than was Gwen of the feelings Meredydd entertained for her.

And the knowledge did not pain her. It seldom does. Rather the reverse. There was to her a sweet consciousness of happiness she had never felt under the more gallant attentions and florid courtesy of ap

Gwenwynwyn. They had appealed to her pride, but Meredydd's more thoughtful, if less forced, attentions appealed to her heart, and she soon came to know and to feel that, even apart from the fidelity of the one and the treachery of the other, her heart would have been won by Meredydd if placed in fair competition with ap Gwenwynwyn.

In this state of mind she landed at Aber. Meredydd, with the thoughtful kindness which marked all his actions where Gwen was concerned, had insisted upon not permitting her to undergo the excitement of an audience with Llywelyn till the morrow. He undertook to convey all the necessary information to the Prince at once, so that no danger could possibly result from the postponement of her audience with him until the following day.

Happy in her escape from the dangers to which she had been exposed, happy in the sense of security she now felt both for herself and her mistress and her prince, and happier than all in the thought that she and they owed all this to Meredydd, Gwen sought congenial company in the beauties of nature outside the palace. While, therefore, Meredydd was holding audience with the Prince, she wandered down the wooded slope which led to the beautiful river below, and, seated on the mossy trunk of a fallen tree, allowed her thoughts to linger lovingly on the brave and faithful heart to which she owed so much.

Like all her nation – naturally poetic, if not romantic – her thoughts soon found expression in words, and, in a charming contralto voice, she sang:

THE MAIDEN'S CONFESSION
Midst earth's fairest countries there is none to me
That can be compared, dear Gwalia, to thee!

Stout hearts are thy warriors, inspired thy bards
Each garden an Eden, all win my regards.
Thy beauties so charming,
My heart aye entrancing,
With joy overflowing my heart laughs aloud.

Sweet home of my childhood, my own fatherland
What wonder that I should still cling to my land?
Oh dearest Cymru! My centre of love!
Oh! List to my secret, my heart's tale of love.
And now in confessing
I seek for thy blessing.
My heart all too willing
Hath been given to a Cymro, a son of thine own!*

Hardly had she ceased singing when she felt herself seized from behind, and clasped in a pair of strong arms,

---

* The original of these lines, taken from the Drama-cantata *Llywelyn Ein Llyw Olaf*, is as follows:

CÂN GWEN

Ymhlith gwledydd y ddaear, ujd oes un imi
A ddeil ei chystadlu â Chymru mor gu;
Dewr galon pob milwr, llon awen pob bardd,
Pob gardd fel Paradwys, pob llecyn fel gardd
    Mae'r cwbl o'i swynion
    Yn denu fy nghalon,
A'm calon yn burion yn llawen a chwardd.

Magwrfa fy mebyd a chartref fy nhad,
Ai syn fy mod innau yn caru fy ngwlad?
O! Gymru anwylaf! Canolbwynt fy serch!
Clyw nawr ar gyfrinion o galon dy ferch.
    Clyw un o'm cyfrinion.
    Mae un o'th feib dewrion
    Trwy rinwedd ei swynion
Yn berchen fy nghalon – yn nesaf i'm gwlad.

while bearded lips were passionately pressed upon her own.

Believing it was Meredydd who had thus unexpectedly heard her confession of love, and overcome with confusion at the thought, she hid her blushing face in his bosom, while he poured his kisses on her flushed cheek.

"My own!" he said.

And lo! The spell was broken!

She looked up in dismay.

Instead of the tender, loving eyes of Meredydd beaming upon her, she met the burning glance of admiration from those of Gruffydd ap Gwenwynwyn.

Chapter XXIX
Disappointed Hopes

*Oh that a dieam so sweet, so long enjoyed,
Should be so sadly, cruelly destroyed.*
— MOORE, *Lalla Rookh*

Gruffydd ap Gwenwynwyn had been out hunting all that day, and so had been unaware of the arrival of Meredydd and Gwen. Finding on reaching the palace that the Prince was engaged, and not caring with whom, he had himself strayed down the very path which Gwen had taken half-an-hour previously.

Suddenly catching a glimpse of her through the trees, he had been for a moment seized with a panic of surprise and fear. How had she come there, and what could be her business? Had his treachery been discovered? Had any secret negotiations passed between the Prince and the King, and the Lady Eleanor been released and honourably escorted to her future home? And the Prince in consultation with some one? Who could it have been? How he cursed his forgetful folly in not instituting enquiries!

How could he repair the mistake? Should he approach Gwen, and greet her as though surprised to see her, or should he dissimulate again and pretend that her arrival and that of her mistress was expected, and possibly hint that this change for the better in their condition was due to his personal influence?

He never doubted but that the Lady Eleanor was there as well as Gwen, for how could the maid have arrived without the mistress?

It must be acknowledged that the situation was a most embarrassing one, even for such a diplomat as ap Gwenwynwyn.

However, as not infrequently happens, fate favoured the traitor, and Gwen's song gave him, as he supposed, a clue to the situation, and offered the means whereby be might get out of the difficulty in which he found himself so unexpectedly placed. He did not doubt for a moment but that her song referred to him. And, to do him justice, a less self-confident man than Gruffydd might have been excused for thinking so under the circumstances. The tender passages which had occurred between them at both the French and the English courts, and that so recently, although there had been no actual avowal of love, fully justified him in the conclusion he very naturally arrived at.

Forgetful of the dangerous ground he had lately trod, carried away by the maiden's avowal of affection for him, knowing himself to be favoured by the Prince, trusted by the Lady Eleanor, and loved by Gwen, his imagination pictured to him an early future of unalloyed happiness, and a satisfied ambition. Leaping forward, he had therefore seized Gwen in his arms, and rained upon her the passionate kisses which were indeed the honest expression of the feelings which filled his heart.

Gwen, as we have said, at first supposing it to be Meredydd, had hidden her face in his bosom. His voice, however, effectually dispelled the charm. No sooner did she recognise him than she forced herself free from big embrace, and stamping her little foot on the green sward, she burst out:

"How dare you, sir! How dare you!"

Thinking this was but the natural effect of her finding that she had betrayed her secret, he advanced smilingly towards her, saying:

"Come, Gwen, come! Thou hast surely no cause to be ashamed! The feelings thou hast expressed delight my heart more than words can tell. Thou knowest, ah, too well, how well I love thee."

As he advanced she drew back.

"Come, Gwen," said he, "this maiden coyness is surely unnecessary. Thou surely dost not resent an honest kiss from the old playfellow of thy childhood. Bethink thee how oft have we played together, and romped together, in those distant days. Thou didst not use in those days to be as chary of thy kisses as thou art today. It is nothing new to thee that I love thee, and though I had hoped it, I never knew till now that thou didst repay my love."

A shade crossed her face.

"I did but mistake mistake thee for another," she said.

"For Meredydd ab Ednyfed, I suppose?" he asked lightly. "Tut, let not the thought of him interfere with our happiness. Listen, Gwen, I have that to tell thee which will I trust fill thy cup of joy to overflowing, as it hath done mine."

She vouchsafed no reply, but stood as though waiting to hear what he had to say.

"Thou dost stand high in the favour of the Lady Eleanor, but not more so than do I in that of the Prince. I have been able to render him a great and invaluable service. In good truth, a greater service was never done him than that I have been fortunate enough to perform since last I saw thee. The Prince, as thou knowest full well, is generous, and he hath rewarded me even beyond my expectations. In a short tune I shall be the most powerful chieftain in the whole of Wales, the Prince himself alone excepted. With thy influence upon the Lady Eleanor, and with mine the Prince, we can hardly place a bound upon our ambition. And Gwen! Oh Gwen! Believe me when I say that what crowns my happiness, what in very truth maketh my cup of bliss to overflow, is the sweet knowledge thou hast this day vouchsafed me that thou dost love me. All that I have is thine, and in thy sweet companionship, and with every wish of my heart and of thine gratified, we can indeed look forward to a future such as we had not dared to picture to ourselves but some short while since. Come then, sweet love, come," and again he approached her and seized her hand.

For a moment she allowed her hand to remain in his. Then suddenly withdrawing it, with an evident shudder, she said:

"No; I have told thee that I did mistake thee for another."

"Mistake me for another? For whom? For that base-born Meredydd ab Ednyfed?"

She flushed to her temples.

"No," she said, "I mistook thee for the innocent and admired companion of my childhood's sports. I thought thou wert the Gruffydd ap Gwenwynwyn who spent with me on the banks of the Ithon so many happy days in the long gone by. I thought once thou wert he, and thought I could be happy with thee as thou hast just said, Sir Knight. But I see I was mistaken," and she averted her eyes as though it pained her to look at him.

"Gwen!" he cried, in deep alarm. "Listen, Gwen, dear, it is indeed I, I, Gruffydd ap Gwenwynwyn, who spent those happy hours with thee so long ago, and who hath loved thee honestly ever since, from that day unto this."

"No, no!" she cried, in deep agitation. "Tell me not so! Thou art not he!"

A terrible fear seized him. Had his sudden

appearance upset her reason?

"Oh, Gwen!" he pleaded, "Do but look at me! Look and remember. Remember who was ever at thy side at the court of France, who lost his blood to protect thee on the seas, who did all he could for thy comfort and that of the Lady Eleanor at King Edward's court. Look, Gwen, look, I am he."

She looked upon him, but with a different light in the eyes which now burned with anger and disdain.

"Yes," she said, "I see thou art he. But thou art no more the honest Gruffydd ap Gwenwynwyn I once knew than yonder creeping serpent is the harmless dove."

"What meanest thou?" he cried, an undefined dread beginning to possess his heart.

"What mean I?" she asked contemptuously. "Ask thine own heart, base traitor that thou art. Thou, lose thy blood to defend me on the sea! Say rather that thou didst suffer a single scratch that thy blood might the better hide thy dastard treachery!"

"Gwen!" he cried.

"Speak not my name with thy false tongue!" she cried in reply. "Double-dyed traitor that thou art! Betrayer of defenceless damsels entrusted to thy care! Traitor to thy country and thy Prince! Be thou accursed of all honest men and women!"

Overcome with dismay, he allowed this torrent of invective to pour forth unopposed.

Her voice softened somewhat as she said:

"In memory of the old days of my childhood, I would see thee safe. Go, therefore, now, while thou hast yet the chance. Seek safety in instant flight, for Llywelyn is even now being made aware of thy past treachery. Fly now from his presence lest his anger should fall upon thee. In remembrance of my childhood I will intercede for thee with the Lady Eleanor, and possibly even yet secure thy pardon."

His anger now blazed forth. "And thou wouldst make me the object of thy charity and of his?" he asked. "Thou hast far mistaken the man thou hast to deal with. I will fly, Gwen, but fly to seek that aid which will lower Llywelyn's pride; but I will not fly without thee. If I lose my estate I will not lose my bride."

Springing forward, he seized her round the waist in his strong arms. Weakened by her recent trials, she was able to offer but little resistance. Shriek after shriek rent the air, until be placed his disengaged hand upon her mouth to stifle her cries, and hastened with her in the direction of the boat which had borne him thither.

Chapter XXX
An Unexpected Rescue

Meredydd ab Ednyfed having obtained audience of Llywelyn, and having executed his message of warning – naturally to the no small surprise and anger of the Prince – returned to the apartments he had provided for Gwen. He had arranged with Llywelyn that no sign should be shown ap Gwenwynwyn that they were aware of his crime, until Gwen should herself have audience with the Prince on the morrow, when the traitor could be summoned to face her, and be possibly thus led to acknowledge, in his first dismay, the treachery of which he had been guilty. Meredydd had therefore been instructed to warn Gwen against showing herself, lest Gruffydd should be made suspicious, and flee before justice could be meted out to him.

Intent therefore upon this message, Meredydd arrived at Gwen's apartments, only to find that she had gone out. Induced to seek her by other considerations than that alone of obeying the mandate of his Prince, Meredydd soon discovered that the maiden had been seen taking the path which led to the river. Following this path the sound of voices soon struck his ear, and glancing through the trees he was more than surprised to find Gwen and her old, though treacherous lover apparently deep in earnest and friendly conversation. Foolish, jealous Meredydd was almost ready to believe that Gwen had either played him false in pretending to be so very displeased with ap Gwenwynwyn's treachery, or that the honeyed words and plausible manner of his rival had once more given him the ascendancy in her mind and affections. As he gazed, too far away to understand the words, whose murmur alone reached his ears, he saw the fancied lover seize the hand of his mistress and press it to his lips. He either did not, or would not, see the shudder with which she withdrew her hand from his clasp. His heart was filled with bitterness, and, cursing the weakness which had induced him to place his affections upon one evidently so unworthy, he turned and retraced his footsteps up towards the palace.

Poor Gwen! Had she but known how near to her her true lover was while her false love so vainly pleaded his cause, how her heart would have bounded with joy!

Meredydd made his way moodily up the steep path, and had almost reached the top when be fancied he heard a scream. Pausing to listen, he became convinced that a muffled or stifled scream came from the direction in which he had last seen Gwen and Gruffydd.

The truth flashed upon his mind. Gwen was either being murdered by the vengeful chieftain, who had been made aware that she possessed his secret, or she was being carried away. Cursing now the jealous folly which had led him to depart rather than suffer the pain of witnessing what he had thought was a lovers' interview, he made up, to some extent, in rapid and energetic action for the remissness of which he had lately been guilty. Through a break in the trees he, from his elevated position, saw ap Gwenwynwyn hastening towards the beach, bearing Gwen in his arms. The sight filled him with fury. Heedless of all obstacles, he dashed down the steep slope in a straight line to intercept the fugitive.

On his part Gruffydd ap Gwenwynwyn had been too intent on making good his retreat to his vessel without loss of time to notice the commotion made in the wood above him by Meredydd's headlong progress, and he found himself suddenly and unexpectedly confronted on the path by his rival, whose drawn sword and flashing eyes were sufficient evidence of his intentions.

With a muttered oath, ap Gwenwynwyn, seeing his retreat cut off, dropped his burden on the ground, where she lay inanimate.

"False Welshman and base villain that thou art!" cried Meredydd advancing upon him, "Thou hast sealed thy fate."

"Boast not till thou art sure!" was the fierce rejoinder, and the other's ready sword leaped from its scabbard ready to meet the onslaught he expected. In justice to him be it said, Gruffydd ap Gwenwynwyn was neither a novice nor a coward, but could handle his sword with the dexterity of a practised hand and with the determination of a bold heart. Under ordinary circumstances be would have been perhaps a match for his present opponent. Now, however, Meredydd's impetuosity was such that, heedless of danger to himself, he rushed on the other, beat down his guard, wrested his sword from him, and threw him at full length on the green sward, almost before his opponent had time to be in doubt as to the result of the combat!

At this moment Gwen revived from her swoon, and saw Meredydd standing with his left foot upon the breast of his fallen rival, with his sword point at his throat.

"Take thy last look at the sun, and utter thy last prayer to heaven, ap Gwenwynwyn," said Meredydd. "Thou hast already lived too long to commit treachery, as hath been thy wont since thy childhood upwards. Praised be the saints that to me is left the pleasure of ridding my country of so unworthy a son."

The other looked sullenly upwards, recognising that his last moment had arrived, and yet either too proud to ask his life of his rival, or all too conscious that any such appeal would be futile. In any case be remained sullenly silent, overcome more with disappointment that his bright hopes had thus been shattered than by fear of his impending doom.

"Oh, Meredydd! Meredydd!" cried Gwen, rising and running up to him, "Spare him, spare him!"

"Spare him?" cried the other, "To work further treachery and harm to Wales and our Prince? No, Gwen, no, though even thou askest this of me, it cannot be. I should be a recreant myself did I but let him escape?"

"Nay, but," she pleaded, "remember thou did'st promise me to spare him his life this once."

Meredydd looked his disappointment. "The Prince," he said, "will never forgive me if I let him go. Thou knowest he deserves to die the death."

"Yes, I do know; but I know, too, that thou wilt keep thy word. Thou didst promise to spare his life."

"Well, so be it, then. Though it goes hard against the grain, and my good sword thirsts for his blood. There is, however, one comfort; I spare him his life only to hand him over to the care of those who will see that he does not much harm again."

"Nay, Meredydd, thou doest not things by halves. If thou sparest his life, thou wilt also let him go free, whither he likes and as he likes. 'Tis not sparing him to keep thine own sword from taking his life, if thou dost employ the swords of others to do the same work."

"But, Gwen, I never promised – "

"Meredydd! *Dear* Meredydd! If thou didst promise, thou wilt do so now, for my sake," and the look she gave him was irresistible. The honest fellow gave up the unequal contest, and, addressing the prostrate man, said:

"Go, then, traitor, and thank Gwen for thy life. Yet, ere thou goest, listen. I swear that – were Gwen ten times as dear to me as she is, and were she to plead as she never pleaded before – even that will not save thy life from my sword if ever again thou dost cross my path by laying finger to touch her."

"Threatened men live long," said ap Gwenwynwyn, as he got up and made his way towards the beach. What impulse made him turn to look back as he left the wood? Whatever it was, he cursed himself for it, for the sight he saw was more bitter even than death itself. Gwen, resting her head on Meredydd's bosom, her white arm around his neck, and with upturned face accepting the kisses so fervently poured upon her lips and cheek.

"And is *this* the end of my scheming?" he asked himself, as he ground his teeth together in impotent rage. "Shall he whom I have hated since the days we were boys together, shall he reap and enjoy the rewards I had purposed for myself? Gwen and fortune smile upon him now, and doubtless he expects to occupy with her in Wales; and Llewelyn's favour the proud position I had pictured to myself as filling soon. But no! Let me be calm and think. It will indeed be strange, unless I can hit upon some plan which will help me pay my debt to both Gwen and Meredydd. The first thing is safety. Then revenge," and he hurried to his vessel and departed with all speed, lest some messenger of Llywelyn's should intercept him, even at the last moment.

Chapter XXXI
An Unexpected Proposal

The next morning Meredydd was summoned early to attend the Prince. He hardly knew how to comport himself, whether he should bluntly confess that he had connived at the traitor's escape, or take it for granted that ap Gwenwynwyn was still within reach.

He was not long left in doubt what to do. As soon as he entered the Prince's chamber, Llywelyn said, "Meredydd. Gwenwynwyn hath escaped us. I have just had a letter from him."

"A letter from him?" exclaimed Meredydd, in unassumed surprise. "Hath the traitor ventured to write again to you, my lord?" Doth he excuse or deny his treachery?"

"He doth not deny it, but gives me cause to believe he could excuse it had he but the opportunity for doing so. He hints at some disappointment in love. Ha! Thou needst not blush, and canst, I believe, well afford to be merciful. To put the matter shortly, his letter amounts to this: he acknowledges he did connive at the King of England's base action in intercepting my betrothed on her passage to Wales. Yet he points out very properly that he had abundantly proved his repentance therefore by discovering to me that other plot whereof I told thee last night."

"Why, then, should he flee?"

"That he also explains. Knowing Gwen's recital of the share he took in preventing the arrival of the Lady Eleanor here would set me against him, and possibly induce me to take extreme measures before he could explain himself, he thought it better to place himself out of harm's way. Nay, do not laugh, but listen to the whole story. He offers me sufficient proof of the change in his feelings towards me. Thou knowest he had told me of this last plot against my life. Of the share taken by my twin brother Dafydd, and others, in this plot, he hath abundant proofs in writing at Castell Tre'r Llyn,* and these be offers to hand over to any trusty messenger whom I will send there for them, on the sole condition that this messenger must be a man whom I can trust with so important a secret."

"And for himself?"

"For himself he asks nothing but a safeguard for himself to pass through Wales to England, such safeguard to expire in seven days if I so see fit. What thinkest thou?"

Meredydd paused. An undefined and indefinable suspicion possessed his mind of Gwenwynwyn's honesty in this. And yet what was there suspicious in it? Did it not appear, indeed, to be the work of a man who had seen the futility or the error of his past treachery? His attack on Gwen last night might have been the result of an ungovernable passion at the moment, and it was certainly neither fair nor chivalrous that he, Meredydd, should allow his personal enmity to stand in the way of Llywelyn's getting to the root of that dangerous conspiracy which threatened his very life.

"I think," said he at last, that from any other man such an offer would require no second thoughts, but should be accepted at once. Coming from one who hath proved himself so frequently a traitor, it requires more caution. Yet, if he be honest, and I admit it is possible be may be – if he be honest, that service he offers to

---

* Welshpool Castle. (10)

render by giving up those papers is indeed a great one, and should atone for many past errors."

"So, too, do I think. The matter is well worth trying. We do not lose much in any case. Even if the information prove not so valuable as we hope for, we, after all, only lose the sorry satisfaction of doing away with a traitor. If these documents be of no value, he will never dare show his face in Wales while I live. In any case he is safe from pursuit now, so that I am inclined to do as he asks. Wilt thou, Meredydd, undertake the journey?"

Meredydd started. Could this be the object of ap Gwenwynwyn? To get his successful rival in Gwen's affections effectually within his power?

A shudder passed through his frame ae he thought of this possibility. But then, again, he thought how could ap Gwenwynwyn possibly have surmised that he, Meredydd, would have been the one fixed upon by Llywelyn for this important and delicate commission? Then, again, was it fair that he should allow his personal jealousy to interfere in any way with the interests of his Prince? For he could not help confessing to himself that his enmity to Gruffydd was certainly intensified by, if not indeed mainly due, to their lifelong rivalry.

All these thoughts flashed through his mind, and though they occupy some time in reading, they were instantaneous in presenting themselves to him. Indeed, the pause before he replied to Llywelyn was so slight as to be hardly perceptible.

"Yes," said he, "I will go."

Four simple words indeed, but full of meaning. Full of meaning to Llywelyn – for they practically represented the placing of proofs of the treachery of the conspirator in his hands. Fuller of meaning to Meredydd, for he know they represented the possibility of placing himself entirely in the power of his most deadly enemy.

"And when wilt thou start?" asked the Prince.

"As soon as you provide me with the necessary authority, and the safeguard for ap Gwenwynwyn," was the reply.

"Good," said Llywelyn. "But thou wert ever ready, and believe me thou wilt not regret this readiness to serve me now."

This, however, Meredydd could not help doubting, but though doubting he at once made his arrangements for his departure.

Chapter XXXII
A Treacherous Act

Without doing more than simply informing Gwen that he was called away for some days on duty, Meredydd made his preparations for the journey which he felt was of so much importance. He had thought it best to kept Gwen in utter ignorance of his destination and of the object of his journey, lest her fears might be aroused, and her anxiety for his safety be unnecessarily increased. Feeling, too, the importance of making all possible speed, he did not even wait for Gwen's audience with the Prince, but hastened away with his half a dozen companions as soon as he had obtained the necessary documents from Llywelyn. The adventures he met on his road to Castell Tre'r Llyn were only such as were incident to the state of the country and the customs of the age. Such was the speed with which he and his party travelled that they arrived at ap Gwenwynwyn's stronghold almost simultaneously with the fugitive chieftain himself.

The meeting between the successful and the defeated rivals would have been, to most men, embarrassing. But whether it was that Gruffydd ap Gwenwynwyn had indeed at last seen the error of his ways, or that his powers of dissimulation were of an exceptionally high order, he, in a way, threw himself so entirely upon the generosity of his more fortunate rival that Meredydd felt he could not but meet the advances of his late opponent.

Meredydd was, in the first instance, ushered alone into the presence of ap Gwenwynwyn. The latter advanced with outstretched hand, and with no traces of the fury which had possessed him at their last interview, saying:

"Meredydd! I have to ask thy pardon for my late folly. Put thyself for a moment in my place. Think that I had loved Gwen from our childhood upward, aye, with a love as warm and honest as thine own, and then think what it was to bear her confess that she loved thee and disdained me. That were surely sufficient excuse for the folly I was guilty of in endeavouring to carry her away, and for the fury I showed when thou didst oppose me. I think thou canst well afford to forgive me now."

Meredydd was doubtful how to regard this apology, whether as an expression of honest feeling or as a mere blind to throw him off the scent of ap Gwenwynwyn's real feelings.

"Even," said he, disregarding the still outstretched hand of the other, "even if thy love for Gwen could excuse thy endeavour to carry her away against her will, how can it justify thy treachery to the Lady Eleanor?"

Ap Gwenwynwyn flushed to the temples, and paused a moment ere he replied.

"It should be some proof to thee how anxious I am to retrieve my past follies that I place this restraint upon myself now, and do not strike thee as thou standest for speaking thus to me."

"Methinks thou hast had too rough an experience already of the fruits of striking me to feel wishful to repeat the experiment," said Meredydd bluntly.

"That was not spoken like a generous foe to remind me of my sorry defeat, nor was it spoken like a wise man, standing alone within the walls of my castle, where the slightest signal from me would bring a score of men upon thee. No! Stop!" he said, as Meredydd was about to interrupt him, and proceeding with greater dignity than he had yet exhibited; "I wish not to bandy words with thee. Thou hast asked for an explanation, and I am ready to give it. And I tell thee plainly, I give it more as a token of my desire to repair the wrong I have been guilty of than because I admit thy right to ask me. Now, hadst thou not been to the Court of France before we? Hadst thou not seen and spoken to Gwen? Hadst thou not had cause to think she cared for thee? These things I soon found out. Now I ask thee again – what chance would there have been for me against thee had I allowed her to return to Wales? Did not my sole chance of winning her rest and depend upon keeping her from thee? And how else could I have done this than by consenting to the proposal of the King of England? Tell me not that my duty to my prince should have led me to do otherwise. Love such as mine was knows no duty but that of attaining its end. Hadst thou loved as I did thou wouldst have been better able to sympathise with the passion which led me to forget all save Gwen."

He paused, and then proceeded. "Up to the last moment I fondly believed I might win her over. At the English Court I thought I saw signs which I might interpret as being in my favour."

Meredydd winced, but ap Gwenwynwyn proceeded as though he had not observed it. "These tokens of her favour led me on to hope that I might ultimately succeed if only I could keep her long enough from thee. This eased my conscience, which at times troubled me, and made me satisfied with the course I had taken. Her arrival in Wales, and thy meeting with her, however, not only upset all my plans, but also opened my eyes to the self-deceit I had practised in believing she could care for me. Once my calm judgment fully convinced me that she cared only for thee, my reason regained its ascendancy over my passion, and I have given the best proofs of it. To Llywelyn I have proved it by the offer I have made him. To thee, Meredydd, have I proved it by giving thee this explanation. Thou knowest my temper and my pride, and must know too what it costs me to say this. However, I do say it, and thou art not the generous, open-hearted Meredydd ab Ednyfed I once knew if thou refusest now to clasp the hand I over thee in friendship."

Carried away by the earnestness of his rival, Meredydd took the proffered hand, saying, "I take thy hand, ap Gwenwynwyn, as much in proof of renewed faith and friendship in thee as of gauge of my determination never to believe thee more shouldst thou to thine own eternal shame now deceive me or Llywelyn, our Prince."

"That then is enough," said ap Gwenwynwyn, with more approach to gaiety than he had yet shown. "And now to business. Thou art come, I suppose, from Llywelyn?"

"Yes. He received thy message, and sent me to answer it. I have here the authority to receive the papers to which thou dost refer."

"And the safeguard?"

"That also have I, and herewith I hand it thee."

"That is well," replied the other, taking the documents from Meredydd's hand; and now to hand over to thy keeping the papers I promised. Come with me."

Calling for a torch to light them, and carrying it himself, he led Meredydd from the apartment through numerous narrow and tortuous passages. Soon their path led them downwards, evidently to the neighbourhood of the dungeons.

"Art thou afraid to follow me?" asked ap Gwenwynwyn, turning round with the torch in his hand.

"I am afraid of nothing," was the reply, "but it strikes me thou dost keep thy deeds and documents in a strange strong-room."

"The deeds and documents, as thou knowest, were not of a nature to bear the light of day," laughed Gruffydd, "and, certes, hadst thou as much cause to hide them as I had, thou wouldst admit that I acted with great wisdom in placing them where I have. But here we are. Wilt thou hold the torch while I unloose these bolts and bars?"

Meredydd took the torch while his companion proceeded to undo the numerous fastenings which secured the door. At last he opened it.

"There," said he, "in this room thou shall I learn more than thou ever didst before. Mind the steps as thou goest down, and light me to follow thee."

Meredydd proceeded cautiously to descend the broken steps, and having reached the bottom turned to light his companion.

What, however, was his surprise, and indeed his dismay, to see the ponderous door swinging to and closing with a clang.

The truth flashed upon him in a moment. He had been duped, and led with his eyes open into a trap skilfully laid for him, and was now a prisoner in the hands of his most bitter enemy. With a cry of rage he rushed up the steps to the door, which he endeavoured in vain to open. The clanging of bolts drawn and bars falling, accompanied by his rival's mocking laugh, all too plainly indicated how futile would be his attempts. Unfortunately, too, in his frantic rage he had struck the torch against the door, and extinguished it, thus leaving him in total darkness, and unable to make any examination of the cell in which he found himself imprisoned.

At first it seemed to him that he was enveloped in total darkness. Not a ray of light could be discovered. As his eyes became more accustomed to the gloom, he found that though no direct ray of light fell into his cell, yet that there was a faint reflection of light. This, however, tended rather to make the darkness visible than to dispel it.

Overcome by his feelings, he sat down on the bottom step of the broken stairs, which he had again descended, and bowed his head between his hands. How bitterly did he repent now, when it was too late, that he had not informed the Prince of the occurrences of the evening of ap Gwenwynwyn's flight. Had he done so, some precautions might possibly have been taken.

A mocking laugh above his head at length aroused him, and, looking up, he discovered his enemy peering at him through a grating in the wall far beyond Meredydd's reach.

"And how dost thou like thy new quarters?" asked Gruffydd. "My hospitality exceeds thy expectations, does it not?"

Meredydd disdained replying, but perceiving by the light of the lamp which his captor held in his hand that a rough stone bench ran along the far side of his cell, he went and sat down there, apparently heedless of his enemy's words.

"That is right," said ap Gwenwynwyn, "I prithee make thyself at home. There is none to say the nay. That bench is thy table, thy seat, and thy couch, and thus thou seest thy apartment is well furnished. I daresay thou wouldst desire company. Mayhap the rats which generally visit this place will hardly be to thy taste, and yet they will not be said nay to. Gwen would doubtless be more welcome company, but I can hardly promise thee that she shall come there. However, I am not without hope of being able to show her thee at this grating shortly, and she will doubtless enjoy with me the sight of her would-be lover in this plight."

Even this taunt failed to move Meredydd, and the other continued:

"Well, I never saw thee pout like a spoilt child before. I begin to regret that I have given thee such welcome. Harder fare and worse lodgings would, mayhap, bring thy tongue loose once more. It did not use to be so rusty as it seems today But the best of friends must part, and I must leave thee. I have business elsewhere, and seeing thou hast ever been so warm a friend of mine I shall favour thee with the secret of it. Thanks to the safeguard thou didst give me but a while since, I am free to come and go among Llywelyn's men as among my own. 'Twas kind of thee thus to think of me. I shall therefore, in the first place, endeavour to make good my promise to let thee see Gwen here. Methinks I have a bait wherewith I can catch her. That being done, I make my way to London, where I shall complete those arrangements, which I have as yet only begun, to secure the downfall of Llywelyn."

Finding that nothing could rouse Meredydd to pay any apparent attention to his taunts, Gruffydd ap Gwenwynwyn, with a muttered curse, turned and left his prisoner once more alone.

Had he seen him shortly afterwards – seen first of all the terrible outburst of furious anger to which he gave way, and then the despondency which succeeded it when he saw how utterly hopeless his condition was – even ap Gwenwynwyn's malice would have been satisfied.

As it happened, however, this pleasure was denied him. Meredydd remained impassive until the sound of his enemy's footsteps had died away in the distance, and he was satisfied that whatever display of feeling he might indulge in would not be seen by any human eyes.

While thus Meredydd gave rein to his feelings, ap Gwenwynwyn was busy making his arrangements. His first care was to secure the followers of Meredydd. This was easily done, for in an enemy's stronghold the opposition of the half-dozen men who had accompanied Meredydd would have availed but little even had they known what to expect. They were, however, seized singly and disarmed before they even doubted the genuineness of the hospitality extended them.

Ap Gwenwynwyn rightly conjectured that Llywelyn would take steps to search for his ambassador when he found he did not return. The wily chieftain had therefore taken measures to stock his castle and to garrison it strongly to withstand any ordinary attack which might be made upon it. Having done this, he gave strict orders that upon no account was the castle to be surrendered, whatever might happen, and directed the commandant whom he left in charge to put Meredydd to death if it became evident that the castle must fall.

"But of that," said he, "there is little fear. My men are numerous enough and brave enough, and thou art sufficiently well provided with food to withstand a twelve weeks' siege. Long ere that I shall have returned to Wales at the head of an English army, and then we shall see whose head will be highest in Wales."

Chapter XXXIII
Hurried Efforts

Gwen, after the hurried departure of her lover, found time hanging somewhat heavily on her hands. The day of his departure passed much more wearily than time had been wont to pass with her lively nature. She could not enjoy the merrymakings in which her companions took part, and of which she would formerly have been the ruling spirit.

In this mood she was summoned the following morning to the presence of the Prince. The conversation naturally referred almost exclusively to the position of the Lady Eleanor at the English Court, and to the unhappy events which had brought her journey to Wales to so unexpected a conclusion. The picture Gwen drew of her mistress's feelings towards the Prince was, we may be sure, such as would be pleasing to a lover's ears, and raised still higher Llywelyn's wish to see his betrothed.

"I am not without hope," he said, "that a way may be found sooner, indeed, than perhaps we think, for bringing home to Eryri the Lady of Snowdon. And Gwen, when that time comes, when my hopes are consummated, then will also the hopes of another be consummated."

The maiden looked up inquiringly. The Prince smiled as he proceeded. "Meredydd ab Ednyfed hath been a true friend to me and to thee. Nay, girl, blush not, 'tis no shame to him to have fallen in love with thy pretty face, and no shame to thee to have been won by his sturdy figure and faithful heart. It beseems both me and thee that we should suitably pay the man to whom we owe so I much."

"My lord," she said, "I shame not to acknowledge my indebtedness to him, but I am I as ill-able to repay him for what he hath done me as he is to feel that his Prince owes him aught."

"I can believe the latter part of thy pretty speech well enough. As for the first part, he will, I am sure, consider the granting him thy hand a sufficient reward for anything he may have done or could have done for thee, and I much mistake if thou wilt say him nay the day the Lady Eleanor saith aye to me. I feel my debt is great, and would be glad to suitably repay him. That, however, I can never do. What I can do, that will glad be done, and no man in Wales shall stand higher in my favour than he. The estate of Glyn Ithon will be made over to him when he returns. I had once thought of seizing ap Gwenwynwyn's lands and transferring them to Meredydd, but the unexpected submission of Gruffydd makes this difficult. We shall see when Meredydd returns whether his old rival hath kept his promise."

Gwen felt a sinking at her heart. "Pardon me, my lord, for asking, but hath Meredydd any commission to do which will bring him into contact with Gruffydd ap Gwenwynwyn?"

"I fancied he would have told thee of it, girl. Shortly, it is this. Ap Gwenwynwyn, by some means as yet unknown to me, found out that I had been made aware of his treachery, and fled. The next morning – that is, yesterday – he sent me a message expressing his deep contrition, and explaining matters better than I had deemed it possible he could. As a token of his repentance, he offered to place in my hands, at his castle of Tre'r Llyn, documents which would prove the share taken by others in this last conspiracy against me. None but a man who wished to stand well with me would have offered to do this. Nay, child, thou needst not fear," – for Gwen had become pale as death – "though I may pardon him later on, and even perhaps permit him to return to Wales, he will never equal Meredydd in my regard."

"Not that, my lord, not that, but Meredydd's danger," she managed to say in broken terms.

"Meredydd's danger?" asked the Prince, not understanding her meaning. "Thou thinkest ap Gwenwynwyn will be apt to do Meredydd a wrong when he finds him in his power, because he hath won thee from him? Thou needst not fear. Ap Gwenwynwyn knows not of thy return, nor, if he did, of the terms on which thou standest with Meredydd."

"Oh, my Lord, save him!" she cried, falling on her knees and clasping her hands beseechingly. "Gruffydd knew I loved Meredydd. He endeavoured to carry me away the night of my return here, and it was Meredydd's strong right arm which hurled him to the earth and saved me. And I, I have sent him to his death!" and the poor girl moaned in anguish of spirit.

Llywelyn leaped to his feet. A new light burst upon his mind. The traitor had indeed outwitted him. By his cunningly-laid bait he had got Meredydd, his rival, completely in his power, and had at the same time secured his own safety by the safe conduct from Llywelyn of which the unfortunate son of Ednyfed had been the bearer.

"Come, lass, come!" he cried, "If this be so it is time to act and not to weep. I will this moment send a courier after him, who shall make all speed man and horse can make. Mayhap he will yet overtake Meredydd, though thy lover is, in good sooth, no laggard, and his desire to return to thee would hasten his footsteps even if he were."

Gwen rose to her feet. "And – and if he be too late?" she asked, quiveringly.

"Even if that be the case, I will provide for that also. Orders shall be given for a strong force to march at once for Tre'r Llyn, a force strong enough to invest the place until we can bring up sufficient men to take it by storm. Thy brother himself shall be their leader, so that thou mayest be satisfied not a moment will be lost unnecessarily. Keep up thy courage, brave lass, keep up thy courage," he said, and hastened out to give the necessary orders, leaving poor Gwen overcome by her feelings.

"The foolish fellow!" said the Prince to himself. "Why did he not tell me when I gave him this commission? I would not have sent him, no, not even for the certainty of getting those documents. But my brave Meredydd himself fancied perhaps that though there was danger, there was, too, the possibility of doing me real service. As ever, forgetful of self, he was ready to sacrifice himself for me and mine, aye, for the bare chance of being able to serve me. But he shall be repaid a thousand tunes over – that is, if he be alive – and if not, he shall be terribly avenged."

And thus saying, and with his features hard set in deep determination, he ordered first of all a courier, and then Eynon ap Llywarch, Gwen's brother, to be summoned with all speed to his presence. In a short time the courier appeared.

"Ha, Rhys, it is thou?" asked the Prince. "I am glad thou art here, for it is not for nothing thou art called Rhys Gyflym, and if ever there was need for speed, it is now." (11)

He then briefly related the facts, and explained Meredydd's peril.

"Thou wilt not linger by the way. Spare not thy beast

nor thyself. Stop at no danger. If any man meets thee and bids thee good-morrow, stay not to answer him. If thou canst overtake Meredydd, were it even at the gates of Castell Tre'r Llyn, turn him back there by this order," handing him as he spoke a paper he had in the meantime prepared.

"Good, my lord, it shall be done. If thou should'st have need to recall me thou must summon one of the eagles of Eryri, for no four-footed beast can overtake mine, and no man can overtake me when there needs haste."

"I know that full well. But one word more. Here is another paper. If thou findest thou art too late to prevent Meredydd entering this lion's den, return not, but hasten forward beyond Tre'r Llyn. To every man thou meetest whom thou canst trust proclaim Gruffydd ap Gwenwynwyn a traitor to his prince and country, and say that a price is set upon him. He must on no account be slain, but taken alive. If it cost the lives of a score of men to seize him unharmed, he must be so seized. Woe betide whoever harms him. Let this be spread far and near, beyond Tre'r Llyn, and on every path that leads out of Wales. This is thy authority," and he handed him another document. "Now, go!"

The courier bowed, and without speaking a word left the presence of the Prince. In five minutes he was galloping with the speed of the wind in almost a bee-line for Meredydd's destination. Rhys Gyflym's boast that no man could overtake him, and no horse compete with his, was no vain one. Yet, though he spared neither himself nor his beast, though he hastened over almost impracticable paths at a speed which others would have considered good on a well-beaten road, he found that his efforts had been in vain, and that Meredydd's progress had been so rapid that he had entered Castell

Tre'r Llyn some hours before the Prince's messenger arrived in the neighbourhood.

Scarcely had Rhys left Llewellyn's presence when Eynon ap Rhydderch was announced. The instructions given him by the Prince were as concise and as much to the point as those given to Rhys, and showed the foresight of an accomplished warrior. His choice, too, of a leader was, of course, a good one. He knew of the personal friendship which existed between the two, quite apart from any connection with Gwen, while the sister's influence on the brother would certainly tend to still further exertion being put forth to reach the end in view.

The instructions were briefly these: to hasten towards Welshpool with as strong a force as could be mustered at short notice, and to demand the attendance of all bodies of armed Welshmen and of Welsh chiefs and their retainers he might meet with on the way. Ap Gwenwynwyn's safe conduct was, of course, withdrawn, and if he should be seized by anyone, he was placed unreservedly in Eynon's hands, to do with him whatever seemed best and most advisable. If Meredydd's safety was assured, or if it was found that he had been slain, ap Gwenwynwyn was to be brought back to Aber. If, however, Meredydd was a prisoner, and if an interchange could be effected, ap Gwenwynwyn was to be set at liberty and allowed to retire into England the moment Meredydd arrived in Eynon's camp. Castell Tre'r Llyn was to be at once invested, and stormed as soon as a sufficient force could be gathered for that purpose.

In a very short space of time indeed the rescue party, under Eynon's leadership, left Aber on its forced march for Welshpool.

Chapter XXXIV
The Prisoner

Ignorant of the efforts being made to effect his release, poor Meredydd had an unhappy prospect before him. He was too firmly convinced of ap Gwenwynwyn's enmity to entertain any hopes of favour at his rival's hands. A lengthened incarceration was the least he could expect, and the prospect, to one of Meredydd's temperament, was little better than death. He could only look forward to two chances of escape. One was that he might find among the jailers who brought him his food someone who for the sake of reward might be influenced to connive at, if not assist in, his escape from Casted Tre'r Llyn. Another hope which he would not abandon was that his lengthened absence might induce Llywelyn to make inquiries, which would undoubtedly lead to his discovering what had taken place, and result in some energetic steps being taken by the prince on his behalf. Little did he think that even then these steps had been taken, and that a very strong detachment under Eynon ap Rhydderch was making all possible haste to reach him.

The door of his prison had not once been opened since he had entered the dungeon. His food was handed in through a small opening above the door, affording him but very little opportunity of endeavouring to make any advances with the view of coming to an understanding with his attendants. He did indeed endeavour to open a conversation with the first man who brought him his food, but met with only a surly response, and a recommendation to keep his breath for some more useful purpose.

Brave though he was, he felt his heart sink within him. If all who came in contact with him were like this man, there would be but little chance indeed of his succeeding. His second and third attempt with others were equally unsuccessful. Then came again the turn of the man who had first visited and first repulsed him. Meredydd recognised him by his voice rather than his features, for the place was too dark to enable him to recognise the lace. As before, too, this man was accompanied by an attendant, whom he now ordered to hand him the food he carried for the prisoner, and to go back to fetch something which had been forgotten.

The repulse Meredydd had met with in the first instance from this man had led him to give up all hope of being able to influence him, and he had determined to speak not a word to him.

Whas was, therefore, his surprise to hear the man say in in an eager but carefully-lowered whisper:

"Sir Meredydd! Sir Meredydd!"

"What wouldst thou?" asked the prisoner in no little surprise.

"Hush!" came the reply, "Not so loud! Not so loud! I answered thee surily enough yester-ee'en when thou didst speak to me, as I knew it would do thee more harm than good to be supposed to hold any communication with any of us. I was born on the banks of the Ithon like thyself, and would not willingly see thee come to harm."

"Good friend, I thank thee, and the heaven that sent thee to me," replied Meredydd. "How shall I address thee? By what name shall I call thee?"

"The name matters little. It is after all only a cloak which a man may put on or throw off at pleasure.

However, I am called Deio, and in my old home was known as Deio'r Llannerch."

"Of Llannerch?" asked Meredydd. "Then, though I know thee not, I know those that belong to thee."

"Aye, that thou dost, as they know thee and thine, was the reply. "Many is the kindness I and they have received at the hands of those that are of kindred blood with thee, and for the sake of these memories – l would not see thee harmed."

"Good Deio! I thank thee – from my soul, I do. But tell me what can be done?"

"That is a difficult question to answer," replied Deio. "But this do I know, that the orders given about thee are more strict than any that have been given here for many a year."

"Aye," said Meredydd, bitterly, "thy master is determined to keep me safe now that he hath got me in his power. And well for him that he doth so, for he knows what would await him were I free once more."

"Whatever the cause he hath against thee, I know he is more bitter than he hath ever been. He hath given orders that will ensure thy safe keeping."

"If he can guard within, he cannot guard without," said Meredydd. "And it will not be long at the worst before Llywelyn finds means to unlock my prison door."

"That will avail thee but little, I am afraid," said Deio.

"Whas meanest thou?"

"Ap Gwenwynwyn before he left gave orders that should there be any prospect of the castle being taken thou wert to be put to death. So that if thy door be unlocked, thy friends may find thee, but not as they hoped to do."

Meredydd muttered a curse upon his enemy's vindictiveness, and was about to address the other again when Deio said:

"Hush! Here comes my companion. He must know nothing of this. Come along, fellow!" he called in an angry tone. "Thinkest thou I have nought to do but kick my heels in this place waiting for thy laziness?"

"I came with all possible speed," replied the other, "but could not find the key where thou didst say."

"Aye. I warrant thou wilt find some excuse. Here, Sir Prisoner," he added, reaching the coarse food in through the opened giving, "here is thy share, and dainty fare thou wilt find it, I doubt not."

"Dainty or not, friend," said Meredydd, "it is better than being without, though I will say I could well be content with more of it, and of a better sort."

"Ay; that is the thanks thou givest, like the rest of them. But thou wilt be long ere thou dost see a better. But I come not to prate with thee. If thou dost want this water take it, else I return it whence it came," said Deio roughly. As he spoke he handed the pitcher in through the grating, and a silent hand pressure passed between the two unseen and unsuspected.

After this Meredydd bore his incarceration with more equanimity. He had now something to look forward to, though the expectation of a return of his gruff friend made the time appear even longer than before.

The second night of his imprisonment passed away. On the occasion of Deio's third visit he had important news to give.

"The prince," he said, "hath proved as rapid and decided in action as ever. There is already a strong force within sight of the castle, and were it not that we have made unusual preparations of late to strengthen our defences, and to provide ample food, we should be soon in sorry plight."

"Llywelyn doth act when the need arises," said Meredydd proudly, "and I shall soon be free again."

"That I know not," said Deio. "For in the first place, as I have said, we are in a position to withstand a larger force than now threatens us. And again, should the place be in danger of falling, ap Gwenwynwyn hath provided for thee."

"Aye! Curse him!" cried Meredydd. "But canst thou not think, good friend Deio, of some means whereby I may yet be able to defeat his object?"

"The only way is to get thee out from this dungeon in good time, and outside the castle walls. Though how that is to be done exceedeth my comprehension."

"Canst thou not manage to leave my door unfastened some night? I will then, with my good sword which I yet have by me, render a good account of all who oppose my passage to freedom."

"Thou wouldst, I fear, have but little chance in such a case. If thou didst kill a dozen or a score, thou couldst not kill all the garrison, and excepting myself and perhaps three or four trusty friends of mine – who might befriend thee for my sake – there is not a man in the whole garrison but would readily obey the command to kill thee. And then as to opening the door, it is locked as well as barred, and the key never leaves the commandant's girdle. I have been trying to think how it can be done. The only way is to get possession of the key, and then to take thee out myself as though thou didst belong to the garrison. Tonight I will risk the matter of the key, and when the commandant sleeps will try to secure it, and place another in its stead. Pray thou, Sir Meredydd, that he notes not the difference between the two." With this understanding Deio once more left his prisoner.

Eagerly Meredydd listened to find if he could

discover any token of an assault being made, but whether it was that he was out of the reach of any bound from without, or that no actual assault had yet taken place, he heard nothing. Early the next morning, however, he heard hasty steps approaching, and the next moment Deio's alarmed face appeared at the grating.

"Sir Meredydd!" he cried, "I bear thee ill news."

"Let it come," said the other. "Be what it may, I will bear it."

"I have no time to wait. It is this. A messenger hath just arrived bearing a despatch from ap Gwenwynwyn, in which he orders thy instant execution."

Meredydd was too surprised for a moment to speak,

"So be it," said he at last. "But they shall find I can sell my life dearly. Thanks, good friend, for the warning. I will benefit by it."

"Be of good cheer," said Deio, in a broken voice. "Whatever can be done to help thee will be done. When the door is opened, bear thyself like a man, and strike the first who enters. Mayhap thou wilt have help when thou dost not expect it."

With that he disappeared. In a few moments Meredydd heard the tramp of an armed band approaching. He knew they were his executioners, come to do the bidding of Gruffydd ap Gwenwynwyn.

Chapter XXXV

Gaily rode Gruffydd ap Gwenwynwyn away from Castell Tre'r Llyn on his way to England and safety. (12) Though his plans as regards Llywelyn had fallen through, fortune had favoured him almost beyond his hopes in placing his rival within his power, and he was determined that, come what might, and at whatever cost, Meredydd and Gwen should never again be re-united. If he could not gain her for himself, at least his rivals would not enjoy her. Of that he was fully determined. It was with that view that he had left such strict orders with his lieutenant that if there seemed a probability of the castle falling into Llywelyn's hands, Meredydd was to be put to death.

It was, therefore, with a feeling of almost unmixed satisfaction that the perfidious Gruffydd rode away to take refuge in England, confident that even if the worst came to the worst, he would have the satisfaction of knowing that his rival at least should not enjoy any benefit from his absence, nor even from his downfall. Turning now to his esquire, he said:

"Thou didst hear me, Alan, give my commands ere we left the castle to have the prisoner put to death in case there appeared any danger of the castle falling into Llywelyn's hands?"

"Yes my lord. And 'twas a wise foresight of thine, for of a surety Llywelyn will not rest quiet under this new insult."

"Thou sayest wisely. But I wish to guard against every possibility of this man's escaping in any way. I have not spent all my life in plotting without knowing somewhat of the feelings of others, and without seeing beforehand what may happen, and providing therefore. Now I hold the Prince's own safe-conduct to the English borders, but still an accident may happen. Some stupid fellow may, perchance, doubt its being given by Llywelyn, or some other difficulty which I have not foreseen may arise which will delay me, and perchance place me again in the power of mine enemies."

"What, then, is my lord's intention?"

"My intention is to make the death of Meredydd ab Ednyfed certain in any case."

"That might have been done very easily before you left the castle this morning."

"Yes, but that would have put an end to his sufferings all too soon, and would have placed it beyond my power to enjoy the pleasure of knowing that he suffered. No, no, good Alan, I lay my plans better than that. I arrange to keep him there while I am safe and while the castle is safe, but as soon as there is any danger of his escaping through my danger or that of the castle, I ensure his immediate execution."

"But how can that be done, my lord?" asked Alan. "I can see how easily it is done in case the castle be in danger. But in case you fall into Llywelyn's hands by any mishap, the knowledge that you are a prisoner, and thus placed beyond the power of calling the governor of your castle to account, may induce him to do the very thing you would guard against, and let Meredydd free."

"Ay? Thou canst see thus far, but no further. Well, now listen. I hand thee this letter which is addressed to the governor of castle. It contains an order under my hand directing the immediate execution of this Meredydd. This letter thou art to take at all hazards to the castle, and see it executed, as soon as thou art fully satisfied I am a prisoner with no hope of escape."

"Ah, my lord!" cried Alan in unmistakable admiration of his master's foresight. "You deserve to succeed in whatever you undertake."

"Well, I must say I believe with thee, my good Alan. But remember this. The charge I entrust to thee is an important one. It must not be acted upon unless thou art thoroughly convinced that I am hopelessly at the mercy of those who will not be apt to show me mercy. There is, indeed very little chance of its being required at all, but I wish to leave no single door of possible escape for Meredydd. I could not die if I believed him alive. Thou dost thoroughly understand what I expect thee to do?"

"Thoroughly, my lord, and you may rest satisfied that I will act as you would wish me to do. Nothing but the direst necessity will induce me to use this power you have placed in my hands, and nothing but death itself shall prevent my using it when it becomes necessary to do so."

"That was well spoken, Alan, worthy of thee and of thy tried fidelity, and hath taken indeed a heavy load off my shoulders. Now let us on briskly."

They rode on for a couple of hours, their sprits rising as they advanced towards the English border and certain safety. Suddenly the keen eye of ap Gwenwynwyn perceived the glitter of arms between the trees in front of them, and, cautiously advancing, discovered a party of Welsh soldiers approaching.

"Now what shall we do, Alan? If we turn from the path we may be seen, and, if seen, we shall certainly be followed. Would it not be the better plan to take the bull by the horns, and by advancing boldly disarm suspicion, and join with these Welshmen in apparent amity? In any case the Prince's safe conduct is sufficient security for us."

"I must say, my lord, that the less we have to do with Llywelyn's followers until we meet them on equal terms, the better I shall like it. At the same time I fully see the force of what you say, and am inclined to think with you that we can do no better than appear totally unconcerned. So be it, then let us on to meet them boldly like honest men," said ap Gwenwynwyn.

Another ten minutes' riding brought the two fugitives face to face with the party of Welshmen, in the leader of which Gruffydd was not over well pleased to recognise Tewdwr ab Ednyfed, Meredydd's brother. Putting, however, the best possible face on the matter, he advanced boldly, and, holding out his hand with apparent cordiality, greeted the chief. The other, however, under pretence of subduing a restive horse, did not take the outstretched hand, and responded rather coldly to ap Gwenwynwyn's greeting.

"Methinks that thou are not taking the direction which loyal Welshmen who are attached to their prince should be taking just now," said Tewdwr.

"And why so?" asked Gruffydd, smiling.

"Simply because in the present crisis it behoves every Welshman to gather round his Prince."

"And think you not, friend Tewdwr, that we may serve our Prince afar as well as near? And if it hath pleased him to send me on an embassy of importance, and if that embassy be, as it probably will be, the means of weakening the army which Edward brings against Llewellyn, I am sure that Tewdwr ab Ednyfed is not the man who will blame Gruffydd ap Gwenwynwyn for doing so."

"Thou art right. Tewdwr ab Ednyfed is not the man to blame thee nor any other man for doing his duty to Prince and country, but he must first of all be convinced that thou art doing thy duty."

Llywelyn 217

"Why, what a suspicious fellow art thou," said Gruffydd. "Come aside with me a moment. I have that for thy ear which suits not to be spoken to all. I am sent on a special message of importance by the Prince himself. Here is his personal safe conduct, in which all whom it may concern are commanded to expedite my journey. I am sorry I do not feel at liberty to tell even thee, Tewdwr, loyal Welshman as thou art known to be, what is the object of my journey. It is enough that the secret is Llywelyn's and the work mine."

"Then have I to ask thy pardon for my bluntness," said Tewdwr, with more heartiness than he had hitherto shown. "The fact is, a rumour had reached us that all was not well between thee and the Prince, and – and – "

"And therefore thou didst suspect me of treachery. Nay, never be ashamed, man, to own it! Thou hadst some cause. And let me tell thee this, or rather let me whisper it in thine ear. Llywelyn had an object to serve in spreading the report. I am glad the rumour has preceded me. It will help me in the work I have to do. And now I must haste me on my way. I should have been pleased to spend an hour with thee, but duty first hath ever been my motto. When next we meet thou wilt understand me better."

The hand he now held out was not refused, but Tewdwr gave it a hearty clasp, saying, "An' thy journey be as thou sayest, in the interest of the Prince. Then may God speed thee, and I am not the man to hinder thee."

Thus with mutual expressions of goodwill they parted, Gruffydd ap Gwenwynwyn – followed by his esquire Alan, who had been quaking in his saddle – riding away to the English border more gaily than ever. Scarcely had the traitor disappeared than a man, whose travel-stained and torn dress showed the speed with which he had journeyed, came running breathlessly up.

"Your leader?" he asked, in Welsh, of the first man he saw.

"Yonder. Tewdwr ab Ednyfed," was the reply.

"The very man!" cried the stranger, who pushed his way, heedless of all opposition, to where stood Tewdwr ab Ednyfed.

"Tewdwr ab Edynfed," said he, "hast thou seen Gruffydd ap Gwenwynwyn?"

"Who art thou who speaks thus?" demanded Tewdwr.

"One who hath no time to stand upon ceremony, and if he had time hath no need when speaking to a man whose brother's life may be in jeopardy through his carelesness. I am the Prince's courier, Rhys Gyflym, Hast thou seen Gruffydd ap Gwenwynwyn?"

"He left my camp but a short while since."

"Then thy brother's blood be upon thine head!" cried Rhys. "The traitor ap Gwenwynwyn hath him shut up in Castell Tre'r Llyn."

"Impossible!" cried Tewdwr. "Ap Gwenwynwyn had the Prince's safe conduct."

"Look, then, at this!" cried Rhys, showing the Prince's order withdrawing the safe conduct, and commanding the capture at any cost of the fugitive traitor.

"To bring thee this in time I have ridden my good horse to death, and all but run myself so also."

"Woe's me! And I have let him slip through my fingers when I had him in my hands!" groaned Meredydd's brother.

Chapter XXXVI
A Defeated Plan

It would be impossible to describe the disappointment of both Tewdwr ab Ednyfed and Rhys Gyflym when they realised the fact that though their prey had been in their grasp they had allowed him to escape them, and had thus practically sealed the fate of Meredydd. In this emergency, however, Rhys fully justified the trust the Prince had reposed in him. With him, to think was to act. Turning to Tewdwr he asked:

"In what direction travelled ap Gwenwynwyn?"

"Straight on, making, as far as I could judge, directly for the English border," was the reply.

"Then, unless he doubles upon us, we may even yet catch him. Let me have a horse, and half-a-dozen of thy men well mounted, and we shall, mayhap, catch him in his own net."

"How dost thou propose to act? To follow him now would only be to warn him and send him off the quicker."

"Just so; and, therefore I go to meet him."

"To meet him?"

"Aye. Didst thou but know this country as I do, hadst thou been obliged as I have to travel it as the crow flies rather than as the water flows, thou wouldst know that a man in a matter of life and death can cover more distance in a mile properly chosen than an ordinary traveller could in two miles. Let me have these men of thine, and in an hour's time I will meet him face-to-face."

"That thou shalt right ready, and I will lead them

myself."

"Nay, not so. Thou must perforce remain with thine own men."

"What? Thinkest thou I will permit him who is in spirit, if not in actual deed, my brother's murderer to be captured by another hand, when I can reach out mine own to seize him?"

"I know thou art not the man to risk the failure of this scheme by thy foolhardiness. Thou wouldst not frighten our wolf from the trap into which he is going blindly. Seest thou not this? When he sees half a dozen men approaching him from the direction of the English border, he will remember how easily he slipped through thy fingers, and that very ease will induce him to come blindly forward right into our arms. Wert thou, however, with us, he would recognize thy burly form a mile away, and seek safety in his horse's heels."

"But there is the possibility he may likewise suspect thee and thy men, and attempt to flee."

"That is possible, but not like to happen. But even if he did so, where could he flee in first instance but away from us? And away from us would of necessity be towards thee and thy party. Therefore, when we have been gone, say half a mile's distance, do thou and thy men follow on the heels of ap Gwenwynwyn, so that if he doth flee from us he will fall into thy hands."

"So be it then," said Tewdwr, "and the sooner this be done the better, for already my blood boils within me when I think of poor Meredydd shut up in that castle, and my hands crave to be at this base traitor's throat."

No time was lost. Rhys Gyflym was supplied with a horse, and, accompanied by half-a-dozen picked men excellently well mounted, he started off, taking a course almost at right angles to that pursued by Gruffydd ap

Gwenwynwyn. Rapidly he rode forward, heedless of obstacles before which any less bold a heart would have quailed, and which no ordinary traveller would have dared to face. Fortunate it was for them that his followers were equally well mounted with himself, and that the example set them by him made up for any deficiency in boldness which they might have. Obstacles which appeared to them to be insurmountable were proved by him to be such as might be overcome, and what he had done his followers could hardly fail to attempt. Thus it happened that after an hour's hard tiding the party found themselves once more on the beaten track.

Here Rhys dismounted, and, after examining the ground carefully, said, in tone which betokened his deep satisfaction, "I thought so! He hath not yet passed this way, and unless some spirit from Annwn help him we shall have him safe enough. Let us on to meet him."

A quarter of an hour's hard riding proved his surmise to be correct, for reaching the brow of a small hill, they perceived, preparing to descend the declivity on the opposite side, a couple of horsemen whom they had no difficulty in recognizing as Gruftydd ap Gwenwynwyn, and Alan, his esquire.

It was evident that Rhys and his men were perceived by the fugitives at the same time, for both stopped for a moment as though hesitating what to do. Apparently they were discussing the advisability of retiring or proceeding.

"Let us go forward, boys, as though we had no special object in view," said Rhys. "No hurry, nor any token that we expect so find in them any but ordinary travellers whom we can meet any hour of the day. Let us proceed as though we had abundance of time at our disposal."

This timely precaution cooled the ardour of one or two of the men, who would have hurried forward at the first sight of their prey.

The leisurely descent of the hill on the part of Rhys and his party seemed to have settled the question with the others, for they did not retreat. They remained, it is true, for a moment longer, as though undecided what to do, and then likewise slowly continued their journey downwards. The consequence was that the two parties found themselves face to face about two-thirds of the distance up the slope down which Gruffydd ap Gwenwynwyn and his esquire were descending. But Rhys, keen of vision and quick of action as he had been, had overlooked one thing.

He had forgotten that his features were familiar to the traitor he had come to capture, and that ap Gwenwynwyn had seen him at Llywelyn's court the very evening of his flight. When, therefore, the two parties came so near each other as to enable them to recognise each other's countenance, Gruffydd saw with dismay that here, facing him, was a man in the confidence of the Prince, and whom he had left at Aber with Llywelyn when he fled for his life.

Conscience makes cowards of us all, and the Welsh proverb says that the guilty flees before he is pursued. (13)

So it was now. The traitor at once expected that a trap of some kind awaited him. There was no time for consultation, not even time for consideration. The only thing left him to do was to act. To go forward meant certain captivity. To return the way he came offered possible safety.

"If Alan," said he hastily, "an' thou lovest me and art a loyal man, keep these men at bay at whatever cost till I reach the top of the hill."

So saying, he turned his horse's head up the hill, and spurred madly away, leaving Alan alone to cover his retreat.

Chapter XXXVII
Caught

So unexpected was ap Gwenwynwyn's flight that Rhys and his men paused for a moment in surprise. This pause was sufficient to afford Alan time to make his preparations, and the opposition he presented to the pursuers when they tried to pass by him was so stubborn and determined that the fugitive had already reached the crest of the hill before his esquire had been knocked from his saddle. Leaving him lying insensible on the earth, Rhys and his men pressed forward in pursuit of Gruffydd, who had now disappeared over the crest of the hill. When they themselves reached the top they paused to look and to listen. Sight served them no purpose, but hearing did. Loud cries ascended from the depth of the wood below.

"He hath fallen into Tewdwr's trap," cried Rhys joyfully. "Let us on to see."

A few minutes' gallop brought them on the' scene of the late strife, and there they found Gruffydd ap Gwenwynwyn lying on the earth, with Tewdwr ab Ednyfed's foot on his breast, while the uplifted sword in the hand of Meredydd's brother seemed about to descend upon the fallen foe.

"Hold!" cried Rhys, flinging himself from his horse. "Hold, Tewdwr! On thy life harm him not!"

"And wherefore should I not harm him?" asked Tewdwr roughly. "Base traitor to his Prince and murderer of my brother as he is!"

"The commands of the Prince are peremptory," said Rhys, "and thou must not harm him."

Gruffydd ap Gwenwynwyn, who had thought his last hour had surely come, again mustered courage at this unexpected reprieve. He began to think he had acted foolishly in being frightened by the presence of Rhys at this place, and now thought that very possibly the comer might have been sent by the Prince on a very different errand. The peremptory commands of the Prince could only, he thought, refer to the safe conduct granted him. Under this idea he now got upon his feet, and with an assumption of dignity turned to Tewdwr saying:

"Thou hast cause to be thankful that urgent business on behalf of our Prince prevents my remaining to chastise thee as thou deservest for thy unknightly interference with me. When I return I will again call thee to account for this. What ho, there! My horse!"

Tewdwr grasped the situation at once, and with all his native love for fun he determined to carry on the joke for a while.

"Nay," he said, "thou wilt surely not leave us thus."

The other looked at him disdainfully, and again called for his horse.

"Nay, but," urged Tewdwr again, "of a verity I cannot permit thee to go thus. Thou wilt remain a while with us. Tut, man, bear no grudge for the fall and the rough handling thou hast had. We must all take our share of such fare as that nowadays."

"I can understand that thou art already sorry for thy behaviour towards me," said Gruffydd, willing to appease the other if that could facilitate his departure. "I am ready to believe too that thou didst labour under a mistake when – "

"Nay," said Tewdwr once more, but this time with a more dangerous look in his eyes. "It is thou who dost labour under a mistake."

"Well, let it be so," said the other, anxious to avoid any new cause for dispute which might lead to his further detention. "I am willing to let bygones be bygones, and will bear thee no malice. But as thou has heard, the Prince's orders are peremptory, and I must be gone."

"It is because the Prince's orders are peremptory that thou must stay," replied Tewdwr.

"What meanest thou?" asked the traitor. "Did I not show the special safe conduct given me under and by the Prince's own hand?"

"Aye, so thou didst, but the hand which gave can also withdraw, and he who ordered the gate to be left open for thee has since ordered it to be shut and barred. Base traitor that thou art, thou hast been found out and caught in good time, and think thou not thou wilt again escape. Here, boys, bring a halter, and fasten him on his horse's back. I will take good care he escapes not again."

"By what right do you treat me thus?" cried Gruffydd, now greatly alarmed. "Beware what ye do."

"For such as thee it would be enough to answer that I do this by the right of the strongest, the right thou didst exercise when thou didst throw my brother to rot in a dungeon at Castell Tre'r Llyn. But for mine own honour I tell thee we act under direct orders from the Prince."

"But I have the Prince's own safe conduct."

"Yes, obtained by fraud, and recalled since. But we are only wasting time here in this useless talk. Bind him on his horse," continued Tewdwr, turning to two of his men who had now approached with halters for that purpose.

"Tewdwr ab Ednyfed!" cried ap Gwenwynwyn. "I appeal to thy knightly chivalry. Is it seeming that a knight of as high an order as thine own should be bound like a common felon? These halters shall never bind me!"

"Chivalry should not be mentioned in the same breath as thou, and as a felon's fate awaits thee I see no reason why a felon's bonds should be spared thee I would fain fasten thee by the halter to yonder bough in another way, but that my orders are to bear thee to Eynon ap Rhydderch. So come; if thou dost feel inclined to mount of thine own free will, well and good, and we will make thy bonds as little irksome for thee as we may. For any other man I would take his word as a sufficient bond; thine, thou well knowest, having been forfeited is worth naught."

Realising that resistance was now useless, he submitted with the best grace he could, hoping almost against hope that he might even yet have an opportunity for escape.

Now it was that Rhys remembered the squire who had been left lying bleeding and senseless beyond the hill. He sent a couple of his men at once to look for him, and to bring him, if yet alive, along as a prisoner after the master. When, however, the men reached the spot, Alan had disappeared.

Rhys and Tewdwr attached but little importance to this. Confident in their numbers, they feared no effort at a rescue, and accordingly hurried forward as rapidly as possible.

Little did they dream how much turned on the escape of Alan! Had they secured the esquire with the knight, they would have found on him the order for the execution of poor Meredydd ab Ednyfed. As it was, Alan had recovered from his swoon, and managed to hide himself in the wood before the searchers arrived at the spot where he had fallen. Discovering that his master had been made a prisoner, and realizing that there was for him no hope for escape, Alan had made all haste to give effect to his master's commands respecting Meredydd.

Thus it happened that at the very time that Gruffydd ap Gwenwynwyn was handed over by Tewdwr to Eynon, Gwen's brother, Alan handed Meredydd's death warrant to the governor of the castle, who lost no time in putting the orders given him into execution.

Chapter XXXVIII
Bride or Country

Meanwhile matters had not gone well with Llywelyn. In his anxiety to rescue Meredydd he had weakened his forces elsewhere. Not only had he sent all the available men at Aber under the command of Gwen's brother, but he had despatched couriers to several places along the northern marches and elsewhere calling for powerful contingents.

Edward, too, had happened to seize upon this moment for pushing forward more vigorously than ever the campaign against the Welsh. In obedience to the king's orders, the lords marchers had made several attacks upon the Welsh in their vicinity, and as the forces of the mountaineers had been weakened by the drafts sent to assist Eynon ap Rhydderch at Welshpool, it was a task of much more than customary ease to overcome the resistance offered. Thus courier after courier reached Llywelyn at Aber, informing him of numerous ravages and inroads. At the same time, too, be was informed that the king in person, at the head of a large army, was pushing forward by way of Chester, bent upon the subjugation or the annihilation of the Welsh.

Under ordinary circumstances Llywelyn would have laughed at this as he had at many a previous threat. His past experience of English inroads into Wales had been the arrival of a large army determined upon conquering, but departing under very different conditions. The day they crossed the borders into Wales their numbers began to dwindle. Whether by desertions, or by the cutting off of small detached parties, or by the unusual hardships they had to undergo, the imposing force had from day to day become more and more weakened and more and more demoralized, and finally marched back from Wales in very different guise from what they had shown when entering the Principality.

Then, however, things were very different from what they were now. Then Llywelyn had his forces at his command, and under his own direct supervision, ever hanging on the flanks of the invaders, and pouncing down upon them at every available opportunity. Now his forces were more scattered than they had been for years, and his strongest force was for a time unavailable, being gathered around the walls of Welshpool, leaving the north of the country practically open to the march of the enemy. Then, too, though a few chiefs might be disaffected, Llywelyn well knew who they were, and knew whom to trust. Now the recent revelations of Gruffydd ap Gwenwynwyn had assured him there was a widespread conspiracy against him. How wide it was he had no means of knowing until the papers promised him by the arch traitor ap Gwenwynwyn were placed in his hands. He hardly dared venture to issue a private order of any importance, as he had no guarantee but that an order issued to a trusted friend might not be received by a secret enemy. Meredydd, his best counsellor, was a prisoner in Castell Tre'r Llyn. Eynon ap Rhydderch, Tewdwr ab Ednyfed, and others of the chiefs on whom the Prince knew he could always rely in any emergency, however great, were either on their way to Welshpool, or already gathered around its walls. He was not without some ground for suspecting that the few chiefs who had now gathered around him at Aber were either in the pay of Edward or inclined to favour him so far as they dared to do.

When already placed in this dilemma, a terrible temptation was placed in his way.

One morning a messenger informed him that a knight from the English camp desired audience of him. On being admitted, he handed the Prince a letter, which Llywelyn recognised at once as coming from Eleanor de Montfort. Glancing hastily over it, he found it to contain, among expressions of warm affection for himself, intelligence which tended to cause him much anxiety. His betrothed, whether from being too closely confined or from pining for her future husband and home, was in ill-health and longing to see him, and to enjoy with him the free air of the county over which he ruled. The letter gave him grave cause for apprehension, an apprehension which was not lessened on finding, by inquiry of the knight who had brought the letter, that she was indeed much worse than she herself admitted. The Court physicians, said the knight, declared her to be in a critical state, and that nothing short of a miracle could save her life unless she gave over brooding as she had been doing now for so many months.

"And now, Sir Prince," said Edward's ambassador, "I am authorised by our gracious Sovereign King Edward to make thee a very fair offer. He is grieved that his ward and cousin should show signs of a malady which hath oft proved deadly, and would gladly give her her liberty and free permission to come here to thee. He hath, however, sworn that she shall never see thee, nor any belonging to thee, and never be again her own mistress until thou hast made thy submission."

"And call you this fair chivalry, Sir Englishman?" cried Llywelyn, starting to his feet. "Must your king war with defenceless ladies because he dare not face the lances of their knights?"

"Nay, nay," said the other, interposing, "let us not

come to hard words, which lead to something harder. Whatever may be said of the action of the king in this matter, none will deny that he is ever ready to meet his enemies on the open field. Indeed, his having already penetrated thus soon so far into Wales is sufficient answer to such a charge. He, however, regrets deeply having done what he hath done with the Lady Eleanor, but, having taken the vow he did, he is now bound by his vow and by his regard for his own honour not to yield to the more kindly feelings which now fill his breast towards her and towards thee."

Llywelyn remained silent. The ambassador, after a pause, again continued.

"This being so, and the King being so well disposed to thee and to the Lady Eleanor, in all justice and fairness it must be said that, whatever wrong he may have done in the past, he is now prepared, nay, desirous, to right that wrong. It follows that if the proposal he now makes thee be rejected by thee, it must be thou, and not he who continues her captivity. Nay, I would venture to say more. If her present illness, which may at its present stage be so easily remedied, be allowed to take deeper hold upon her, and should it, as there is some cause to fear, prove fatal, her death must not be laid at the door of him who is ready to give her her liberty; the rather must it be placed at his who from a perverse spirit would needlessly continue her captivity."

"And what be the terms Edward offers?" asked Llywelyn.

"They be only such as a king may ask and a prince may grant. I go not now into details of them. I only say that he is willing to acknowledge thee as Lord of Snowdon and Prince of North Wales – thou, however, paying him fealty in form; then thy opposition hath been so long, and thy success so great, that a certain sum must be granted him as an indemnity; still, to show that he is anxious to place as little pressure as possible upon thee, the payment of this tribute will be only a matter of outward form, and will not be demanded after the payment of a first instalment thereof. Being anxious that the peace made should be lasting, it follows that a full and free pardon must be given on both sides to subjects of either country who may have been guilty of assisting the other. Thou wilt grant a free pardon to all Welshmen who have at any time aided him, and he will grant similar pardon to all English subjects who have favoured thee. The day thou agreest to this, and dost swear formal allegiance, that same day will terminate the bondage of the Lady Eleanor, and make Wales more truly thine than it is now. As things are now, thou knowest Wales is only thine in name. The reality is already gone from thee. How many chiefs are there to whom thou canst to-day issue an order to advance against Edward with any certainty that they will not join his standard at thine hour of need? Thou mayest say, and doubtless wilt think, that to bribe thy chiefs thus to betray thee is not right. But thou must face things as they are, and not as thou wouldst wish them to be. If thou decidest to reject the terms our lord the king offers thee in amity, what is there left thee to do? To whom wilt thou apply for help against him? To thy brother Dafydd? He would gladly see thee fall that thereby he might rise. To Gruffydd ap Gwenwynwyn? Thou knowest he hath leavened the chieftains of North and of South Wales in favour of Edward. To Meredydd ab Ednyfed? He is shut up in Welshpool Castle, and it is only the king's leniency which hath kept his head on his shoulders till to-day; and that head falls when thou rejectest the offer I now make thee. Wouldst thou call Tewdwr ab Ednyfed or Eynon ap Rhydderch? They are sitting down before the walls of Welshpool, and before they could reach thee to give thee help, Edward's army would have overwhelmed all opposition, and what then could the few thou canst trust do for thee against him? Listen therefore to the voice of reason. Edward offers thee thy friend's freedom for the day thou acceptest these terms; that day will orders be sent to Welshpool for the release of Meredydd. He offers thee a real power and authority for the semblance of one which thou now hast. He imposes no burden of debt upon thee or upon the Country, for he will forego all payments but the first, which will be taken as an outward token. Above all, he offers thee that for which thou couldst well afford to sacrifice thy country itself: the love of thy bride, the preservation of her life, the security of her happiness. Throw not therefore these great things from thy hand. With Edward supporting thee, thy fickle subject chieftains will return to their allegiance. With thy bride at thy side thou wilt be able to face a brighter future than thy past has been."

Llywelyn felt the full force of the reasoning of Edward's ambassador, and remained plunged in thought.

"Let me have," said he at last, "till the morrow to decide. This is not a matter to be lightly weighed or unripely considered."

"Thou sayest wisely," said the ambassador, well pleased to have succeeded so far. "Calm judgment will, I am sure, direct thee in the right path."

So saying, he bowed himself out of the apartment. Llywelyn, thus left alone, found himself the prey to sad thoughts. All that the ambassador had stated was true. His friends, in whom he could trust, placed beyond the power of helping him. Those who surrounded him possibly already in the pay of the English king. His nearest blood relations ready to seize upon his downfall as a stepping stone to their own elevation. And worse than all, his bride, his beloved Eleanor, around whom all his heart's afflictions were centred, pining to death in captivity, while a word and a stroke of the pen from him would serve to give her liberty, and with liberty, life. Then his thoughts wandered forward to the future. With Eleanor at his side he would, he felt, be able to face any troubles which might come again to meet him. The thought of her would strengthen his arm, now weakened by the thought that nothing he could hope to do would ever give him back his bride; her presence would clear his brain, now darkened by the hopelessness of securing her for his own, unless he consented to the course proposed.

Mixed with this, too, was a natural feeling of satisfaction that he would have once more in his hand undoubted power in Wales, and that those who had deserted him would be only too glad to curry favour with him. This, however, was only a passing thought. His soul was torn with the conflicting emotions raised by the one great question.

Bride or country?

Which should it be?

If he decided upon the latter, he would certainly lose the former for ever.

If he chose the former, there was the possibility of his retaining much and possibly regaining more of the latter.

Under these circumstances he at length yielded, and Edward's ambassador returned with Llywelyn's signature to the one deed which marked the ebb of Welsh independence during the Prince's lifetime.

Chapter XXXIX
Friends and Foes

As Meredydd had anticipated, the tramp of armed men, which had sounded so distinctly in the corridor, stopped at the door of his dungeon. He had but little time in which to make up his mind as to what to do. If he fought his executioners, what chance would he have against so many? If he yielded without a struggle, his fate was already sealed. Too well he knew the malignant enmity of Gruffydd ap Gwenwynwyn would have left him no possible loophole of escape. It was evidently his duty to sell his life as dearly as possible.

Then there was, too, the possibility of his gaining some outside help. The castle was so closely invested – and the attack upon it likely to prove so energetic – that, if he could hold out for a little while, his friends might have mastered the situation, and he himself be restored to safety. But how could he do this? He had no means of barricading the door – no means to prevent their opening it. How he wished that Deio'r Llannerch had been able to carry out his first plan, and have abstracted the key of his dungeon. But that was now out of the question. Still, there was Deio's distinct promise of help, and Meredydd counted upon finding among these assailants at least one or two friends to help him. With the help of these he might even yet cause his would-be executioners no little trouble.

These thoughts flashed through his brain as the party halted at the door and prepared to open it. Grasping his sword firmly in his hand, he stood at the foot of the steps determined to strike the first who entered the dungeon. The plan he had resolved upon was this – to offer all the opposition he could to their entrance into his dungeon, and when finally compelled by force, of numbers to give way, to retreat to a corner, where, with his back to the wall, he would have all his enemies in front of him. With a beating heart he heard the key put into the lock, and expected to see the bolt shoot back, and the door open. It soon became apparent that there was something wrong. The door remained closed, and the bolt unmoved. Though he could hear the sound of voices, the sounds were too indistinct for him to make out the exact words. He, however, understood that something was being said about the unforeseen difficulty in opening the door.

What actually took place was this. The governor of the castle, on the arrival of Alan with his master's written order for the instant execution of the prisoner, had immediately set about obeying the mandate. A guard of soldiers was ordered to attend him and Alan, and taking the key the governor handed it to one of the soldiers to open the door. The man tried to turn it, but in vain, and turning to the governor said:

"The key will not turn."

"Tell me not that it will not turn!" cried Alan. "It is thy want of skill or of power. While we linger and dawdle here the enemy may gain the walls, and our master's last orders after all be set at naught. Get thee aside and let me open it."

So saying he pushed the soldier to one side, and placing the hilt of his dagger into the handle of the key to serve as a lever, gave it a wrench, which, after a slight resistance, seemed to prove sufficient, for the key turned round.

"There!" cried the esquire, "said I not so? And now undo the other bolts and bars." These were quickly removed, and the door pushed inwards.

Still, to the surprise of all, it remained immovable, apparently as sound as ever With a muttered oath, Alan gave it a kick with his iron-shod shoe, with no other effect, however, than to cause the door to rattle, and to prove that the obstruction, whatever it consisted of, was of a very substantial character.

"Can the prisoner have barricaded the door from within?" asked Alan.

"That can hardly be," said the governor, "for he had not, to my knowledge, the wherewithal to do so. Didst thou unlock the door?"

"Unlock the door! Didst thou not see the key turn? See!" and he seized the key, which still remained in the lock, and turned it so as to re-lock the door. What, however, was his surprise to find that some resistance offered itself within the lock to the re-shooting of the bolt, and turning with a laugh to the governor, he said:

"See! I have unlocked it so effectually that it will not lock again!"

Without saying a word the governor gravely took hold of the key and, drawing it forth from the lock, held it up to the light. Alan looked, and gave a cry of dismay. It was broken! He had exercised such strength that the key, massive though it was, had broken in the wards. The governor re-echoed Alan's cry, but his own was more of surprise than of dismay.

"This," he cried, "is not the right key! How could I have been mistaken? It seemeth very like, too, but still it is not the right one. No wonder the hole would not shoot! Run thee, Tom, and fetch me the key thou wilt find hanging up in my room."

The man thus addressed hastened away, while Alan fumed and raved at the delay thus occasioned. The man remaining away longer than was expected, another was despatched to hasten him. When both returned Tom was the bearer of ill news. The key was not to be found. With a deep oath Alan ordered the door to be burst open.

This was, however, easier said than done. The combined force of the party had apparently no effect upon the massive door, which formed an effectual barrier between them and their prey.

"This will never do!" cried Alan. "Run and get something to serve as a battering ram."

Some of the men hastened away, with this purpose. Before they returned, a message was brought to the governor that a flag of truce stood at the gate, with a communication for the governor of the castle.

"Let the herald be admitted, and his business asked," said the governor.

"Hadst thou not better see him thyself, Sir Governor?" asked Alan. "I will see to that being done here which is necessary."

"Then I leave thee to do it," replied the governor, "for to tell the truth, I stomach not the executioner's work too well."

As the commandant left, the men who had gone in quest of a battering ram returned with a heavy beam of wood, which answered the purpose well. A few well-directed blows from the ponderous beam, swung by a dozen willing arms, caused the door, massive and iron-bound though it was, to shake and rattle, and, finally, to burst open. No sooner, however, was this done than a voice from within the dungeon cried out:

"I give ye fair warning that the first who crosses these steps falls by my sword!"

The soldiers, who were pushing forward, paused.

"What?" cried Alan, "Are ye cowards all, and all afraid of one man? Follow me, or be for ever branded as cowards," and so saying Gruffydd ap Gwenwynwyn's esquire leaped in with up-raised sword upon Meredydd. The Welshman was, however, fully prepared for him, and with one terrible blow felled his assailant to the earth.

"On him!" cried Alan, faithful even to death to the charge entrusted to him. It was the last word he uttered. Meredydd's sword had been all too certain in its work, and before the soldiers could obey him, Alan sank back on the stone floor, dead.

"The next man meets a like fate!" cried Meredydd, menacingly.

The danger was too great and too real to be lightly faced, and the men paused irresolutely.

"It is too bad," cried Deio'r Llauerch, who formed one of the party, and was indeed now its chief remaining officer, taking advantage of this fortunate pause, "It is too bad that we should be asked or expected to risk our lives to take that of a brave man who hath done us no harm."

"But the governor's orders are strict," protested another.

"In ordinary times and in ordinary circum- stances I would go with thee," said Deio, "but I see no need why we should now rouse the anger of those other Welsh devils outside higher against us. It is plain enough that we cannot hold out much longer against them, and if we can – by giving up their prisoner alive to them – get better terms for ourselves, I see no reason why we should throw away the chance. What say you?"

"I think with thee," cried one of the men whom Deio had already enlisted in his favour.

"And I!" "And I!" cried two or three others also in the secret.

The influence of example is so great that it is no great matter for surprise that the other men, one after another, should have fallen in with the plan proposed.

"What say you, Sir Knight?" asked Deio. "Will you go with us peaceably to the gates, and speak your friends outside fair on our behalf?"

"If ye give me your word, as men, that ye will not take unfair advantage of me if I accompany you, and if ye promise to support me against those who may wish to oppose my way to freedom, I will readily go with you, and can promise that whatever befalls the rest of the garrison, those who now favour me will not only be spared, but will amply be rewarded. For this I pledge my word as a knight."

"There! Said I not so?" cried Deio. "And now, men, if ye promise, we go together in a body, shoulder to shoulder, with this brave knight as our leader, and we force our way to the gates. The officer there is my own brother, as ye know, and will render us every assistance. What say ye? 'Yes' means safety and reward for ourselves and the knight, 'No' means certain death to us ere nightfall. For my own part, though I stood alone among ye all, I would accept the safety thus offered us. What say ye? We serve ourselves and our Lord ap Gwenwynwyn at the same time, for he is now a prisoner in the hands of the Welshmen outside the walls. The saving the life of this knight will certainly make the lot of ap Gwenwynwyn easier. What say ye, my masters?"

With one accord, the men who now regarded Deio as their leader, and who felt the weight of the argument both as regarded themselves and their lord, ap Gwenwynwyn, agreed to the proposal thus placed before them, and the next moment Meredydd found himself in the midst of his late assailants, all with drawn swords ready to shed their own blood in his defence.

Scarcely, however, had they left the dungeon door than they saw approaching them, in evident haste, the governor of the castle, followed by a fresh relay of armed retainers.

Chapter XL
The Page

Gruffydd ap Gwenwynwyn, notwithstanding his capture, and the consequent defeat of all his fondest hopes, had still some cause for satisfaction. He had been somewhat anxious until he obtained news of Alan's fate. When, however, the men sent in search of the esquire returned with the news that he was not only apparently not dead, but that he had evidently made his escape, the traitor felt that one of the bitterest pangs of his own captivity had been greatly alleviated. As to his ultimate fate he had little apprehension. He felt no doubt that, however much angered Llywelyn might be, he would not care to proceed to extremities with a man who had obtained such influence throughout Wales as he had done. Then, too, Edward of England would intercede on his behalf, and by offering an exchange of prisoners, might, and probably would, secure ap Gwenwynwyn's release. And while thus confident about his own fate, he had the satisfaction of knowing that Meredydd's fate was sealed. He had too much confidence in Alan's fidelity to doubt for a moment that he would fail to execute the important commission with which he had been charged. How well founded was the Knight's trust in his esquire's faithful execution of orders we have already seen.

The game in which ap Gwenwynwyn had been engaged was, however, necessarily of such a nature as prevented his forecasting with exactness what might take place. There were possible combinations of which he could have no foreknowledge. His calculations were liable to be upset at any moment by occurrences he could never have foreseen. Admitting that he were once delivered into Llywelyn's hands, and that his friends were once permitted to open negotiations directly with the Prince, then the forecast of ap Gwenwynwyn would have been a fairly correct one. Whether the circumstances in which he actually found himself were such as he imagined them to be, we shall shortly see.

The party lost no time in hastening forward to join the forces before Castell Tre'r Llyn, under the command of Eynon ap Rhydderch. the brother of Gwen. When they arrived, ap Gwenwynwyn had the satisfaction of seeing that the place still held out. He would now, he thought, be able to make terms for the surrender of the castle after assuring himself of Meredydd's death. Tewdwr ab Ednyfed immediately took his prisoner to the tent of the commander of the forces, and formally handed him over to Eynon. Gwen's brother was attended by a number of other chiefs, and standing near him, in the centre of the tent, was a youthful-looking page, who appeared to be in deep converse with him.

"Ha!" said Eynon, when ap Gwenwynwyn had been introduced, "and so the fox hath been caught in his own trap. It is well, for we know how to deal with him."

"I am pleased to hear thee say so," said ap Gwenwynwyn, with an attempt at bravado. "I feared thy knowledge of the customs of chivalry would have been as scant as that of this coward who hath bound me like a serf."

"Speak not thou, of all men, of the customs of chivalry," said Eynon. "Thou hast forfeited every right to chivalrous consideration. And well it is for thee that thy position just now prevents Tewdwr ab Ednyfed from calling thee to account for the word 'coward'."

"Aye," replied Tewdwr, with a laugh, though there was, too, an angry beam in his eyes, "Aye, we all know the proverb, 'Drwg ei hun a debyg arall' (He who is himself evil thinks evil of another)."

"But we have no time to spare in parley," said Eynon. "I ask thee, Gruffydd ap Gwenwynwyn, where is Meredydd ab Ednyfed?"

"Why ask ye of me where he is? Am I his keeper?"

"So said Cain, when asked of his brother's fate," said Eynon, gravely. "I trust the comparison will not go further. We know he entered thy castle yonder, and we know he hath not left it."

"Then why ask ye of me if ye know already?" demanded Gruffydd.

"Simply because we would fain think that thou dost already regret the treachery thou hast been guilty of. Therefore I ask of thee again for information respecting Meredydd."

"And I," said ap Gwenwynwyn, "refuse to answer thee. I do not acknowledge thy authority, but demand to be taken before Llywelyn, whose safe conduct under his own hand I hold."

"Aye, and which thou didst receive from Meredydd ab Ednyfed when he came to thee on the Prince's own command, and which thou hast forfeited by the treachery thou didst contemplate in asking for the safe conduct, and didst execute when once thou had'st it in thy hand. But I have no time to dally here with thee. An' thou wishest not to answer, I will not compel thee. Ho there without!"

At this an attendant at the door entered.

"Hath the gallows been erected, as I ordered?"

"Yes."

"Exactly opposite the chief gate of the castle?"

"Yes, and within all but a bowshot of it."

"That is well. Bring in half a dozen men, and lead the prisoner to his proper place."

Ap Gwenwynwyn had listened to this conversation in mingled wonder and anxiety. He could scarcely believe that the gallows was seriously intended for him, the scion of one of the most powerful houses in Wales; and yet, when he looked upon the dark and lowering countenances of the assembled chieftains, in all of whom be recognised either Llywelyn's most faithful adherents or Meredydd's most intimate friends, his heart began to sink within him.

"This," he cried, as the soldiers approached and seized him, "I will never submit to."

"We do not ask thee to submit," was Eynon s cold reply. "Thou hast no choice in the matter. Take him and hang him up, that all his men within the castle may see him, and know what will be their fate unless the castle be delivered up ere noon this day."

"This is murder, cold-blooded murder," cried the traitor, now thoroughly alarmed.

"Thou art such an adept in calling things by their wrong names, that to call this murder is the best proof that it is justice," said Eynon. "Away with him, men, and we will accompany you to see that the act be properly done."

This last utterance of the leader of the Welsh forces led ap Gwenwynwyn to hope that the whole thing was nothing but an attempt to frighten him, and so with an assumed bold step and upright bearing he accompanied his captors to where the gallows had been raised.

It was only a rough structure, consisting of merely two trunks of trees firmly fixed perpendicularly in the earth some two yards apart, and with a strong bough of one left growing horizontally out, and fastened at its end to the upright trunk of the other. From the centre

Llywelyn

of this bough was suspended a strong rope, ending in a noose.

Not until he found himself actually on the spot, and bade to ascend a rough and shaky platform for the purpose of having the noose fastened on his neck, did he really believe that his captors were determined to proceed to extremities. Until then he had maintained an appearance of dignity which he knew well how to assume. Now, however, this assumed calmness left him, and he became visible as the abject, cringing wretch he really was.

"Eynon!" he cried, "Eynon! Do not this great wrong. I would, indeed, save Meredydd if I could, but I cannot."

"Thou canst not? And why?"

"Because he is already dead," replied ap Gwenwynwyn.

"Then heaven have mercy on thy soul," said Eynon solemnly, "for die thou must. Thy only chance of life was that Meredydd might yet be alive, and that thy written order might bring him back here in safety."

"Oh ten thousand curses on the head of Alan, my esquire! Had he but waited a little longer!" cried ap Gwenwynwyn. "But give me the chance. Here, send this ring to the Governor of the castle, and tell him it is my command that Meredydd be released."

At this the page already referred to sprang eagerly forward, and seized the ring from the trembling fingers of the craven knight.

"Haste thee, sir page! Haste thee!" cried ap Gwenwynwyn, as the page, accompanied by a herald, left the little bank on which the gallows had been raised, and hastened towards the castle gates.

"Thou needst not fear as to the haste of the messenger, said Eynon with a smile. If the governor of thy castle be as speedy as my messenger would have him be, all will be well. Yet do not foster any false hopes, for as certain as that the sun is now approaching its meridian, so certain will its midday beams fail upon thy corpse if Meredydd ab Ednyfed be not here then safe and sound."

Meanwhile the page and herald, as we have already seen, reached the castle and obtained audience of the governor. The sight of the ring, and, above all, a glance through the window at the gallows erected since he had gone to bring Meredydd out for execution, convinced the governor that both in his lord's interest and in his own he could do nothing better than release Meredydd forthwith. He accordingly hastened, accompanied by the page, who pressed him to use all speed, to Meredydd's dungeon, calling at the same time for a dozen personal retainers who, he thought, might be required to convince Alan in his headstrong adherence to his master's orders that the only course left open for them was to release Meredydd.

No sooner did they come in sight of the band, headed by Deio o'r Llannerch and Meredydd, than the page leapt forward, and casting himself on Meredydd's breast, exclaimed:

"Thou art safe and free!"

Meredydd gazed in surprise, and found that the page, overcome by his feelings, had fainted.

"Poor boy," said the governor, "I never saw anyone so eager and anxious for the safety of anyone as this page of thine. Had he been thy ladylove instead of thy page he could not have been more afraid of being too late to save thee. Now haste thee and secure the safety of my lord by showing thyself among thine own people. Leave thy page in my charge. I will see to his having every care."

"Nay," said Meredydd, pushing back those who

would have taken the limp form of the poor boy from his arms; "nay, no hand but mine shall tend him. Let me bear him to the open air, and that will help revive him."

And so saying, tenderly and lovingly he bore the precious burden in his arms through the grim castle gates to the open air and freedom beyond. Then, and only then, did he imprint a passionate kiss on the ruby lips of the face upturned towards him.

Never to living soul did he say that it was Gwen who had herself released him.

Chapter XLI
All Hope Gone

The scene is changed. Wales has been left far behind. Llywelyn, with his leading chieftains, has gone up to London to do the formal homage agreed to in the terms of peace to which he had consented when he placed bride before country.

Before this, however, he had sent Gwen, under a strong escort, to London to be once more with her mistress, so soon to be her princess. Gwen's arrival with the information that Llywelyn was shortly to follow did more for the recovery of the Lady Eleanor than all the physic of the skilful leeches Edward had ordered to attend upon her. Gruffydd ap Gwenwynwyn, too, had been released, chiefly by Gwen's intercession with her brother. The joy and satisfaction of all at having Meredydd once more free and safe was so great that little opposition was offered when Gwen entered her plea for mercy for the traitor. Eynon felt, too, that he was in a manner bound in honour to release the man who had done Meredydd such great wrong, as that wrong had now been righted. Thus it happened that Gruffydd found himself again at the English court, but little the worse for the rough handling he had undergone in the Welsh camp.

Gwen was herself unaware of his presence, and, passing along a lonely walk in the palace gardens one day, suddenly and unexpectedly found herself face to face with the man who had tried to do her and those she loved the greatest wrong. She would have passed him, but with a malicious smile he stopped her, saying:

Llywelyn

"Not so fast, fair maiden. It is such a long time since I had last the pleasure of speaking to thee that I would now fain ask thee to spare me an hour's quiet chat."

"There can be no pleasure to thee nor to me in any talk with each other," said the maiden, though greatly alarmed, "so I pray thee let me pass," and she made as though she would pass him by.

"Nay, by my soul thou shalt not!" cried he. "Think not that thou hast here, as thou hadst in Wales, thy lover at thy call to aid thee; though in good sooth I wish he were but here that I might teach him, too, the lesson he so sadly needs. If thou comest not with me of thine own free will, I know the way to make thee come of mine own choice! Come!" he said, harshly, "I brook no more folly of thine. Since thou wilt not come of thine own free will, thou must come as I wish thee, and be what I wish thee."

She was too breathless to call for help, and her whilom lover felt that he had her completely in his power, for the part of the palace near which they found themselves was that containing the apartments allotted to his use. Seizing her therefore in his arms, he bore her into the corridor which led to his room.

So saying, he made a grasp at her dress.

With a loud scream, however, she eluded him, and, darting with the speed of the startled fawn past him, she rushed towards the palace, which loomed between the trees in front of her. With a muttered imprecation Gruffydd ap Gwenwynwyn followed, and, though her flight was rapid, the sound of pursuing footsteps soon told her that she had no chance in the race against him. Indeed, in a very short time, and while almost with her hand upon the door to one of the entrances to the palace, he overtook her, and, placing his hand on her shoulder, he roughly shook her.

Poor Gwen felt that she had now indeed no hope. Her capture had been made without an eye perceiving them, and too well she knew that, once within his own rooms, her fate was sealed for ever.

Chapter XLII

When Gwen had given up all hope, succour came from a source quite as acceptable as unexpected. (12) The door of Gruffydd ap Gwenwynwyn's apartment had already been opened, and he was on the point of bearing his helpless burden within, when a deep imprecation was heard, and the next moment Gwen had been wrested from his grasp, and he himself hurled to the ground.

The poor girl, who had become almost unconscious, no sooner found herself released from her captor than, without waiting to thank her unexpected champion, or even to see who it was, rushed screaming away to the apartments of her lady.

The Lady Eleanor and Llywelyn were enjoying for the first time since their separation in France the pleasure of mutual companionship, and, engrossed in each other, were oblivious to all else, until their privacy was suddenly broken upon by the frightened Gwen, who had lost all her self-possession. All she could do was to mention the name of ap Gwenwynwyn, and point to the corridor along which she had fled.

Without a word Llywelyn, seizing and unsheathing his sword, rushed in the direction she indicated, and soon heard the clashing of arms, which convinced him he must be on the right track. Reaching the apartments of ap Gwenwynwyn, a strange sight presented itself to him. When ap Gwenwynwyn found himself so unceremoniously treated by his unexpected assailant his rage knew no bounds. Leaping to his feet, he drew his sword and rushed upon the intruder.

When, however, he saw who it was he paused and drew back.

"Aye," said the other, "well mayest thou pause, double-dyed traitor and false coward that thou art. But, didst thou draw back more, thou shalt not escape me. Did I not swear that when next thou didst cross my path thou shouldst surely die? As truly as I said it shall it be, and I thank heaven that thy folly hath placed thee once more within reach of my weapon."

Ap Gwenwynwyn laughed aloud. "Thou speakest bravely, indeed," said he, "and crowest as loudly as though thou wert on thine own dunghill in Wales. Thou needest a lesson which my dungeon at Welshpool failed to teach thee but which my good sword shall now do. When thou art disposed of, I shall have time to settle mine own account with the would-be coy maiden."

Without further parley he rushed upon Meredydd – for it was indeed he who had come so opportunely to the aid of the maiden he loved so well.

Fortunate was it for Meredydd that he was on his guard, for the attack of Gruffydd was so sudden and so fierce that had his opponent been less skilful or less prepared, the result would have been immediately decided. Even as it was he felt obliged, in consulting his own safety, to fall back before the fierce shower of blows which the other rained upon him, and which he with difficulty warded or parried.

The first fury of the attack having been exhausted, Gwen's lover found himself on more equal terms, though he felt himself bound to acknowledge that whatever might be ap Gwenwynwyn's other faults, never had Meredydd ab Ednyfed met a foeman more worthy of his steel, if worth be measured by skill, ability, and blind courage. Indeed, the outcome appeared to be for some time doubtful, and even Meredydd began to feel anxious as to the final result. Soon, however, he began to feel reassured as he felt the fury of the other's attack slackening.

After the first mutual challenge neither of the combatants spoke a word. They had each enough to employ them in the work they had in hand. They could not afford to waste time in speech. Their swords were their only tongues, and spoke the mutual jealousy and hatred of the combatants quite as effectively as human tongue could have done. No sooner did Meredydd feel the efforts of the other slackening and weakening than he plied him hard in return, and forced him back step by step to the far end of the apartment, where the wall prevented his further retreat. There they were as Llywelyn entered the room. By a dexterous combination of skill and strength Meredydd at this moment beat down the other's guard, and plunged his sword to the hilt in the traitor's breast.

Gruffydd ap Gwenwynwyn fell to the ground, the blood spouting from the wound, and be-spattering the clothing of his opponent as well as of Llywelyn, who had rushed forward. At this moment steps were heard, and the next moment the King, who had been attracted by the noise, entered the apartment. Ap Gwenwynwyn proved himself true to his deceitful nature to the very last. Seeing the entrance of the King, he half rose upon one elbow, and pointing with his finger to Llywelyn, he said:

"Sire! I demand justice! This false prince, angry at the part I have taken in thy service, and desirous to rid him of me, hath, in company with his follower, attacked me. I call upon thee to avenge me!" The exertion of doing this proved too much for him. The blood poured from his mouth, and with a dying groan, and with a lie on his lips, he fell back, dead.

Edward's passions were never remarkable for being under control, and the scene he had witnessed and the words he had heard raised his anger to the highest pitch.

"Cousin!" said he sternly, "I am grieved to see that thou dost so ill-acknowledge the clemency I have shown, and dost so badly observe the mutual conditions to which we agreed. It was stipulated that all past misdeeds by our subjects should be forgotten, and that no man should suffer in person or in estate for any part he might have taken in the past. And yet I find thee here, with this knight of thine, attacking and slaying a man whose only fault appears to have been fidelity to me. But I will uphold my rights, and my court shall not be thus suited by evil actions unrestrained. What ho, there! Half a dozen of ye, take this knight," pointing to Meredydd, "and string him up on yonder oak tree. In good sooth, 'twill be the biggest acorn it hath ever borne."

"Methinks," said Meredydd, placing his back against the wall, "that I should have a word myself in that arrangement, and I have a very strong objection to the course your Majesty hath advised. Back, sir! Back!" he cried, pointing his sword at the breast of the officer who was advancing to arrest him. "Back, I say, or by heaven thou shalt suffer the same fate as this traitor," and he spurned the dead body with his foot.

"Dost thou dare to oppose my will?" cried Edward.

"I know not what may be thy will, Sir King, but I oppose the swords of those who would fain give me, a sworn knight, the fate of a felon. Whoever advances upon me doth so at the peril of his life."

Llywelyn turned to the King and said:

"Sire, I pray you think not of doing my friend such great wrong as what is now proposed to be done. I would – "

"Thou wouldst harbour a traitor, it seems," said the King roughly. "Thou hast good cause to be thankful, Sir Prince, that thou dost not bear him company to the gallows."

Llywelyn's nature was as haughty and as hot as that of Edward himself, and this veiled threat roused his ire.

"An' you think that, Sir King, it beseems me to give you some cause for it, and so I e'en join my good friend Meredydd, and I give fair warning that whoever attempts to seize us will have his death upon his own head."

So saying, he sprang forward and placed himself by Meredydd's side,

"Well," cried Edward, "an' that be so, 'twould be a pity to spoil your sport. Seize them both, and while the Prince's passions cool in a dungeon, let the other be hung."

This was, however, much easier said than done. Not only were the Prince and Meredydd already well and widely renowned for their skill in arms, but the sounds of altercation had attracted others to the spot, among whom were the majority of the Welsh chieftains who had accompanied Llywelyn to London. No sooner did they understand how matters stood than they pushed forward, and formed by the side of their prince, offering a terribly menacing phalanx, which Edward's practised eye assured him would not be broken without great loss.

Now he began, when too late, to regret the precipitancy with which he had acted, and wished he had taken more time to consider his action. Still, there was no means by which he could withdraw without compromising his own honour.

He was on the point of giving the order to advance when another interruption occurred. Two ladies pushed forward and stood between the contending parties.

They were Eleanor and Gwen. The former was too overcome by emotion to speak. The latter, who had now quite recovered her self-possession, and who had been given to understand that her lover and protector were one and the same, and that he was now in danger of his life for having saved her, felt no delicacy in addressing the King.

"Methought, Sir King," said she boldly, "that it was the custom of chivalry to protect ladies, and to honour those who do so."

"What hath that to do with us, or what hast thou either? Get thee gone."

"I will get me gone when I have said my say, and not before. Thou wouldst be false to thine own oath, Sir King, didst thou carry out thy threat upon this brave man."

Then in a few hurried words she explained how she had been attacked and carried away by ap Gwenwynwyn, how Meredydd had appeared and rescued her, how she had hastened to her lady's apartments, whence Llywelyn had proceeded to aid his friend.

"And because this brave knight defended me, and thus obeyed the calls of the duty of that chivalry of which thou wouldst fain be an ornament, thou wouldst condemn him to a traitor's doom. If you, Sir King, must have a traitor, there he lieth; hang him up, and honour this brave knight even as he deserves."

The king laughed.

"Well, then," said he, "be it so. Thou hast taught me a lesson, and I will not soon forget it. I had been misinformed, but have now been enlightened. I know how to value a brave knight when I meet with one, and this I now do," and he stepped forward, holding out his hand to Meredydd, saying: "I thank thee for having saved the honour of my court, which would have been for ever sullied had yon traitor carried out his scheme. In token of my esteem, I invite thee to the feast to which my cousin Llywelyn, with his future bride, will now accompany me."

"I thank you, sire," said Meredydd, "but as I owe my life to this fair maiden, I must e'en ask to be allowed to bring her with me, else the feast will be gall and bitterness to me."

"So!" said Edward laughing, "Sets the wind in that quarter, doth it? Well, thou art worthy of her and she is worthy of thee, so come together."

The incident which had threatened to end so tragically turned out most happily. The party which met around the royal table that evening was a happy one, and to Meredydd and Gwen at least the knowledge that Gruffydd ap Gwenwynwyn would never more trouble them added materially to their enjoyment.

In a short time afterwards Llywelyn's hopes were realized, and Eleanor de Montfort was made the Lady of Snowdon by being united in marriage with the Prince. On the same day Gwen and Meredydd were united, and the party which returned to Wales soon after did so with every hope of a life of comfort, of peace, and of prosperity.

THE END[*]

---

[*] As intimated at the commencement of this tale, the life of Llywelyn presented far too many incidents to be compressed within the compass of a single story. We, therefore, close this portion of it here with the attainment of one of his life's objects – the hand of Eleanor de Montfort in marriage. The story of his life will be continued in *The Widowed Prince*, a sequel to the present story.

Notes

(1) This was true at the time *Llywelyn* was written in 1886-7. A statue of Llywelyn by English sculptor Henry Alfred Pegram (1862-1937) would later be unveiled in 1916 as one of ten statues of Welsh heroes to adorn Cardiff City Hall. The subjects of the statues were chosen by a popular ballot. A second monument to Llywelyn in the form of a substantial standing stone was erected in 1956 at Cilmeri, Powys, near the site where he was killed; and his grave at Cwmhir Abbey is also now marked with a stone.

(2) Gogleddwr (Northman) or Deheuwr (Southerner).

(3) Dragons are a symbol of leadership and nobility in the earliest Welsh poetry and are associated with ideas of Welsh nationhood and identity in some of the tales referred to (somewhat inaccurately) as the Mabinogion. Llywelyn himself is referred to as a dragon in his famous eulogy by Gruffydd ab yr Ynad Goch. However, Beriah's suggestion that Llywelyn would have worn a dragon – especially on green and white silk – is anachronistic. Llywelyn's banner was that of the house of Aberffraw, four lions in red and yellow. The earliest Welsh leader known with certainty to have used a dragon banner was Owain Glyndŵr in the 15th century, though his was white and gold; the red dragon on green and white now familiar as the Welsh flag has its origins as the flag of Henry Tudor.

(4) Whilst Welshmen under Llywelyn did indeed sack De Clare's building site at Caerphilly in 1270, this was prior to the construction of the imposing fortress which now dominates the town. Beriah's suggestion here that it was that enormous stronghold which fell into Welsh

hands is inaccurate.

(5) The 'Drama-cantata' *Llywelyn ein Llyw Olaf*, staged in 1884, was one of a number of musical-dramatic collaborations Beriah would complete during his prolific career. Though Beriah is right to attest in his next footnote that the words lose something in translation, it must be admitted that the original is only slightly less soggily sentimental. Alaw Ddu (William Thomas Rees, 1838-1904 – his bardic name means 'Black Melody'), like most Welsh composers of the 19th century is almost completely unknown today, but worked tirelessly to raise musical standards in his country and briefly edited the musical section of Beriah's magazine *Cyfaill yr Aelwyd*.

(6) Tradition holds that the leek was associated as a symbol of Welshness as far back as the seventh century, so it is at least vaguely plausible Llywelyn might have used it as a calling-card in the thirteenth; more so in any case than that he would wear a red dragon.

(7) The Albigenses are perhaps better known these days as the Cathars, a Gnostic sect in southern France which were massacred in the twelfth century, with the encouragement and approval of the Pope. Gnosticism refers to a set of non-canonical beliefs arising from Christianity and yet which purport that God, whilst benevolent, is not omnipotent, and thus ascribe the problem of evil to the actions or indifference of another being known as the "demiurge." It is unlikely Beriah would have had any direct philosophical sympathy for Gnosticism, though he may have enjoyed the opportunity to present the Catholic church as oppressive.

(8) Annwn is the 'otherworld' of Welsh mythology in which dwell various magical and mysterious creatures and beings. The concept likely has continuity with pre-Christian Celtic beliefs, although any definite claims about what form such beliefs might have taken should be treated very cautiously.

(9) Abergwyngregyn, historically Aber Gareth Celyn, a short distance east of Bangor, Gwynedd, was long a seat of the princes of Gwynedd and Llywelyn's favourite of his palaces. No remains can be seen today, but a wonderful reconstruction of one of the princes' other courts, at Aberffraw, can be seen in the magnificent outdoor Museum of Welsh Life in St. Fagans, near Cardiff.

(10) This is Beriah's original footnote as are all the footnotes in this book. "Tre'r Llyn", Town of the Lake, survives in the alternative form Trallwng which is Welsh name of the town known in English as Welshpool. The castle in question is better known today as Castell Coch (Red Castle) in Welsh, and in English as Powis Castle. The impressive fortress-turned-stately home that bears that name today would not yet have been built in Llywelyn's time, though it is built on the foundations of ap Gwenwynwyn's previous castles on the site.

(11) Rhys Gyflym – Rhys the Quick.

(12) Chapters XXXV and XLII are untitled in the original publication.

(13) "Yr euog a ffy heb neb yn ei erlid," *lit.* The guilty flees without anyone chasing him.

Also available from www.melinbapur.cymru:

T. Gwynn Jones
The Great Deed of Gwilym Bevan

"No, they'll kill me too. Shh, here they come, they're breaking down the door. Oh, have mercy, have mercy, save me!"
"So you're scared of dying? Flee then, run for your life!"

After being rescued from a suicide attempt in London, Gwilym Bevan returns home to Wales and finds work in the local quarry. His wit and charisma mean he soon finds himself elected a leader among his fellow workers, but the spectre of unrest is already on the horizon...

The hard-hitting political novel *Gorchest Gwilym Bevan* by T. Gwynn Jones was one of the first Welsh novels in either language to portray industrial unrest, and was a bolt from the blue when first published in Welsh in 1899. This English translation provides a unique opportunity to sample the prose of one of the great Welsh thinkers and artists of his day.

"A novel with a social and political message... a socialist novel that speaks out for workers' rights..."
—*Alan Llwyd*

Also available from www.melinbapur.cymru:

Beriah Gwynfe Evans
Bronwen:
Chwedl Hanesyddol am Owain Glyndŵr

"Ond eto un gair. A ydyw y telerau hyn yr wyt ti er dy anrhydedd, Syr Frenin, yn caniatáu i ni, yn gyfyngedig i ni ein chwech, neu ynte, a awdurdodir ni i'w cludo ar flaenau ein gwaywffyn, yn ôl i'n gwersyll, ac yno i'w cyhoeddi yng wyneb haul, llygad goleuni, i bob Cymro yn ddieithriaid?"
"Gydag ond un eithriad," ebe'r brenin.
"A'r un hwnnw?" gofynnai y Marchog.
"GLYNDŴR!" oedd yr ateb...

Mynyddoedd y Berwyn, 1400. Mae'r cadben dieflig Syr Philip Marglee wedi'i anfon gan ei arglwydd, de Grey, i feddiannu darn o dir ei gymydog. Ychydig a ŵyr neb mai'r sgarmes fechan hon fydd dechrau gwrthryfel a fydd yn llyncu'r holl wlad.

Beriah Gwynfe Evans (1848-1927) oedd un o Gymry llengar mwyaf gweithgar ei oes. Ysgrifennodd nifer fawr o nofelau yn y Gymraeg a'r Saesneg, llawer ohonynt yn portreadu digwyddiadau a chyfnodau o hanes ei wlad mewn ymgais bwriadol i efelychu yn y cyd-destun Gymreig yr hyn yr oedd Walter Scott wedi'i wneud yn yr Alban gyda'i gyfres o nofelau hanesyddol.

www.melinbapur.cymru

Dilynwch ni ar:
F

X (@melinbapur)
Facebook (@melinbapur

www.ingramcontent.com/pod-product-compliance
Lightning Source LLC
Chambersburg PA
CBHW061215070526
44584CB00029B/3839